114161

THE UNIVERSAL WORD

THE
UNIVERSAL
WORD

*A Theology for
a Universal Faith*

by Nels F. S. Ferré

THE WESTMINSTER PRESS · *Philadelphia*

STANDARD BOOK NO. 664–20852–5
LIBRARY OF CONGRESS CATALOG CARD NO. 69–12907

PUBLISHED BY THE WESTMINSTER PRESS ®
PHILADELPHIA, PENNSYLVANIA

PRINTED IN THE UNITED STATES OF AMERICA

To

Millard G. Roberts

Preface

THE UNIVERSAL WORD is my lifework. Almost everything in this volume is new and different from my previous books; yet it seems that all my life has prepared me for this work. It started out under the title *A Theology for a Universal Faith*. My intention has been right along to minister to the need of a coming age when we must be open to all faiths without neglect of our own, or rather, with the fullest possible appreciation and acceptance of our own. During a year's lecturing in different universities and colleges throughout the world and from probing conversations with both Christian and non-Christian leaders of thought I became convinced that there is a fulfilling dimension of truth that can minister to all faiths, within them, among them, and beyond them. THE UNIVERSAL WORD is an attempt to give expression to this conviction.

In particular I believe that we live in an age when philosophies based both on substance and on process can be corrected and expanded in the light of a new framework for thought generated by the reality of spirit, love, and the personal. This framework allows these philosophies to have their say up to their point of highest efficacy and yet also to find fulfillment for their main contentions within a more adequate set of categories. Part One, The Analytical Word, is thus regulative for the entire work. Some readers of the manuscript, however, have been even more excited about the new material presented in the last chapter, on consummation.

In previous works I tried to show that Agape solves many ultimate problems with which substance and process thinking cannot fully cope. Lately I have come to understand, however, that adequacy requires a fuller picture. THE UNIVERSAL WORD, inadequate and fragmentary though it be, is my present answer. Better scholars and more persuasive writers must complete the work. My vision has compelled me to begin the search, and I feel I have discovered some true pointers in the needed direction.

In the autumn of 1966 I went to Britain to give lectures on this topic at King's College, University of London, at the invitation of the theological colleges of the University. Afterward, Principal Charles Duthie, of New College, had arranged for me to lecture at Oxford, Cambridge, Edinburgh, and Glasgow. I am thankful to Principal Duthie and to all who generously welcomed me. At Oxford, after a lecture on how to get beyond the categories of substance and process by substituting spirit and love, lively discussions ensued. At one of these, members of the Oxford University faculty of theology suggested that I return upon the completion of the manuscript of which the lecture was a foretaste. Later the Chairman of the Board of the Faculty of Theology, Principal John Marsh, of Mansfield College, confirmed this invitation most cordially in writing. When I finished the manuscript of THE UNIVERSAL WORD, consequently, I returned to Oxford to become a willing target for creative criticism.

For two weeks I listened to the response to the ideas that constitute the heart of this book, such as the development of spirit and love as the framework for a universal faith, a multidimensional view of God with its consequent contrapletal logic, and unimunity as a new social theory. One evening the members of the Senior Common Room of Mansfield College ("the faculty," in American parlance), who had prepared for my coming by reading the chapters I had sent in advance, helped me with a most penetrating discussion. On another occasion, faculty members of several colleges had a "real go" at my proposals in a concerned but genuinely challenging analysis and appraisal. I cannot mention by name or ever thank all the scholars who participated in these evenings or in the many personal discussions at several colleges with one or two members. At the end I was gratified that my proposals had weathered well, and was pleased that some suggestions could be incorporated in the book. I came away thankful to have had the chance to test out my new ideas on eminent scholars. I am, of course, especially grateful to Principal John Marsh, who took much time and trouble to be of effective help. It is always a joy to return to Mansfield College, where I spent a year as Fulbright Lecturer.

I have had help from many readers throughout the writing of this book. My son, Professor Frederick Ferré, has as always been both a sympathetic and a rigorous critic. Others who have read sections of the manuscript have been my colleagues at Parsons College, Professor Floyd Crenshaw and Professor Robert Brank Fulton. Professor Wallace Gray and the Reverend John Davis have also offered criticism of parts of preliminary drafts. My wife has continued her interest in my work, but this time I did not let her see what I was doing until I had completed three drafts. This did not discourage her, however, from finding ways of improvement! The bulk of the typing of several drafts was done by Myrna Marie Read and Dianne Tuttle; Susan Allen and Suzanne Ihrig also helped. I am thankful to them all. I appreciate especially the far-seeing encouragement of the staff of The Westminster Press.

I have dedicated the volume to Millard G. Roberts, former President of Parsons College, whose generosity in providing time, place, and secretarial help for these years of concentrated writing, gave me a privilege so great as to make me feel both deeply thankful and continually humble. My three years at Parsons College were climactically happy.

Above all, I am thankful to God for the chance to work for a better day, in theology and in life. God's new age cannot come until men find the faith that unites both thought and life. I send THE UNIVERSAL WORD on its way in trust that it will contribute to that end.

The College of Wooster   NELS F. S. FERRÉ
Wooster, Ohio

Contents

Contents

Part One

THE
ANALYTICAL
WORD

Behind and Beyond
the Ontological Argument

AUTHENTIC THEOLOGY must deal with the Universal Word. Theology involves ultimates, and ultimates are universal. Strictly speaking, therefore, a theology for a universal faith is an analytical statement.

In some sense, no doubt, theology can never deal with its subject matter, at least in primary perspective. God as God, the ultimate as ultimate, God as *theos*, remains hidden. *Theos* we know only as *logos*. Or we know God only through meanings which for us must remain proximate. These meanings, moreover, depend necessarily upon God's revealing his nature and his purpose, or, at least, his nature *or* his purpose. Theology is man's study concerning God, his will, his deeds, his promises. There can thus be no authentic theology except on the presupposition that *theos* is revealing reality, that man can know because of this fact, and that he can know only because he can in some manner participate in or learn from the *logos*, the Word which God speaks. Behind these assumptions lie innumerable presuppositions which we cannot discuss in this work, and which, indeed, we have developed at length elsewhere.

Nor can we for our purposes here go into the reasons for assuming an ultimate at all. New ways of conceiving of the ultimate should, of course, throw fresh light on the issues with which we are concerned. The fact that the ultimate is analytically universal, or alone related to all and every aspect of existence, does not mean, of course, that there can be no unique relations to the ultimate. It means, rather, that the ultimate is related to all there is in a primary sense. We shall consider this problem at some length in the two chapters devoted to the universal and the unique. What is involved for our purposes now is the fact that if the ultimate is universally related, any revelation concerning the ultimate at its center must constitute a universal word. Consequently, revelation at its full heart cannot be limited to or by any historical faith. A universal faith engendered by the universal word must by nature be open to all truth. It must at least be unfinished.

Thus when Karl Jaspers in his *Philosophical Faith and Revelation* avers that philosophy alone can be fully open to truth since theology must necessarily be limited by and to concrete historic revelations, he fails to see that authentic theology requires analytically that it be universal and as such completely open to all truth from whatever quarter. Calvin, indeed, defended such openness as alone consistent with the definition of the Holy Spirit as the Spirit of truth. Genuine theology at its center must therefore go beyond every concrete religion. It must be not only beyond all religions as the greater truth but also ahead of all religions as historic realization. Revelation, no matter how centrally true in and from the past, necessarily points ahead, waits for a fuller speaking from the future.

Revelation, then, is not only interfaith but ahead of all faiths and traditions. Ever since writing *Faith and Reason* I have been pressured by the power of this fact.

For our purposes in this work we need to include the full gamut of the Universal Word, from the Analytical Word through the Historical Word to the Potential Word. We shall find that the very nature of universal revelation requires the dimension of the future, "the eschatological": that creation bespeaks consummation.

Once while lecturing in the Philippines I was taken to task for centering my theology in the "selective actual," a historic Event. A brilliant and profound young theologian insisted that the presuppositional task for theology was to analyze the meaning of reason and of being in order to show the need for, and the explanatory power of, any claim for incarnate truth, or revelation in history. One of America's foremost theologians also sternly advised that no solution of theological problems can be accepted until the integral relation between thought and being is understood and clarified. Such doing justice to the givenness of the world we find must precede any bypassing of elemental problems in theological terms. With my training and lifelong concern for philosophy I thought that I had truly satisfied this requirement in *Faith and Reason* and later in *Reason in Religion*. Finally I came to see that the question involved the very categories of thought, or the most basic way in which we organize and understand our experience. THE UNIVERSAL WORD is the result.

There is an Analytical Word, I believe, a givenness of truth. Paul Tillich is superbly right that no responsible thinker may avoid the problem of what ultimately is. But this givenness, I now see, is not in terms either of being or of reason as ultimate or as presuppositional categories. Making being ultimate, as Western thinkers have persisted in doing, not only at the expense of becoming and nonbeing, but also and especially, at the sacrifice of spirit, love, and personal purpose, has bedeviled in every way the entire intellectual history of modern man. Tillich, toward the end of his life, was rightly shifting from the categories of being to those of spirit. Modern and historic rationalists alike, moreover, have mistakenly made reason central, giving as their ground for so doing that man's only means of interpretation is reason. The fact that man must use reason even to examine the competence of reason, as Hegel stressed, does not mean, however, that he must make reason central to knowledge since what he finally comes to know may not be reason. What we know does not have to be the same as what we know with; what we see does not have to be all eyes because we see only with our eyes.

Nevertheless, there is some truth behind the natural tendency to make being a central category because man cannot escape the question what it means to be. Similarly, there is profound truth in the drive to make reason of central importance since to know at all man must use reason. Whatever truth these positions affirm, however, must be seen in proper proportion and within as full a context as possible. Later we shall consider a third candidate for an ultimate, namely, process. Thinkers in Asia long ago developed process thinking. New theologies by process theologians in the West, moreover, are not only impressive but exceptionally relevant.

Christian theologians should find it natural, it seems, not to make being, reason, or process into an ultimate category. Surely such categories as spirit, love, and life (or spirit, love, and the personal) should offer themselves as primary candidates. After all, the claim of Christian faith has been that the God of the New Testament is ultimate reality and he is defined precisely as spirit, love, and "our Father." This book attempts to understand why, then, reason has rightly been deemed of such importance in relation to being, why being has tended to be thought of as substance or process, while the categories of spirit, love, and the personal, in fact, help solve the philosophical problems that arise when substance or process are made the ultimates. I am mystified when I ponder why Christian theologians have never dared to take as statemental fact the claims that Christ is the truth and that the Holy Spirit shall lead us into all truth. To be sure, the ultimacy of spirit, love, and purpose cannot be limited to any historic faith, but freely works ahead of all concrete religions to fulfill them. It is indeed strange that "the truth that enlightens every man that comes into the world" has been forsaken by Christian thinkers while they have continually been frustrated in trying to express their faith within alien philosophical frameworks.

As I launch this project I feel that I am laboring to fulfill the depth intention of Karl Barth's *Fides quaerens intellectum,* the climactic change to spirit in Tillich's strivings, the constructive stress on spirit in Berdyaev, the feeling for love and spirit as ultimate by Robinson and Altizer beyond substantive supernaturalism and traditionalistic theism, in fact, the intention of all those who, like Harvey Cox, can neither accept traditional theology nor let go of the universal truth they feel in Jesus. I seek to universalize Bloch and Moltmann by showing man's true hope from the future. THE UNIVERSAL WORD fails of its vision unless its Analytical, Historic, and Potential Word are consummated within such universal truth as will speak fulfillingly to man's most honest seeking and his most critical and creative finding.

This chapter will deal with the importance of reason in relation to being and show that reason can find its fulfillment only in terms of faith, that while the ontological argument will not do for proving the existence of God or for the knowledge of God, nevertheless the drive underlying "the argument" indicates the nature of the most warranted faith stance concerning the ultimate. We shall also discover that the good constitutes an often silent but important partner in this dialogue concerning ultimates, that it is in fact generally presupposed. Then we shall devote a chapter to the definition of time, because process thinking has as one of its main dimensions the understanding of reality within the dimension of time. We shall try to define time directly in terms of our most adequate ultimate.

Following this discussion we must deal with identity and distinction in terms of the categories of spirit, love, and the personal as they supplant substance and process. Such a procedure revolutionizes the whole framework of thought. The pioneering thrust of this volume will no doubt be rough and partial, but I hope it will start a direction that will prove ever more rewarding as those equipped in many fields of knowledge and those with more competent analytical and systematic skill will take over the fuller task. We turn, then, to our first question concerning the persistent drive to equate reason and being, which is the depth drive or the basic "instinct" behind the ontological argument.

In order to get at what the drives toward being and reason stand for we are obliged, indeed, to search for the basic instinct behind the ontological argument. Why did the classical tradition assume the adequation of thought and being, or shall we say of true thought and of genuine reality? Why did this same tradition also in large part include virtue as constitutive of knowledge? Ever since Plato, at least, true knowledge was not so much virtue as virtue the nature of true knowledge. To know was not necessarily to be good but only the good man could truly know. For the classical tradition it is not true simplistically that mere intellectual knowledge comprised virtue. Knowledge was virtue only when knowledge involved the realization of the good. The Buddhists similarly distinguish between superficial acquaintance with and knowledge as the realization of a state of being. They speak of truth-reality.

My own understanding of the knowledge of the good and of the equation of knowledge with virtue is on this level rather than on the level of the prior isolation of knowledge from the whole of being and value, and then of the identification of such knowledge with either being or virtue. If we can get at the instinct behind this holding together of reason, being, and value, we shall begin to see both the natural strength of the classical equation, the loss of which is the fundamental problem of modern man, and also the inherent weakness in it which gave a new line of thinkers legitimate grounds for their ruthless and excessive dissolution of the equation. The point of our analysis in this section dealing with the Analytical Word is to recover the truth of the equation apart from the falsehood which at present renders ineffective the truth contained in it.

The main drive behind the ontological argument is man's conviction that true thought and eminent reality should go together. The strongest instinct behind the classical adequation of thought and being was precisely this inner urge that right reason should find reality. Connected with this vague conviction and this depth urge was the feeling that only good reason could lay hold on reality. Somehow man sensed that reason in depth is in the service of man. Thus right reason needs good motivation. The instinct behind the ontological argument found favor as long as this ultimate identity rested on a general and broad, but vague, faith judgment. The equation, in fact, depended upon the total presuppositions of classical civilization which for the most part took it for granted. Philosophers subsequently tried to put this faith in terms of knowledge, so that at least from the ambiguous Anaxagoras on, and the more obvious Parmenides, there was some overt acknowledgment of the identity of truth and reality. The mind itself began hesitantly to be made a key to the understanding of the world. Arthur O. Lovejoy has traced "the great chain of being" in detail up to the breaking of it by Hume and Kant. The chain they broke, however, was the weak chain of knowledge. They showed that from within man's historical situation such an equation could not be proved. How could it be, in the light of the evils of experience and of the unfinished stage of the pedagogical process?

The instinct behind the ontological argument, instead of finding favor in a new age which stressed empiricism rather than the classical understanding of ultimate reality, became frustrated but could not be killed. Marxism, for instance, for its part gave nerve to history by believing that there could be a new age of the people. Marxism posed its conviction, that the meaning of things could be known and could be realized, in terms of scientific knowledge, but its messianic contention can no more be proved than could the classical equation of thought, being, and virtue. The difference was that Marxism stressed the historical as the medium of solution. Dialectical materialism became a faith based on the nature of history in terms of inevitable historical development. Marxism is a faith in an ultimate nature of things, but instead of attempting knowledge of the ultimate directly, the knowledge of what must be, Marxism endeavored to prove that history afforded us such knowledge. By shifting its approach into line with the Christian upbringing of the Jewish Marx, Marxism introduced not only history directly but also the potential indirectly.

Methodologically Marxism would have been stronger if it had not claimed scientific knowledge for its position but had rather called it a warranted faith, but psychologically and historically it strengthened its case by claiming to be based on scientific knowledge. Marxism is a faith bolstered by its confused and illegitimate reliance on knowledge. Its kind of knowledge is, in fact, of the same nature as that of the classical philosophy which assumed the ultimate union of true thought and being. Science and dialectical materialism, the Marxists believe, support each other. Actually Marxism introduced also the element of virtue as essential to the equation by insisting that Marxism can be finally understood only from within the concrete involvement of the historic struggle for the victory of the people. The objective facts are there for all to see, but the unwilling will not see them!

In the same way Freudianism, for another illustration, assumed that knowledge of the repressed past, and the ability to accept it, would release man from his subconscious evil. Man's natural drives of the subconscious id and man's drives from his parental and racial superego would have to yield to the knowledge by the conscious self of the depth nature of his malady. Freud also wanted to call his ideology scientific knowledge, but obviously the most he could have claimed was a warranted faith, unless, indeed, all men had finally been cured by his method. What Freud did was to change the classical stress to the historical and to the potential through which man must learn what the nature of things really is!

Generally speaking, few thinkers would today subscribe to the possibility of any objective knowledge of the classical equation of the ultimate coincidence of thought, being, and virtue, but modern man still keeps presupposing it in many hidden forms. A direct survival and brilliant restatement of the classical position is Charles Hartshorne's *The Logic of Perfection,* but his case is weakened because he too far disregards both history and the cosmological potential and fails to see that man cannot within process go beyond warranted faith to knowledge in terms of demonstration and proof. Only the conclusive consummation of process can do that! Accordingly only what John Hick calls "eschatological verification" will do. Hartshorne's profound contribution would be deepened by a fulfilling dimension of eschatology.

The fact is that man must live in a situation where his best knowledge of ultimates can never exceed the status of warranted faith. Freud even acknowledged the need for virtue along with knowledge by holding that apart from man's willingness to face up to or to accept his past he could not be rid of its oppressive power over him. Thus he, too, had to come full circle in his indirect acknowledging that knowledge, healing, and virtue go together. He defined them in his own way, but the result is the same. To be sure, he never worked out the universal implications of what free, mature selves would find for truth, but he did indict our entire kind of civilization as oppressive and needing to be transcended or transformed as coming generations of children would be less saddled by the inhibitions of our present era. There was in Freud a kind of mysticism underneath his scientific shield. In modern clinical psychology, moreover, even beyond the works of Jung and Adler, there is an increasing acceptance of logotherapy. Viktor Frankl's form of it is only one sample of the modern turning to some indirect acceptance of the ultimate equation of thought, being, and, in some manner, virtue, which underlay the classical equation and the later explicit formulation of the ontological argument.

The trouble with the classical equation of "the great chain of being" was that it aimed at a statement of the position in terms of knowledge when in fact it was, for the most part, a general presupposition of classical thought, which functionally was a matter of faith. The attempt to formulate the position was attributable to man's craving for a *warranted* faith. Thus a basic confusion of faith and reason lay in the very inception of the classical position. On this confusion Hume and Kant jumped with power. But they in turn—although they both acknowledged the need for faith and its place in man's life of understanding in its wider sense, whether in terms of Hume's more direct and forthright stressing it or in terms of Kant's more indirect resort to practical postulates or to legitimate convictions that could not, nevertheless, claim the status of knowledge in the narrower meaning—left a heritage of agnosticism and positivism which, to be sure, is less their own fault than it is occasioned by the general mood and presuppositions of the modern age. They have been both used and abused.

Hume and Kant are even now more accepted as symbols than for the full intention of their concrete thinking. They are taken more on faith than because of an objective full-scale examination of the adequacy of their philosophical frameworks. In some circles they are practically taken for granted as the bringers of a new era. Few thinkers plow deeply enough to find how near the surface the profitless hardpan is. Modern philosophies almost always assume the legitimacy of the frameworks of Hume and Kant, as both existentialism and linguistic analysis particularly demonstrate. They all too often assume an ultimate linguistic agnosticism. *All* frameworks of interpretation, to be sure, are in the final analysis faith judgments, but it is better to acknowledge them as such and to strive to have faith become as warranted as possible rather than to declare what in fact is faith to be knowledge. If we do so, we can begin to grasp what relation faith and reason have to the conclusions of great thinkers like Hume and Kant, and especially to the false and partial use of their positions.

We need to try to formulate positively and forthrightly the truth that drove man's depth instinct to produce the classical equation of right reasoning, the really real, and virtue. The instinct explicitly behind the ontological argument and implicitly behind the equation of thought, being, and usually also virtue, in the classical tradition, was that *truth can be trusted.* Some philosophers, to be sure, mistakenly tried to turn faith into a matter of provable knowledge rather than having it remain no more than warranted faith for thought and life. Or we might put the matter in a different way: Knowledge became too far connected with what could be analyzed or demonstrated. Knowledge tended to lose its fullness.

With Plato there was a strong bond between thought, being, and good-ness, and Aristotle knew that knowledge had to be adapted to the nature of the field in order to prevent false expectations of demonstrable validity where the field, in the nature of the case, could not allow it. Augustine and Anselm, too, kept goodness, even man's openness to God in prayer, a part of the total knowledge situation. Descartes, however, relied on mathematics as a model and thereby courted a misdirected quest for the ontological argument. The Cartesian approach reflected, to be sure, a new feel in civilization and a new mood in method. Nor can Descartes himself be limited to his central scaffolding, in that his total use of the argument outstrips the more narrow intellectualistic equation. After all, he relied on God's faithfulness for the veracity of our knowledge of the world!

In the trusting of truth, however, we have both knowledge and faith, and as a background of both we have the kind of life that can trust. Thus faith, reason, and goodness are combined as a total stance that can then be justified only in its total practice. Seeing and being belong together. But what of the place for goodness? It is necessary to observe even preliminarily that thought and reality, or the knowledge of the really real, must not be divorced from goodness. The rift in the trusting of truth begins at this point and, once riven, reason, being, and goodness usually remain in-effectively apart. The drive behind the classical tradition is precisely the instinct that truth can be trusted, or that there can be a warranted faith. The need for any constructive civilization is to unite all three integrally. Such a union may occur under auspices which, indeed, seem to deny it.

Perhaps the best modern illustration of such a framework is that of the scientific method. Von Weizsäcker in his *The Relevance of Science* claims that the religion of modern man is scientism. Modern man trusts science and acts almost instinctively on that faith. He takes his faith in science as a method to find truth for granted. Confusion sets in only when he self-consciously tries to call that faith knowledge, when he becomes critically aware of his assumption. Faith in science is indeed far more psychological than logical. Man assumes the unity of the universe in the sense that there is a predictable order. Such a total order can never be proved, nor can it be falsified. Such a whole is as unprovable for science as for philosophy and for religion. Scientific theories come and go, but when they are proved separately false the total framework is not thereby declared illicit. Instead, modern man believes that more truth has been discovered. In the total and final sense such a conclusion is an act of faith. Man trusts that we now know more of the nature of the universe than before. No number of startling discoveries as to the previous inadequacy of discoveries count against the faith as to the total reliability not only of the method but of the kind of universe that such a method has to presuppose.

Science as science, as a total method, cannot be falsified and yet people keep believing in what can neither be proved nor falsified. The power of the ontological argument is at work. Man assumes a positive relation between scientific thinking and what can be truly known. Even when the possibility of randomness is introduced, as in the case of the atom or the gene, shaking the very principle of predictability not only in its scope but in its nature, the basic faith in the method of science to find truth persists. The tough-minded prove this by wanting to call randomness a matter of incomplete *knowledge*. Recourse is had to the scientific gods of the gap. Man knows that although science as such can never become a matter of knowledge either analytically or through some total demonstration, nevertheless there is enough reliability both in the theoretical and the practical reason to use science as a *warranted* faith. Instances of error which have been discovered count for, not against, the method. In general, such faith seems justified in its place and scope.

Such is man's unconquerable faith in truth. To be sure, in the case of science the comparative objectivity of the field lessens the personal temptation for self-promotion and self-protection. The method can easily unmask pretension. Science as science seldom deals, and then only marginally and illicitly, with matters that pertain to man's ultimate meanings, nature and destiny. Nevertheless he is naïve indeed who thinks that there are no fashions in science, no schools of thought with vested interest of prestige and power, or that no personal matters of pride and place ever enter scientific inquiry! Einstein, we recall, complained that fashions were nearly as common and disruptive in science as in women's dresses!

But in general modern man's almost universal faith in science, all but taken for granted until quite recently, serves to illustrate exactly the nature of the instinct behind the classical equation of thought, being, and goodness. Man believes in pursuing science even in the teeth of the evidence of possible total destruction at its hands. Modern man has simply narrowed the scope of the equation and has thereby not only increased the possibility of objectivity in knowledge but also impoverished the meaning and total relevance of knowledge. And all too often he has called his faith in science knowledge and has thereby hidden from himself that he was in fact living by faith. The real question is the kind of warrant this faith can have, not whether or not man must live by faith. Faith and knowledge cannot be rigidly separated. When sophisticated modern branches of science like physics speak of limiting our knowledge to phenomenological analysis, leaving the ultimate nature of things beyond knowledge, this *can* be used to combat scientism and to make room for faith, but all too often it still amounts to scientism, to an affirmation that physics has no right to make, to the effect that man cannot know what is ultimately real.

The first point, then, behind the drive of the ontological argument is that knowledge cannot be dissociated from faith. The classical equation of thought and being, or of true thinking and the really real, at times purported to be a matter of knowledge while it was in fact a general trusting of truth. It was a presupposition for both thinking and living. The trusting of truth appeared to the classical thinkers to be an obviously warranted faith. It was the assumption on which community, art, education, religion, and life in general were built. But another point is equally important though less obvious and a less constant factor. Just as the classical equation must not be dissociated from faith, so must it not be severed from goodness. As we have said, in the classical tradition, as centrally represented by Plato, goodness constituted an integral part of true knowledge. To the Stoics, for instance, the world reason and the world soul belonged together. The *logos spermatikos* in the individuation of the world of thinkers, too, was no mere intellectual machine but part of the world ground where thought, being, and the moral belonged together.

Only with the dawning of the modern day did the unity of the total combination generally weaken and make ready to break. Not even in Descartes, however, as we have already suggested, was the break complete, since the knowledge of the world in the final analysis depended upon the faithfulness and the veracity of God. Thought and extension were indeed the critical components of reality but never did Descartes himself reduce them to mere mathematics or mechanical phenomena. His doctrine of God was no mere principle and power of connectedness. God was more evidently real to him than the pineal gland! Therefore, to some extent, both Hume and Kant were tackling straw men when they showed that the ontological argument, on which for Kant all other arguments hung, could not be a matter of *knowledge*. Goodness and God had almost invariably been part and parcel of the presupposition for thought which amounted to a framework of faith.

What harm, therefore, the illegitimate use of Kant's First Critique as the definer of knowledge has caused, not so much in Kant himself—far, far from it—as by the use of Kant's distinctions within a new framework of negativity in general! Kant as a matter of fact stressed morality, and thus goodness, especially in the Second Critique, as the practical basis for knowing ultimates, in terms of his practical postulates; and in his posthumous works he did much to put together again what he had previously severed too severely. As we know, even his rigid bounding of knowledge in the First Critique was undertaken for the sake of "making room for faith." Where? In the total life? Existentially? No, in the total life of the intellect which comprised several kinds of rational normativeness. Secondary interpreters have equated the knowledge of the First Critique with the life of the intellect, and nothing could do more injustice to the very heart of Kant's intention or hurt more the springs of creative civilization.

Can we then restate the truth of the instinct behind the ontological argument? Can we recover the practical power of the deepest drive of the classical "chain of being"? We can do so only if we understand afresh the relation between faith and reason, and between goodness and reasoned reality. The trusting of truth points to the fideistic aspect of the equation; and the truth of goodness stands for the axiological structure within the ontological argument.

The fundamental error, however, was the equation in Western metaphysics of being with substance. In the proper place we shall have to define substance with care. Among philosophers Werkmeister has shown how many senses the term "being" can have. He has delved into the need for deeper categorical analysis of the term "being." Its identification with substance is fatal to adequate thinking. What most fundamentally *is* should be rethought and rephrased in terms of different categories. What *should* go together are thought and spirit, with concern as the variable factor in knowledge. Concern is that vaguer component which guards the reality of freedom in knowing. Man can "not care" or "care not to know."

In the full equation of reality, as we shall see, love needs to stand guard over the need for goodness. The need for love as a principle and power of cognition brings out the fact that there is a justification by faith with regard to knowledge as well as a justification of righteousness by faith. The nature of love precludes any demonstrable knowledge of necessary being either objectively or subjectively. If God could be proved as necessary being, he would not leave us free for the final act of faith. God, indeed, is no supreme substantive being, but the supreme Spirit, and as love he can be known most fully by love. Ultimately, we shall see, like can be known by like only through participation. Are we not, however, inconsistent? Did we not previously claim that the fact that we see with our eyes does not demand or entail that we see only eyes?

If ultimately, however, as Kierkegaard claims, "truth is subjectivity," a matter of love, spirit, and personal purpose, then such inwardness, such experience, cannot be known as it is except by having it. The marks of it can be noted, desire for it promoted, and change of heart necessary for its appropriation can be generated in preparation, but the inward understanding of it, it seems, must be a matter of participation in its reality. If only those who love God can know God, as The First Letter of John announces, the equation of knowing, being, and goodness comes full round. Is it possible, then, to relate the drive behind the classical equation and the instinct behind the ontological argument in terms of the Christian categories? What *has* driven man to assert some such equation whether of science in the more general sense of the classical past or of science in the more narrow sense of modern man?

Before we attempt a fuller analysis of this depth drive we shall look aside a moment at the philosophical implications of some Eastern religions. We have seen already that the Western equation of thought and reality suffered from an attempt to get at the equation directly in terms of knowledge, and that it did so with no genuine understanding of the historic and the potential. The Historical and the Potential Word were cheated of their rights! Plato's myth of the cave symbolizes and expresses this lack. He depicted graphically reality and shadows, but with no sense of historical reality as either actually or potentially present within the world of the caves. Christian theology, on the contrary, centers in the Historical Word and requires for its fulfillment the Potential Word. The Universal Word, therefore, by the nature of the case can never be a matter of mere direct knowing; for human beings within history there can be no outright equation of thought and ultimate truth.

What, however, of the Oriental approach which has not made substance its category of being, and for which becoming and non-being have both been basic categories? How did Hinduism and Buddhism, for instance, treat the problem of the ultimate nature of things in contradistinction from Christianity? In discussing this question we are naturally aware of the proliferous multiplicity in Eastern approaches within which in its totality almost any position can be found. There is nevertheless a core truth that characterizes most Eastern thought almost like a motif. The instinct behind the ontological argument and its wider drive in the classical equation of thought and being (and usually of goodness, either explicitly or implicitly) can thus be seen also in the Eastern religions. In Hinduism, for instance, what is essential in man and what is ultimately real generally go together. *Tat tvam asi* is defined precisely in terms of *saccidananda:* Thou art that bliss, being and intelligence. Ultimately there is, accordingly, the full equation of goodness, thought and being. The basic difference between the Christian and this Eastern tradition is that the

Christian stresses incarnation as central whereas the latter makes excarnation basic. Eternity does not become historical but the deepest in man is eternal. In the Eastern tradition, moreover, there is no vibrant, creative potential for history within the Ultimate. Only the Christian faith makes Incarnation fully its main approach and even Christian interpreters have generally—yes, almost entirely—shied away from making Incarnation a *general principle* central to human history and to the understanding of nature as pedagogical process. But in worship and in principle, at least, the Universal Word has quite often been made basic to Christian faith, not only directly, but at least in some frustrated forms of implications.

Even before Christianity, however, there were in the Western tradition drives toward the identification of thought and being, at least, as we have indicated, ever since the ambiguous and crude attempts of Anaxagoras, or more clearly, the explicit equation by Parmenides, no matter how severely Plato may later have criticized Anaxagoras for his physical form of *nous* and for not making it into a general principle. The latter development in Plato and the Stoics, for instance, made some of the church fathers think that the Greek philosophers must have learned from Moses! But however inadequate the equation may have been, the main line of Western thought reveals the power of the identification, explicitly or implicitly, so that even Aristotle's removed and remote *actus purus*, the Unmoved Mover, had directive power by emulative attraction whereas in much of the Oriental picture, by sharp contrast, the empirical world as such was *maya*, a world of undependable and unreliable illusion. Most Western thinkers, to be sure, fail to grasp the Hindu empirical understanding of *maya* and to see that it is illusion not so much for life or empirical thinking as such as in the light of the unchangeable *Brahman*. Nevertheless history as such does not participate in *Brahman* nor does it have integral meaning for the understanding of the ultimate nature of what is absolute. Aseity is severed from *maya*. Even so, the roads to release, the *margas* to *moksa,* give a subjective witness to the classical equation; and deliverance in much Hindu thought, moreover, especially in the *Bhagavadgita,* had to come through undivided *bhakti*. Thus goodness is there too!

Goodness and knowledge, as well as work, the three roads to release, moreover, must implicitly at least, have some historic as well as potential power. Without it they would not be effective even as *margas*. If only the equation in the West had been fully understood, accepted, and applied as *faith courting knowledge,* we could now deal more fulfillingly with the fragmenting identification of thought, being, and goodness in the East. The West has long lacked an adequate understanding of the *Universal Word*. It has substituted idolatry, a unique and basically unrelated Christ, for the final Universal Word. In the East the identification between thought, being, and goodness has been too haphazard to affect life and civilization, but it is there! It is there, we have said, both ultimately in Hinduism's *saccidananda* and also suggestively in its subjective approach to illumination. The roads had to be appropriate to the destination. It must be remembered, too, that the avatars were incarnational manifestations. This aspect of Hinduism can constitute a bridge between the Word and its capacity for constant manifestations in human history. In this understanding we have a chance to allow the Christian and the Hindu approaches to be fulfilled by complementariness. The cleft between ex-carnation, the not seeing *Brahman* in the *maya*, can give way to the potential organic relation between possible avatarhood and the general meaning of nature and history. We in the West have much to learn of the deeper truths from within the Oriental vision, and the East has much to learn from our forthright stress on the relevance of the eternal for the world of time, of God for creation. First, however, the overarching understanding to help both sides must be filled in.

In Buddhism, moreover, the subject is exceedingly complex and some-what uncertain. Primitive Buddhists may have denied—and many Theravada Buddhists now deny—that there is ultimately any identification that can be known in terms of our kind of knowledge. Instead of the realization of *tat tvam asi* resulting in *saccidananda* (if we may use dynamic or process terms at all for the finding of reality in the ultimate identification) we have generally in Buddhism the *neti neti* leading to *nirvana*. The "not this, not this" affirms the full chasm between our kind of world and truth-reality. *Nirvana* may mean extinction, the final blowing out of all mean-ingfulness, or it may mean that we must ever remain agnostic from this side as to what, if anything, lies beyond our meaningfulness, or it may even mean the conviction that the identification is too real and too final to be known at all from within our present kind of experience. We know that *nirvana* was a Hindu term indicating the true self, the "true such-ness," as some scholars now call it, beyond the illusory self that could know sorrow, ignorance, and impermanence. The Buddhists may also posit a reality too real to be known behind *anicca*, impermanence, *dukkha*, suffering, and *anatta*, no-selfness or insubstantiality. Winston King has written most persuasively in his *A Thousand Lives Away* to advocate the more positive interpretation at this point of even Theravada Buddhism, and he surely is backed by some contemporary scholars, like Murti, Dean of Benares University, and several Western scholars who agree in this matter with J. B. Pratt, an early Western contender for such an inter-pretation.

As to the identification in the metaphysical, idealistic branches of Ma-hayana Buddhism, there is of course no question at all as to the ultimate equation. There is some question, to be sure, as to Christian influence at the very inception of the "larger vehicle" and also of the basic return ideationally of Buddhism to its Hindu prime well. The fact, however, that even Theravada Buddhists speak of truth-reality and of the realizing of truth rather than of merely knowing it abstractly already indicates a genuine degree of equation of thought and being. The Eightfold Path especially, that leads to final enlightenment, indicates a strong identification. Dean Murti's treatment of the *madyamika,* or the middle way, at this point bears intense studying and intensive pondering. But the fact remains clear that neither Hinduism nor Buddhism had any developed *historic* or *potential* understanding of whatever universal Word either of them approached and accepted ultimately. The embryo, however, is there, and from it can come naturally the child and the mature man. At this point a whole field for interfaith cultivation challenges future generations.

What, then, is the truth behind the ontological argument? What is the authentic upshot in the classical equation of thought, being, and (generally) goodness? How do we appraise the classical formula: Perfection must exist? Not to exist, the claim goes, is to lack being. Therefore being as well as idea belongs to perfection. Such is the crass form of the argument which when connected with substance philosophy becomes peculiarly vulnerable. Existence is not a (necessary?) predicate. There can be a perfect description of something without its having existence. But . . . ! Such analysis substitutes one faith for another. It shows that within its own kind of framework, within its own kind of presuppositions, there need be no necessary existence (as isness) even of perfection. Perfection from within our kind of experience cannot be *known* as existing. Of course! Even perfect existence (isness) is not analytically necessary because existence can never be a matter that is analytically necessary. There is no direct passing as necessary knowledge for us from propositional truth to existence. Such passing involves a *trusting* of truth, the affirmation that true thought and reality belong together. Existence is not a matter of propositional truth, but of empirical factuality. Only empirical factuality, genuinely understood, can occasion a warranted faith.

When existence is defined in terms of substance, moreover, perfect existence cannot be a matter of a universally necessary, synthetic, propositional truth, either a priori or a posteriori. Even if perfection is considered the logical presupposition for all being, it still is no more necessary, for us, than existence itself. Apart from existence we can know nothing about logical presuppositions. Our understanding of existence is, moreover, based on factual observation from within, and, from without, on personal experience of the outside world. Neither experience can constitute analytical necessity. There can be neither analytical nor empirical proof of experience as such. We must take experience itself or, as such, *for granted.* We accept experience. We therefore take experience on faith. It is accepted. We affirm its reality. Such affirmation is the heart of faith.

Buddhist thought may generally deny truth its empirical reality and its reliability for knowledge of ultimates, and then take the consequences for life and for civilization. Such denial is, of course, itself a faith stance. The opposite affirmation is also a matter of faith, nay, *the very essence of faith.* Such positive acceptance, such a trusting of truth, is the foundational faith. Faith affirms the acceptance of meaning and that meaning *means.* That we are, that we can know, that authentic knowledge is veridical, and that knowledge is worthwhile are primary faith judgments that are back of the ontological argument. Of course they cannot be a matter of knowledge! The decision, in fact, whether we are basically pro-universe or con-universe as the approach to truth and life is the vinculum for an effective faith.

Analytically, as a synthetic proposition a posteriori the matter is fully as faulty. When perfection means a perfect supreme being, and being is turned into existence as substance, any competent thinker can show that such a being is limited by other beings and is therefore finite, or if that being is supposed to encompass all finite beings that he then includes also all the imperfections of the world we know. He cannot therefore be known as perfect from within such an inductive approach. Thus God is either limited by other beings or defiled by them, or both. Accordingly synthetic propositions a posteriori cannot prove a perfect God. They cannot attain to the ultimate equation. Such reasoning, however, leaves out of account both the Historical and the Potential Word. It denies or fails to understand that the ultimate can be known more fully because of history and process.

What the whole charge boils down to, indeed, is that God as perfection, the perfect supreme being, can be known neither deductively nor inductively. We agree emphatically. There can be no knowledge of God, certainly not of God as Supreme Being, in terms of proof or demonstration, in terms either of analysis or of inductive logic. That, however, is never the real question. Such an approach is most certainly a red herring. Even to talk of the possibility of such knowledge is to misread the intellectual situation. It is to falsify the evidence. It is to mislead thinking. The real and only question is whether, in the light of the most critical and the most creative interpretation of experience, we can have a warranted faith to the effect that there is an ultimate nature of things and that we can know something of what this ultimate nature of things is. Whoever does not accept that we are and that we can know something reliably thereby puts himself categorically beyond both the need for and the possibility of human communication. His affirmation, indeed, is self-contradictory. Whoever bothers to communicate at all thereby affirms meaning. He thereby agrees to live by faith. It does not follow from such a commitment that he is a continuous person or that knowledge as such is continuous.

It follows only that the communicator believes, at least at that moment, that he can communicate something. It follows also that he believes that it is worthwhile to do so in whatever terms and for whatever reasons.

Obviously no knowledge of the ultimate can be had ultimately. Only the ultimate can know ultimately. Knowledge of the ultimate for creatures must be a matter of faith. Such knowledge depends upon the faith *ab initio* that knowledge hangs together sufficiently to make some sense as a whole, and that there can be a universe of discourse. A universe of discourse, moreover, involves that whatever wholeness a person may see has meaning for others and that it can in some way and to some extent be shared. Thus knowledge within a warranted faith is never merely personal but also communal. If what one then sees as knowledge is not self-explanatory or self-sufficient but calls for something more and other to account for it and to fill out its implications, we can see the need for an ultimate. The mere givenness of experience calls for no ultimate. We can accept it as it is, provided that it seems plausible that such has always been the nature of experience. If, however, what we know has not always been of the same nature but has come to be, if what we see is a process that begs for an explanation, then the need and the problem for an ultimate, at least for "the more and other than," becomes an important matter.

In the nature of the case such an ultimate cannot be a matter of knowledge. Experience itself and its interpretation we must take on faith. If there is sufficient agreement as to what we ourselves find and what others find to constitute some common world of experience, we should accept our faith as warranted to that extent. We tend to affirm what we think others either can or should affirm in the light of the nature of the experience we have had and have examined. If there is agreement that our experience is not a matter of satisfactory life or knowledge, we may seek together for more and better knowledge and for more and better life. We seek even for the fullest or the ultimate nature of knowledge and life. If our analysis indicates that such search is a warranted faith, we can go on from there to determine to what extent we can know the ultimate and what the nature of the ultimate might be. We should seek, in any case, to ascertain what man can know, what he can hope, and perhaps even what he might expect. Such knowledge, in the nature of the case, must be a matter of acceptance of both the fact and the content of knowing. We know that we know and that we know something. Such is the road to the trusting of truth.

The classical equation and the drive behind the ontological argument most deeply mean that man believes deep down that he can know an ultimate, that the ultimate is worth knowing, and that the nature of the ultimate matters to both life and knowledge. The Western, and especially the Christian, instinct is for faith to affirm that at its highest and fullest, at its truest and best, knowledge can be had and is worthwhile. We have seen, however, that implicitly such affirmation characterizes also secular knowledge and the faith of other religions. To make such an affirmation wherever it is made a matter of knowledge, either analytically or inductively, is, however, to misread our situation as men in process, while to deny that such faith is warranted is to reduce life and knowledge to meaninglessness. It is for this reason that what is happening to us now in negative terms, following Kant's and Hume's demonstrations, *on their terms,* that knowledge of perfection as existing is impossible, is such a disaster for both life and civilization. Both Kant and Hume generally defined knowledge in too narrow terms and apart from faith. They thus misconceived the intellectual task and led overwilling interpreters into a dead-end road.

The blocking of man's great desire to know ultimate meanings and tasks has cut the nerve of life. The reason that the Orient has not been vigorous in the development of thought, the exploration of nature, and the purposive promoting of history has been exactly that it has lacked the central nerve that underlies and furthers history. The breaking of the great chain of being has proved disastrous because we have not seen that what was broken was only the false chain of knowledge and substance and not the ultimate relations of faith and knowledge constituted by spirit, thought, and love.

The long tradition of the equation of thought and being has usually insisted as well that the equation is ultimately good and can be known only by the good. The rest do not want to know it, and since it is man and not reason that knows, they will not know. Those who reject the demands of truth use reason to rationalize, so to speak, whereas only the concerned and committed use reason to think properly. Only "the good" want the good and therefore seek and think the good. The others shun it and try to reason it away. The equation then affirms not that it is good to be, but that fully to be and fully to see involves being good. The classical tradition of equating thought and being in the bosom of goodness quietly though vaguely affirms or believes that true thought and genuine goodness go together; and that when they do, and only then, can we find reality. Truth-reality is, therefore, also in some way a matter of goodness-reality. Or truth involves the condition that the more good a man is in life the more he will tend to think that goodness is real. Naturally no mere willingness or openness produces knowledge! It is only a condition for getting to know. Never can even the concerned "know" reality to be good, for he cannot know as God knows, nor can he know as though he were at the end of the pedagogical process, but he can believe warrantedly that faith in no other terms can give him true insight into the meaning of what truly is and what is truly good and how to attain it.

Behind the instinct of the ontological argument, then—and the wider equation of thought, being, and goodness—lies the conviction that ultimately life and knowledge are good in that only goodness can find and illumine either life or knowledge in their deepest and most meaningful dimension. The equation involves the faith that truth can be trusted to be good and that goodness alone trusts truth all the way to its full meaning and full potential reality. Such an attitude is faith in the sense that while the affirmation may be backed by both subjective and objective seeing, and while it may be confirmed by other seers and by their testing of experience critically and creatively, even so the trusting is both anterior to and superior to the warrant in terms of knowledge. The equation is thus more religious than philosophical. It is more life than knowledge. Nevertheless it tries to keep life whole by being open to, and changeable by, the best knowledge. Thus its faith is that far warranted.

When all is said and done, however, there is one sense in which there is an insistent demand on reason to accept the ontological argument. Somehow it seems hard for man to think that his own thinking can go beyond the nature of reality. Can it be more real than reality itself? If he can think the ultimate identification of goodness, reality, and truth, can he then by so doing, go beyond what is the ultimate nature of things? Or can he think so ultimately only because it is so? He obviously can think that the world is better than it is. Why can he not then think similarly that even reality as such is better than it seems in terms of pedagogical process without being mistaken in his view? In order to obviate this inconsistency between a perfect ideal and a faulty world Hindus and Christian Scientists, for instance, have denied that the world is as bad as it appears to be. They put the empirical world in doubt. We see only *maya* or the illusions of mortal thought. The real truth, they insist, could we but see it, is that everything, *when genuinely and fully understood,* is as good as we can conceive it to be, or better. But thus to meet the problem is to deny the facts as they are known by ordinary knowledge. And for that matter even the illusion is bad.

The contradiction, however, can be solved if we distinguish between the actual nature of the world that we know and its potential nature. If we do, we have to take into consideration the pedagogical purpose of the cosmic and the historic processes and, doing so, we immediately introduce into our total picture the historical and the potential categories. If the ultimate can be seen neither as merely indicated by description of what we now experience nor as devoid of understanding in terms of the *maya* of the ordinary world, but rather as working through the present imperfections of creation the intended result of a process of maturation and growth through decision, then there is no inconsistency between our being able to think at the same time a reality better than the reality now judged

in terms of, or in relation to, the actual process and the realistic acceptance of the world as it is for what it is. The ontological argument is then
not a sure proof of knowledge, but the affirmation, a faith stance, that
reason can think reliably along the lines of the truest maturation indicated by the nature of the process. What ultimately is, then, is indicated
by the highest and best that can be thought, even though it cannot be
proved by a process that is not meant at this point truly or fully to represent the ultimate, but only genuinely and potentially to indicate the purpose of the process and the general direction in which it is going.

The eventual equation of thought, reality, and goodness has fallen
apart, to some extent, because of a confusion between faith and knowledge. People have not understood the dual, dynamic relation between
trusting and *truth*. The equation has also sometimes been undermined by
the removing of goodness from the equation. The final belonging together
of true thought, of what is really real, and of genuine goodness can never
be made a mere academic or intellectual matter of knowledge, and particularly not when goodness is taken out of the total equation. It has
also been made ineffective by arguments to the effect that the perfect
being in terms of substance, the so-called "supreme being," does not exist.
The attack has been justified, but misdirected. The attack has been on a
false target by illegitimate weapons. Without the right equation of warranted faith, however, the whole edifice of meaningful life and knowledge
is undermined.

Kant and Hume have indeed helped us by breaking the chain of being,
by putting knowledge as such in the limited sense within its proper limitations, for by so doing, they have helped to "make room for faith" in its
decisional place among candidates for knowledge. Hume's *Dialogues Concerning Natural Religion* and Kant's First Critique stand monumentally
as the dethroners of knowledge as ways of knowing God, but they challenge
instead the finding of the deeper and more decisive faith that will be
genuinely open to the testimony of knowledge. The aging Whitehead
tirelessly stressed our need to become "post-Kantian." I am myself convinced that the deepest stress of Kant was on the fullness of interpretation
that also observed the critical canons of thinking. Neither Hume nor especially Kant can be held responsible for their being used *to ward off* warranted faith in the name of knowledge. Jaspers fascinatingly reaches out
for the fuller unity of the transcendent, the encompassing, beyond knowledge, by means of an ever open philosophical faith, and Heidegger in
Discourse on Thinking goes beyond *Gelassenheit zu den Dingen* to "openness to the mystery" which involves *Edelmut*, nobility of mind. The cal-
culative reason for him gives way to the meditative, and thinking ends in
thanking! The best philosophers still seek the deeper and fuller truth
behind and beyond the ontological argument.

Theologians have often been cowed by philosophers of many kinds who have offered spurious and unwarranted lines of reasoning. We need now to clear away the roadblocks to warranted faith in order that life and civilization may flourish once again. There are roadblocks of both false interpretation and of guilt. Christian theology can become strong and man's life of faith effective only when once again man dares to accept and to develop creatively the ultimate and eventual equation of true thought, the really real, and genuine goodness. Man's life and knowledge have to advance to the point where once again he can live in a constructive atmosphere where the presupposition of his life and society are the truths that underlie the instinct behind the ontological argument and the classical equation generally. I believe that the most profound witness of the philosophic tradition as well as that of the great religions of the world is that deepest seeing and truest being ultimately belong together and that goodness must also have its part. The full significance of the basic drive behind the ontological argument, however, can come to fruition only for those who see that the Analytical Word can find full meaning only in connection with the Historical and the Potential.

Time and Eternity

TIME AND ETERNITY have always been puzzling and yet tantaliz-
ing topics. What is time? What is eternity? Can man know eternity
from within time? If he can, what is the relation between them? Are they
congruent or radically separate?

There seems to be no one satisfactory definition of time in the overall
sense. The attempt to understand time encounters all the problems that
beset knowledge in general. Time is both objective and subjective, and
indeed, comes in forms that combine both aspects of experience. Both
Plato and Aristotle thought of time as measurable succession, governed
principally by the movement of the heavenly bodies. We can count on
night and on day, on winter and on summer. Bergson, however, thought
of time basically as concrete duration, the experience of time from within.
The former experience is objective; the latter, subjective. One can be
measured and compared; the other is private and relative.

But, indeed, objective time, as in Einstein's view of it, has its relative
aspect, since we cannot establish at the same time both absolute motion
and absolute position, while subjective experience, on the other side, is
had in an objective, communal continuum. Not only that; time varies
from the astrophysical yardstick of sidereal events to what Whitehead has
called the long second of an inframolecular occurrence. Biological time,
as for example the age of sexual maturation, differs from psychological
time. A girl can be advanced in one age and retarded in the other. The
clocks in her differ. One may run fast and the other slow. Medical age (or
time), again, is quite another matter as the rate of recuperation shows.
People heal at different rates not synchronized with chronological age.

Philosophers, too, speak of *chronos* (clock time) and *kairos;* neutrally
or formally empty time, in the former case, and filled or concretely occu-
pied time, in the latter. These terms might also be applied distinctly to
personal experience and to communal experience; or they might be
thought of in terms of historic epochs coincidental and yet noncongruent.
The subjective scope may vary widely from the objective occasion. Or
philosophers may speak of *telos* as the goal and direction of time. Time,

then takes on a goal-meaning, from within, for the objective continuum. That goal-meaning, in turn, may be defined as the *logos,* the concept, the purpose of time. All these approaches to the question of time are significant and in their own place irreplaceable.

Our approach here, however, is going to be none of these specifically. Our perspective on time for our present purposes is from the point of view of the New Testament categories. We want especially to ponder the implications of the Universal Word for the questions of time. What happens if we try to think of time in terms of love, in terms of spirit, in terms of personal purpose?

From the point of view of love, time is the means and medium for learning love while eternity is the full life of love. Eternity is then fullness of time because it is fullness of love. Time is an aspect of the pedagogical process which provides the occasion for growth in the experience of love. Time is the opportunity for choosing love. Eternity is the living of love. At this point we must be exceedingly careful. We want time definitely to be viewed as adjectival to person and process. That time has no being in and by itself is a definitive assertion. Time has no reality of its own apart from concrete durations of sentient and nonsentient events. Unless we are careful we can fall into the trap of considering time the fields in which experience lies, as with Immanuel Kant, with time then the field of pedagogical process and eternity the field of the mature living of love. In such a view time is at least semireal or semiobjective. It is, to be sure, not separate from and yet constitutive of cosmic process and personal experience. Kant therefore was feeling for some genuine aspect of experience when he called time and space the fields in which experience *lies.* He had no absolute space and time. Newton's *Principia,* in the main, stands for such an objectivist position. Alfred North Whitehead grew lyrical in his prophetic, poetic rejection of this in the lectures on the topic during his last years of teaching. Perhaps Newton's position is less bald or stark than Whitehead's interpretation of him, but his objectivist position, in any case, contrasts sharply with the adjectival process view of George Herbert Mead. Mead placed the locus of time in the present and considered the nature of time the continually stirring, so to speak, of the dough of process. Whitehead's chapter on time in *Adventures of Ideas* is particularly insightful, but for the background of the kind of position we are here developing few works can be more suggestive and stimulating than Bergson's *Creative Evolution* and *Matter and Memory.*

If God is love, spirit, and personal purpose, and if God is ultimate as the eternal Life from which these categories are derived, or so to speak sequestered, then we must arrive at some understanding of time as primarily subjective in nature and meaning, at least as mainly adjectival, even while offering secondarily some objective continuum for the learning and living of love. Obviously, we do not wish to deny or do away with *chronos* as part of time, although it may not be directly or centrally *theological* time. Can we find the clue to eternal time, God's time, *theological time,* which is completely adjectival to his experience, and thus at its heart entirely subjective, and which is yet also intrinsically generative of the semiobjective kinds of time which pertain to pedagogical process? If we can do so, time will be appropriately subjective and genuinely adjectival even while offering all needful objective structures, albeit these structures, in turn, are mostly functional and provisional in character. With Kierkegaard in his *Concluding Unscientific Postscript* and in his *Philosophical Fragments* we view time from the final affirmation that "truth is subjectivity." Our criteriological category of time is adjectival to the eternal Love. And yet such subjectivity is precisely creative of pedagogical order. Such Love, in sharing, creates the proper conditions for learning love. Eternity defines the fullness of time as the fullness of love, although time in the pedagogical sense is both partially of the nature of eternity and partially an objective means to it. Earthly or human time is necessarily a mixed category. Blake poetically calls time "the grace of eternity."

All objective order is, then, adjectival, either as descriptive of the living of love or as the continuum for the learning of love. Time has accordingly only a derived, functional reality or, at most, only a descriptive reality as the experience of the living of love. Eternity is fullness of time; therefore it is mature time and right time. Eternity is ultimate time as to both its meaning and its direction. Eternity is perfection of quality; it is the life of the Universal Word. The Universal Word means the fullness of time in the fullness of love. Since ultimate time is universal time, eternity is both ultimate and universal time. Eternity is time fulfilled by maturity in the experience of love; it is the maturation of time as love. Such love, we have said, is qualitatively perfect. It involves no spatialization. It is not objectified, being beyond finite existence. All love of finite existence is pedagogical and therefore unfulfilled and imperfect. Eternity is the fulfillment when that which is imperfect will be done away. Eternity is God's time as perfect Love, while time involves the imperfections pertinent to God's pedagogy.

Only pedagogical time has a future, in the sense of what is unfulfilled, lacking. Only the learning of love has a focused direction and pedagogical directives. Only love in time has a past. The past is unfulfilled experience, pointing in the present toward the future. Pedagogical time knows the repeating the past forward, which is Kierkegaardian "repetition." Such repetition is needed. Time is the chance to learn love, in Leibniz' terms *"chargé du passé et gros de l'avenir."* Future and past as media of growth belong to time only. Eternity, however, is the consummation of the learning of love in the living of love. In eternity time is fulfilled. Growth in

God, ever, is eternity in time, neither eternity nor time in eternity. The learning of love knows ignorance, error, suffering, and sin. The fullness of time is beyond all pedagogical lacks and distortions of time. Eternity is the end of time without the means. It is the product beyond the process. It is the fullness of experience, the fullness of love, without the pedagogy.

What, nevertheless, can eternity mean in terms of the full living of love? It means, first of all, that what *is*, is defined in terms of love; being, in this sense, is understood through love, not love through being. God is love. The ultimate is love, the full universal reality is love. Western philosophy has deified substance in terms of being. Eastern philosophy has deified non-being. Process philosophies have deified becoming. Deeper, more fundamental, and more fulfilling than them all is love. To be sure, love cannot be understood apart from spirit and personal purpose, which are ultimate factors ingredient to love. They are all intrinsic, ultimate categories of reality. God is love, but he is love as Spirit and as personal purpose. Or God is love as personal Spirit. Eternity, in contradistinction from time, is reality found and reality lived.

Love, then, *is*. Love is, as it was in the beginning, is now and ever shall be. There is no beginning to Love, to God as Love. In the beginning God, Love. There is no ending of Love. Love never ends and never fails, for love is ultimate. Love cannot end, for it has no beginning; it is eternal. Ultimately Love, being eternal, is universal; ultimately love, being eternal, was universal; ultimately love, being eternal, will be universal. Love eternally creates, but creates no eternal beginning. Love is fullness of time ever. There can then be no beginning of time as eternity. There is no filling time full to make eternity. There can be no beginning of God's time, eternity. There can be beginnings *within eternity* in the sense of the creation of pedagogical time; time for learning love. Learning love is time, not eternity; eternity in time, not time in eternity. It is Love that creates and Love is eternal. That Love creates eternally means that there is no time when Love does not create. Or put it the other way, when Love does not create there is no time. We must not spatialize time, time is not extensive; only the conditions of time are a matter of genetic continuity, of chronological extension. What we are discussing is rather time as quality. Love is eternity with the will and capacity for creation. The nature of Love is to create. *Creativity belongs to the nature of Love.*

Love, however, creates freely and responsibly. Love may endow creation with the secondary power to create so that seeds and species are wasted in the eternal generosity of love's creativity. But the higher love moves, the more responsible and selective it becomes. God himself creates directly only on the highest pinnacles of love, not even on the pinnacles of human existence, his children by creation, but only on the level of children by adoption, where Love begets love and Spirit meets with spirit, and where

personal Purpose is recognized and accepted. The secondary creation has
no permanent status; it lacks true being; substance is pedagogical: from
nothing, for something, to nothing. Substance is form of flux for the
temporary purposes of pedagogy. Thus natural creation lacks true time,
the time of love. Even though human history as a whole moves toward
true time, it lacks such time and distorts it. Only spiritual history—the
history that is learning love—partakes of true time directly. Only growth
in love is true time, even pedagogically.

Measurable succession, to think with Plato and Aristotle, is the moving
shadow of eternity. Plato's *Timaeus* is a dynamic flow of creativity. Measurable succession, however, is an order of what is substantial, of what is
objectified, and is therefore actual but not real, appearing for a time and
for a purpose, but not permanently of love. It is actual and, in the final
analysis, actuality is irreal rather than real. Within our scheme of understanding, it is for love in the tertiary sense that it helps provide the
medium and thus the means for learning love, but it partakes neither in
the growth of love as such nor of the final living of love. It is thus neither
of time nor of eternity. To call actuality merely *maya* is, however, to
denigrate the meaning of creation, while, on the other hand, to call such
order real is to substantialize time and to deify not only the creature but
even the means for the creature. Actuality basically is neither illusory nor
real. God has a purpose with nature, but nature as such has no purpose.
Thus there can be no history of nature or natural history in the final or
full sense of any growth of love, of any moral summons, of any decision
for personal purpose.

The indirection of nature is God's needed veil behind which he hides.
The hiding is real for the creature, but not for God. Indirection provides
freedom for man through ignorance (but also can provide freedom
through knowledge), not in the sense that God cannot see through a veil,
speaking symbolically, of course, but in the sense that God turns his back
to allow needful privacy. God turns his back until man, mostly through
the indirections of nature, becomes willing to face him. Thus the order of
nature, in time, is neither *maya*, illusion, nor real *as* time, for or as, love.
Nature is more than *maya*, even conceived of at its highest as empirical
actuality, while also less than the world of I-thou. Nature is instrumental,
not intrinsic. Time *for* love is pedagogically time for growth in love; and
time *as* love is the living of love. Measurable succession is, rather, the
objective condition which occasions the time for love. The time of love
always transcends spatialized succession. It is concrete duration. It is a
direct spiritual relation within an insubstantial reality where relations are
not quantifiable but only qualitatively real.

There can accordingly be no real beginning of time with or in physical
creation. What comes from nothing goes to nothing. Nothing of reality

is added and nothing is lost. This aspect of nature gives meaning to *maya*. Actuality is quantifiable but not real. It serves a purpose for time, but is not in time or for time. It is by eternity, but not in or of eternity. It is not therefore, as such, in or of love. It is not at all of the nature of time or eternity except to facilitate the making of time, the birth of love, which is ever nontemporal. Love transcends time. God never began to create and he never will stop. Such a statement, to be sure, in no wise involves continuous creation. Creation characterizes love, but is not love. Time is not mathematical. It is not quantifiable. Creation adds nothing either to time or to eternity. Love is, was, and ever shall be. It is no fixed quantity. It is no substance. It is beyond process. From the point of view of measurable succession God is always halfway through eternity. If such creation were real beyond being actual, there could be an unsolvable problem of mathematics. On the one hand, any new creation, in the aspect of reality beyond actuality, adds one, and therefore introduces a series, providing the occasion for the logic that calls somewhere for a first creation, but also for a logic within eternity where what is perpetually inexhaustible can never either begin or reach an end. We are therefore left with a logical contradiction, an antinomy that cannot be solved from within time. If the number one cannot be reached, then there is no true new creation, no real beginning. Somehow creation is intrinsic to Love, always without being either accidental or forced. Nor can Love's creation be accumulative without being serial. Yet it is real. What then?

Philosophers and theologians have worried and fought over this issue. Some have maintained a theory of special creation and disregarded the arbitrary status of that creation. Such a creation never defines the nature of God as love, as *by nature creator*, but only sticks out, so to speak, like a sore thumb. Others have opted for eternal creation, but have undermined the status of creation by refusing to consider the logical dilemma of their choice. Such exhaustlessness, where the adding does not involve any retrospective subtracting, stresses the eternity of God but makes eternity itself problematic in terms of quantification. Still others have made God timeless, and thereby have in effect denied the full life of love, his fullness of time, or his timefulness. They have defined God as the absence of quantification, with time as genetic spatialization. Such ways out have felt for some partial truth on the pedagogical level but have failed to find the positive meaning of eternity as the fullness of love. They have forfeited the living God. Such positions have made God timeless rather than timeful and have robbed him of life, of being the living God, the living Love. Others, again, like Gregory of Nyssa, have evaded the final problems by insisting that the problems of time begin with time. Rather they end with time, in time, by time's becoming full, by love's maturing.

There has been truth in all these theories, as we shall see, but none has grasped the heart of the matter. Only the full truth puts the problems in their proper places and shows the measure of any attempt at solution. Only God as love and personal spirit can provide the perspective from which to understand the nature of eternity. Only eternity, the standard of time, defines pedagogical time. Only pedagogical time provides the truth for grasping measurable succession as the means for time, for growth in love.

Eternity, then, is the living of love fully and maturely. Eternal life is the genuine life of love. What matters is not place. What matters is not space. Heaven is the symbol of the fulfillment of life. Heaven is the authentic living of love, or, since true life is the life of love, heaven is true life. Time cannot "get into" eternity. Spatial metaphors must suggest rather than say qualitative relations. We even conceive of "relations" as spatial rather than qualitative. Such are the problem and prejudice of language. Time, in any case, is the not yet of learning love. But eternity must "get into" time both as direction and as partial attainment; otherwise there would be no growth in love. Otherwise love could not be learned in freedom. The partial and distorted cannot be present in the perfect without spoiling that perfection while the perfect, on the other hand, can penetrate the imperfect, directing and correcting it. The perfect can come as the fulfilling reality, through and within the imperfect, both to fulfill it and to end it. Eternity as the fullness of time qualitatively transforms the meaning of time. Eternity categorically transcends pedagogical time. If, so to speak, the sinner enters the community of perfect men, there is no longer a perfect community; but if the saint enters the community of sinners, that community as a whole is still imperfect even though it is now in some respect perfect. In the case of life, however, there is some perfection everywhere in the sense that God has "not left himself without a witness." There is no person or place so dark that God is not there in some sense.

But is God as love necessarily present as love? Yes, and again no. God is nowhere and nothing except love. But he is love both directly and indirectly. He is eternity for time. He is love indirectly as the creator and sustainer of pedagogical processes in nature and persons. Since he is there in some sense that situation is that far touched by perfection. His being there and working there, even through the indirections of Spirit, even as spirit in general, is the outcome of his love. It is the outgo of his love creating the conditions for the outcome. It is the invitation of his love, even indirectly through the long learning process. Therefore even nature and human history at their worst, so to speak, are touched by the infinite compassion and are serving the eternal purpose. Love, at its center, is personal. That is why we call God metaphorically "Father." That is why "abba," as Bishop Robinson has stressed in *The New Reformation?,* is an expression, an outcry, central to genuine Christian worship. But the personal purpose of love prepares through indirection the conditions of freedom which alone can make love to be born and to grow. The preparation is the pedagogical process wherein God is present mostly as spirit. Therefore eternity can be present and is present even in the means and media for time. Eternity is present even in *chronos* to use and to guide its content.

Chronos, or empty time, clock time, is not true time. It is adjectival neither to the perfect, or the mature life of love, nor primarily to the experience of growth in love. *Chronos* never enters life directly. It is the condition for the growth and the decisions of life. Thus *chronos* partakes of the nature of time indirectly, but is never either normative time (eternity) or pedagogical time (growth in love). *Chronos* is the chance to learn love, not the learning of it. Possibly the New Testament had this condition in mind when it called succession, *stoicheion,* an enemy. Mature love always transcends succession. Perfection is completion, not in the sense of being done with living reality, with creative experience. Perfection of love is no flattening of experience, no merely having the problems and evils of life abolished. But mature love, the definition of perfection, never knows the unsatisfaction and dissatisfaction of waiting for the fulfillment. The fulfillment is here; it has come; it is lived.

Pedagogical time knows anxiety. It is touched by restlessness; it suffers from lack of satisfaction. It is spoiled by distortion and destruction. It is longing, touched with fear. Whatever hope it has is only partial and touched with foreboding. Only perfect love can cast out fear. Only full love can fulfill life. Eternity is open to pedagogical time. Pedagogical time partakes of eternity. It is, so to speak, imperfectly distributed, being more received in some than in others, as they are taken up into eternity, or lifted into love. Love, for that matter, is more understood in some than in others. Mere succession in itself is neither good nor bad. As a means and medium for learning love it is part of the stuff of process and therefore instrumentally good. But the instrument can be used for good or for ill. The experience is determined by the choices and the growth of the person, not by the mere succession which is only the occasion for choice and for growth. Love as such always transcends succession.

In full life there is no waiting for the better. In the fulfilling experience of love there is, rather, the experience of perfect satisfaction. It is not only as though this moment could go on forever—for there is no sense of time —but it is also the experience of fulfillment that transcends even the consciousness of time. Time is killed by eternity by becoming timeful

rather than timeless. Love becomes so real and so right, living so satisfactory in the present, that the experience of succession whether as fear or
as hope is quite overcome.

Love is; that is eternity. Love becomes; that is time. When love becomes, full time becomes eternity. Not that time makes eternity but rather
that eternity fulfills time. God is; that is eternity. Man becomes; that is
time. Man becomes man by learning love; in such a process time comes
to the threshold of eternity but cannot enter it. God's love comes down
to man; it comes into human life; that is Incarnation. But Love comes in
condescension, under the conditions of finitude, not as eternity. When
God's finite word becomes full, of course, when the word that comes is
the Universal Word, time has been reached conclusively by eternity.
Eternity has entered time, not time eternity. On the level of the means
for time, on the level of pedagogical process as mere succession, the temporal occasion for choice and growth, there can be neither Incarnation,
nor incarnation. On the level of time, of learning love, there can be incarnation, the imperfect understanding and acceptance of the love of God.
Eternity enters time, then, not as Love but as spirit in general in the
mechanism of clock time as an aspect of nature, as adjectival to natural
process, neither as real time which is historic nor as eternity which is history fulfilled in eternity by the maturation of love. Eternity also enters
time in varying measures as the growth of love. But neither succession nor
pedagogical time as such can enter eternity. Eternity remains sovereignly
eternal, perfection, perfect. Succession and pedagogical time have to stop
on the threshold of eternity; time can enter eternity only by being filled
by eternity. Maturation as the learning of true time (love, God's time, the
living of love) crowds out the conditions and imperfections of time.

What can eternity mean, moreover, in terms of fullness of love? Only
God can know that, and those who have matured within his love. God is
and is eternally love. Finite spirits add nothing (no thing, no substance,
no quantity, no process) when they enter eternity, for they are nothing.
They cannot be quantified; they are not substance; they are finite only
because although they *are* spirits, they *have* being. Their being comes
from nothing and disappears into nothing. Within pedagogical process
or the conditions of time such spirits live an objectified existence. This
existence is subject to addition, to serial addition or subtraction. But
do not personal spirits add to eternity? The objectified disappears, becomes nothing. But does not each spirit, so to speak, add one numerically?
How else can it be if finite spirits are distinct? Far from it! Life in the
spirit is neither substance nor number. It is never spatialized *as spirit*. It is
never a matter of inventory *as spirit*. It is neither extension nor abstract
number. The infinite Spirit is not a matter of being the whole to the
many separate spirits. Such thoughts belong to the realm of either sub-

stance or numerical distribution. Conjunction and disjunction belong to the realm of existence.

When we use finite language in terms of the world we know that we use it only suggestively. Love makes use of the finite order. Love uses physical bodies and brains. Creation is the proper medium for learning love through indirection. But the meaning of love at its center is spiritual, the touch of spirit on spirit, of personal meaning on personal meaning, of personal purpose on personal purpose. But all these spirits, meanings, and purposes are within the one reality of Spirit, transcending all experiences of extension or mathematics, of coordinate extension or genetic succession. They center in life as such; in love; in fulfillment. They most deeply inhere in what the Buddhist calls "true suchness," in *nirvana* or heaven. They reach up to heaven and are reached into by heaven, for into heaven itself they cannot enter until the end of time. Eternity remains eternity, and time, time, until time, by the ingression of love under the conditions of pedagogical process, finally by the process of love sloughs off the conditions and frustrations of process; then time is transmuted into eternity. Life in love is creative experience beyond creation. It is the realization which is the end of all the striving.

This eternal life of love, furthermore, is beyond the dichotomy of subject and object. Even within pedagogical process, incarnation, and preeminently Incarnation, depends upon the possibility of the coinherence which involves the genuineness of cosubjects. Spirit interpenetrates spirit. "I live; yet not I, but Christ liveth in me." "For to me to live is Christ." "I and my Father are one." The works I do the Father within me is doing. Even in human history are thus the beginnings and even some conclusive fulfillment of the congruence of spirit with Spirit. Only when this happens does love reign. Love never reigns externally. Love always reigns within. Love never reigns *over*. Love always reigns *with*. Thus the highest and most satisfactory experiences in human history are the foretaste of eternity. In them eternity is most present. Thus we can at least guess at the radiance of life when there is general fulfillment. What radiance? When love reigns supreme in a community! Then it is not a matter of place but of condition. Not of quantity but of quality. Such a community becomes less and less numerical and more and more a total all-encompassing experience of the unity of the Spirit, of the "one Love," as Jakob Boehme writes, "which is Christ in us all."

In eternity love, spirit, and the personal are, so to speak, congruent or coincidental. This is of course spatial language. There is in eternity no diversity of function for the sake of, or in connection with, pedagogical process. The love that goes out into process, in a manner of speaking, spreads out into the impersonal and the personal, into nature and history; but in eternity, to use the same language, they come together again. They become congruent and coincidental. The nature of true love is to be related without being relative, like the nature of the Trinity. Love is beyond the one and the many. God is the prototype of both aspects of love. We can feel for, but never know from our side of time, what eternity as full love can be.

If the impersonal spirit, the pedagogical medium, is not present in eternity but present only in time, does this fact mean that eternity is through and through personal? Is eternity, to use a current expression, all I-thou and in nowise I-it? Is the full life of love pure consciousness? Is eternity subject to subject? Substance cannot have relations without being relative, but neither can personality confront personality without some division of subject and object or subject *and* subject. Spirit, on the other hand, can be relational without being relative; and personal Spirit can also be related without being relative. Relative in this sense, of course, means deficient or imperfect. The deepest meaning of the Trinity, for example, is surely that God is personal Spirit beyond the limitations of personality. Spirit (and later I shall give a fuller definition) has the capacity to be selfsame while creating and communicating with what is other. Spirit has the capacity to enter and to coinhere the other without being the other. Spirit can be total identity with genuine distinctions. Spirit is the primary power for unity, the principle and power of identity, which yet knows the richness of distinction.

Thus in finite life we know separation. We cannot, to be sure, know complete separation. Solipsism is not a viable doctrine. Obviously it is utterly self-defeating. Nothing is just itself. In some sense everything must be related. Exaggerated separation characterizes the worst contention of substance thinking. But we can know the divisions and frustrations of our kind and measure of finitude. They are actual. They are *there*. Some of this kind of separation is in the nature of creation; other aspects of it come from sin; they are then of our own making. Things and personalities separate. *But* there is unity in the spirit. When we are not in this unity, of identity, we are not in the unity of the spirit; we are not in eternity; we are not *in love*. We are thus out of the spirit, not, to be sure, out of the sustaining spirit of creation, not out of the pedagogical spirit of time, not out of the growing in love, not out of the process of learning love. Nicolai von Hartmann held that consciousness separates while the spirit unites. Both claims, however, are ambiguous. Spirit always unites in itself, but it sustains the pedagogical world where there is division. And in some sense spirit is really there, too. Even though there is separation, especially in substance terms or in terms of personal relations, we cannot deny that the spirit is present in some manner and in some strength. When we enter the personal Spirit of love, there is always identity of spirit and unity of spirit. This spirit defines this mode of being. Distinctions within the identity do not divide; they only enrich.

What then of personal consciousness? Does it necessarily divide? It does, if it is merely an individual consciousness. If consciousness is a matter of a limiting self-consciousness, it must divide by its very nature. It is then numerical in nature. It puts the self over against others and perhaps over against creation. We then have a bald subject-object dichotomy. But self-consciousness can be transcended in such a manner that it no longer divides. The self can be conscious of the other, of the community, of the cause, of God in such a way that he is part of the larger whole. He is not conscious of self as separated. He coalesces in his field of consciousness. He is not conscious of self as divided or over against. The self forms no barrier. He is, of course, *conscious,* for love is on the level of personal reality, but his consciousness in full love is such a total consciousness or such a consciousness of the total, in the quality of its manifestation, that the self is a natural aspect of the field to which it fully belongs. When love is full and when man is not existing in a substantive world, the consciousness of love will no longer be burdened by self-consciousness. Self-consciousness in this sense belongs to pedagogical time. It is of earth earthy. Symbolically it dies with the body. The Buddhists have made much of the fact that full *moksa,* or deliverance, cannot be obtained until the desires of the body have been quenched; therefore death is the point of entering into *moksa* in some sense under the right circumstances in the case where enlightenment has already taken place.

Love, then, is the relation of enrichment in the Spirit which transcends individual and group consciousness in the limiting sense of self-consciousness or in the manner of overagainstness. Love is like being at a great spectacle where the person surely is conscious but is so wrapped up in the occasion that it never occurs to him that he is a self, and where his identification with the group is so real and full that both he and the group are enriched by his participation. Thus we can worship together at a level where consciousness of difference, whether of rite or creed, can quite disappear. A person can be lost as a separate individual in the common reality of worship. Man can be raised into oneness through the one Spirit. Such experiences naturally are only tokens of what can be. The full reality of personal relations in love which are not relative but completely fulfilling and enriching can be conceived of only in terms of the full transcendence of eternity over time. In time we can only experience the temporary transcendence of consciousness. In the consciousness of full love one is not conscious of self or of consciousness!

Tillich has termed transpersonal the fact that being itself is not everywhere personal. Others have accepted this usage. Perhaps transpersonal, however, is a term that can connote what the transcendence of the personal consciousness can mean even where there is no lack of it. Consciousness in earthly experience flickers and comes in drops. William James and Whitehead particularly noted this fact. Consciousness depends upon bliks of experience, to think with Hare and van Buren, ever selective, ever shift-ing. The consciousness of eternal love can be constantly rich and enrich-ing insofar as relation to the whole is never broken, i.e., insofar as per-sonal reference never becomes divisive; but all consciousness partakes of the identity of spirit and the unity of spirit. Thus distinctions enrich without separating. "The sea shall be no more!"

But are not personal spirits finally units? Why otherwise do we use the plural? Is not to be distinct a matter of being different in angle, so to speak, in background, so to speak, in creative contribution, so to speak? No, on the very contrary! Even the concepts of units, of aspects, of angles, are the concepts of the created world. Such concepts pertain to the con-ditions for time, and of time, of seeming substance and of seeming per-sonality. Eternity as the full living of love has no units because there is no substance and no numerical mathematics. Nonsense! Some would shout nonsense! And nonsense it is and therefore true. Not that we have joined Tertullian and Luther in undermining reason but rather that reason cannot finally find fulfillment until it operates within the category of spirit rather than of substance, and spirit knows no things, no sense, as intrinsic to reality. In the reality of nowhere and nothing where eternity lives, where dwells nonsubstantiality, "there!" is fullness of identity, of sameness with the eternal Spirit which yet never reduces sameness to tameness. Identity of Spirit at the core of distinction makes the distinc-tion internal and not external. The distinction is no separate thing, or substance. How then can personal spirits be entities? Are not entities numerical?

Life in God is actually oneness with and in God, a being God at the core of distinction as well as being distinct within the sameness. "I and my Father are one." "That they may be one, even as we are one." Quite true; and such oneness is both real and nondivisible while being genuinely distinct. Spirit cannot be divided like a substance. God feels through every distinction in eternity and becomes infinitely enriched thereby; but every distinction, as distinction, also experiences feeling the whole, while the whole feels the part. Eternal life is life in God, with all life of mature love being in the fullness of life, which is so completely and maturely *Love,* that the One and the Many are One and the Same and yet also One and distinct. Personal consciousness, however much freed from finite limitations and heightened by transformation in eternity, is both real and enriched and yet also in full accord with the sameness of God as the One Spirit. Eternal life is thus equally life in God and life in love. It is life as the One and the many, neither one nor many but coinherently both. A spiritual entity is both one in Love, and truly identical, and yet distinct as a consciousness, a perspectival awareness from within unity and distinc-tion that adds enrichment to the one by the many without becoming a separate individuality. The total inheres perfectly in the part and the part is the total. Such language, however, comes from our world of substance and space and cannot adequately describe the nonsubstantial, contrapletal (I shall clarify the term later) relations of personal Spirit to personal spirits in the identity or unity of Love. Time becomes fulfilled by eternity and as eternity, and thereby ceases to be time as such. Eternal life is man's destiny, and surely, as Tillich did say, it is neither just the cessation nor the continuation of personal consciousness. Quantity yields to quality, contradiction to contrapletion. The basic relation in and among the One and the many is a condition, a quality, capable of becoming objectified, or of creating the conditions for quantification.

What have I said, then, in sum, on the topic of time and eternity? I have said that if God is love and if eternity is God's time, eternity is the time of love. It is the fullness of love. I have also claimed that time as distinct from eternity means the learning of love. Time basically, then, is defined in terms of concrete duration, not as measurable succession, not as genetic experience directionally and not as clock time. Clock time is the means and medium for learning love; it is the occasion for time as nature is the occasion for history. Thus succession is the occasion for time and perhaps as such "instrumental time," but not intrinsic time. Intrinsic time is either preparatory time, the experience of learning love, or the fullness of time, the living of love. Instrumental time becomes bad time when it is viewed as intrinsic time. For this reason I have preferred not even to define the instrumental as time itself, but as an instrument of and ingredient in pedagogical time. The definitions could be otherwise, but it seems preferable to highlight time as primarily adjectival to personal spirit and not to natural creation, to the personal rather than to process. Even as the law becomes evil when substituted for the gospel, although the law is needed in its proper place, even so "natural time" becomes *schlechthinnige Zeit* when it becomes a matter of central theological definition.

I have also said that time can never enter eternity even though eternity can and must enter time. It is the nature of eternity to create, to enter and to redeem time, but pedagogically from within the conditions of time. The manner of this relationship I have yet to discuss both in its context and in the setting of the destiny of man. Eternity enters time as directional and as fulfilling. It can lead man to heaven's door, but time can never enter there as time. When time enters "heaven," time is transmuted into eternity. What goes through the door is eternity, so to speak, having transformed life into love, or having fulfilled a finite life by the maturity of love. Thus what enters is eternal life. The life outside is only partially and distortedly eternal. The life inside is the fullness of love and therefore also the fullness of life. Man reaches perfect maturity. He enters the life of God even as God has now entered and fulfilled his life. None of this discussion, of course, is spatial. It is symbolic, nonsubstantial, qualitative. The directional and the dimensional give way to what is *spiritual*. Our discussion is *spiritward*.

Eternity as love is personal in the sense of universal Word. It is a matter of personal Spirit, of the reality of the personal, of consciousness, beyond any present human comprehension. Martin Buber is surely right in maintaining that whoever is genuinely in the spirit will see the other, not as an "it," but as a "thou," but such seeing in fulfillment becomes a matter of not spiritual personality but personal spirit. Later we shall develop for this kind of relationship the concept of unimunity beyond both individualism and what Walter Muelder calls "communitarianism." Flesh and blood, of course, cannot inherit the Kingdom of God; nor can our kinds of thought and consciousness! There will be the complete transcendence of personality in the fulfillment of the personal. The power of the spirit will so transmute our present experience that the subject-object dichotomy will be done away even as subjects will all be transported into the one unity of Spirit with perfect distinctions. Even distinctions as a plural noun reflects our present existence. We have either the singular or the plural but eternity has neither nor both. There will be relations without relativity.

As in the Trinity, God transcends the dichotomy of the one and the many, being perfect Love, the One, and at the same time also the distinctions which are real. In eternity there will be perfect perichoresis or coinherence. The distinctions, then, are so in the unity of the one Spirit, so identical at the heart of the new nature and consciousness, that there is no numerical separation of the Spirit from the spirits when they are one and the same and yet distinct. When God becomes all in all, even the Son will be subjected, and yet even so the Son will persist as eternally begotten before all ages, the eternal generation of the Son, in the one Spirit which is simultaneously the identity of the one and the many and the distinction of the one and the many. Thus the personal distinction of experience will persist and yet will also be abolished in that fullness of love which is both plural and yet always one, and therefore neither plural nor one.

Love means consciousness of distinction without consciousness of separation; it involves awareness of the other without division. Love is oneness of the many and the many in oneness "without division and without confusion." Perfect love God alone knows in all its fullness; all that creatures can experience, at most, is to participate in that perfect Love. All love is of God and is God. Lives lived in love are of God and are God, not in the sense of sharing the "experience of God" as God lives it, but as sharing it as man can. Love is one in identity, as God is one, and love is for many, as God creates the distinction of the many. Man is thus not

God, in God's sense, even though the heart of man's life at its perfect best is constituted by God's presence. The distinction is there without division. Man is "filled with all the fullness of God" and in this sense is God, without being God in God's sense. Eternal life is eternal love. In this sense God constitutes the inmost nature of man, the identity providing the reality of the manifestation of the many; fullness of time is fullness of love. Eternal life is thus fullness of love. That fullness man can share. That fullness man can know. Such is the faith we have in God as the ever-faithful creator and fulfiller.

What that love can be like we cannot, of course, even imagine. What we mean by perfect love here may only be a foretaste so weak as to do no justice to the reality. God may have thousands of lives more for us to prepare for that love. He may have thousands of pedagogical processes leading to the mature life in eternity. God may even use the billions of possible planets to perfect his work. Man may, even so, find now that he is on the outskirts of that larger pedagogical preparation. Years before the astronomers talked in such a fashion I used to suggest that there may be many preparatory planets, perhaps even with some kind of space-time. Some of them may be characterized by more trying conditions (hell) and some may be characterized by better conditions (purgatory) than earthly existence, depending upon the kind of people we have become through the decisions we have made and the growth we have experienced. For us to think of the perfection of love in God from our present angle of vision, in any case, is not only presumptuous but preposterous. God's way before us is long beyond any belief. We see hardly to the nearest genuine curve in the road of God's pedagogy!.

Tillich's suggestion, already cited, haunts me, to the effect that life eternal is neither cessation nor continuation of our personal existence in earthly terms; it is a transformation of experience unthinkable from our present position of experience. In this life we have hardly learned to add one and one, so to speak, and we think that we can do unknown equations to the nth power! This affirmation is no evasion of knowledge; it is the affirmation of the richness of God. Thus it is rather childish in our terms to speak of the continuity of consciousness and the permanence of the personal. What can the making our consciousness and our personal experience normative to fulfillment *mean?* Eternal life, of course, can be nothing less than the best we know now. Therefore even our highest anthropic pictures must feed our hopes without disappointing us, for what will come will surely include and surpass any and every satisfaction that can be gained from anything we can imagine. When Ramanuja seized upon the upanishadic affirmation that Brahman "is to be served by all" to deny the idea of an undifferentiated ultimate, he may or may not have pictured the prolongation of our characteristic activities, but surely, whatever the picture, it is better than the flat, negative cancelation of man's hopes. And yet *and yet,* how utterly beyond our present imagination the final maturing of love must be!

Why, however, if God is love and if perfect love is perfect joy, should God spoil eternity by the creation of time? If love is perfect in God and if God ever is, if God is the perfect union of the one and the many ("the blessed Trinity," so to speak, which is the prototype of the one and the many, of the individual and the community), why should he ever violate that perfection by creating anything pedagogical? Surely this question is man's most difficult conundrum. Did God create just once in a mood of sentimental generosity (in terms of human foolishness) and that was his one mistake? Is creation an eternal mistake, God's bringing children, so to speak, into the world where there will be more sorrow than gladness? Does God himself have to create and suffer under the burden, suffer guilt from within and involvement without? Does not a onceness of creation seem quite arbitrary and not successful at that? If God can finally perfect creation, will he quit for good, having learned his bitter lesson? Or will God be forever stuck with a creation that cannot be salvaged entirely? Did God have a breakdown in eternity? Or is the glory of the result finally worth the suffering during the pedagogical process? Hedonism can at least be no final standard for *Love.* May God disregard the joy that is part of the full living of love, for a time and for a purpose? Unless love is perfect joy, however, *in some way,* it is not perfect. Was then that joy marred once, by creation, although it may never be again, when once the experiment finally becomes successfully concluded; or does God create by nature in such a way that love's joy is never full, always marred, always waiting for some imperfect creation to be concluded?

The trouble with all these approaches is that they start with consideration of the imperfections of process; they also assume that because man's love, anxious and incomplete, suffers, God's love must suffer as well. It assumes that saints on earth must be so involved and identified with man's suffering that they, too, can have no perfect joy here. Much of this kind of analysis comes from a view of relevance which is condescension. Love goes to the place or condition where man is and becomes as man is! All these views must change if we are to have a true and effective Christian faith and if the Universal Word is to fulfill all faiths, including the Christian. When love becomes incarnate, some think, it shares the human weaknesses even of love. Therefore it becomes weak with human weaknesses, and thus acceptable, but with little power to help. Bonhoeffer at one time developed such an analysis. All such analyses, however, are defective from the start. If a doctor became as sick as the patient and showed only by his involvement in the disease that he cared, he would not help that patient to get well. Sick with the patient's malady, he becomes as ineffective as the patient; remaining well he helps the patient both by his spirit and by his knowledge. Similarly God never helps by suffering like us. For our sakes he must keep "well" and strong, able to make us well under his victorious care.

The same is the case with the relation of God to the world and with the relation of perfect love to the problems and weakness of pedagogical process. Perfect love never loses its perfect joy which is its perfect nature. In *history,* because of its being in imperfect form, love loses its perfect joy and thereby also loses its perfect power. The more love becomes perfected even in human history the more it offers itself; that is its perfect joy, its perfect strength. If God knows what he is doing when he creates, he never regrets his deed. He affirms it with perfect joy. He does not have to approve the abuse of freedom in order to accept the use of freedom. Freedom cannot be used unless it can be abused. If creation is for God's sharing of his love, and thus his joy; if creation is the continual multiplying of God's joy where there is no continuation in the sense of the succession of time, and where therefore such words as "multiplication" speak only suggestively in terms of our human failings; if creation is the love of God becoming many in the one and one in the many—in the ever-throbbing heart of God—God must remain at the same time perfect love and perfect joy. Suffering and weakness can be in history only, and that only as means to the perfect end, "the joy set before." The more God is in history, therefore, the more his love is there as joy, as healing, as growth, as offer of consummation. The more the saints are perfected in the life of God the more they, too, become filled with the love which is the fullness of joy. Thus saints are more and more in eternity and therefore less and less injured and handicapped by the sufferings of love. They stand as doctors, healthy and equipped, to be with and for the suffering patients, but not to be injured by and made ineffective by their sufferings. Bonhoeffer is right rather when he points out that genuine theology must deal from strength.

Eternity, then, means that God is love. Eternity is God's time, its fullness. Time means the learning of love which, when it is consummated, becomes the living of love, which in turn means the living in God. Eternity within time means God's living consummately in the learner. Heaven is eternal love, living in love. Only thus can "God become man," or "eternity" enter "time." There is no descent which is not in fact primarily ascent; eternity in time really means time thus far transformed by eternity. Wherever love is lived, there is heaven. Heaven is a quality of life. God is nonsubstantial. Eternal life is nonsubstantial. Love is nonsubstantial. When God creates time he sees that it is very good.

God uses freedom to develop and to win love. Freedom requires the development of self-being that divides. It requires bodies that separate and lives that learn community as separate individuals. Individuals learn through indirection. They learn in nature through the consequences of their choices. Succession serves freedom by making choice available and the consequence of choice. Measurable succession makes possible the learning through indirection. Succession or *chronos* thus ministers to time, the learning of love. It is ingredient in the conditions for time's pedagogy. Separateness makes for anxiety. Division makes for frustration. Individuality makes for fear. All make possible envy, hate, aggressiveness, defensive dread. All these cause suffering, as well as the inadequacies and injuries of the body in the physical world. Thus succession serves time, the inner meaning of God's pedagogy of which succession is but the outer occasion. Therefore succession is either an enemy or a friend depending on its abuse or use.

Time, however, is never within eternity though eternity "enters" time. Time knows suffering, shortcoming, evil, rebellion, sin, fear, and faithlessness. Time knows these as ingredient in the pedagogy for eternity. But none of these can enter eternity. They are forever debarred at the gate of heaven. But eternity enters time, not as weakness, not as participant of sin, sorrow, and evil, for then, indeed, would time penetrate into eternity. Rather, eternity enters as joy, as healing, as helpfulness, as fulfillment. Love consorts with evil but cannot become evil. In Jesus' life, time was real; eternity entered his life only enough to suggest the peace and the joy which the world, or time as pedagogical, could not know. He was God's pointer. Gethsemane was still in time; Calvary was still in time; only the transfiguration before and the resurrection afterward pointed to the radical reality and relevance of eternity. In this sense of conclusive power eternity entered time, beginning to break time by eternity, or time entered eternity as fulfillment, ready to break away from time into eternity. Time became the accepted candidate for the fulfillment that becomes eternity by demolishing time as time.

When eternity enters time, love learns through suffering. Love learns through its own frustrations sufficiently to head toward its perfecting. God's love in man gives itself for man, but man suffers, being imperfect. He suffers in body; he suffers in spirit; he suffers by identification with the evils of man in time. Such suffering on the side of both the learner and the learner turned teacher—the object of love and the giver of love— is part of the imperfections of time and participates in the needful imperfections of love's pedagogy. But the more eternity "comes in" the more the mount of transfiguration becomes real and the more resurrection becomes effective in the life of the saint. Descent becomes steep ascent; condescension, transformation. Then the sound goes out: Touch me not by your imperfections, for I am still ascending. Eternity must come to you now in different terms. "My peace I give unto you," "receive ye the Holy

Spirit." Time cannot enter eternity, but eternity can more and more interpenetrate time. Eternity can come as rest in work, peace beyond sorrow, joy beyond all suffering. Eternity can never be full in time. Eternity can never enter time as eternity, only as time. From within time eternity is limited, but from within eternity there can be no limitation by time because perfection cannot be spoiled by imperfection.

Thus God creates out of strength. The Christian Scriptures and Plato's *Laws* agree! God shares his life out of love, of joy, of victory. Thus any creation out of eternity is merely the moreness of that which cannot either begin, for it ever is, or end, for it ever is. And that moreness cannot be numerical. Infinity is not added to, for love is quality not quantity. It is no substance, not even a bit, a *small* bit. It is an open and in no way a closed category, although only what is open can enter it.

Will, then, no life make a difference? Is creation after all only *seeming?* Is history *maya,* basically appearance, ultimately illusion? May it not be that the personal is real as experience although ever halfway through eternity, while the personal is never added to and love retains its eternal isness? Is the personal always the personal in being-itself, as Tillich seemed to say? Then have all spirits been before and ever are? Is the eternity of souls, taught by Hinduism and Mormonism, for instance, right after all? Is distinction merely the changing life of God, experienced ever anew through new finite consciousness? Exactly—to a point! The consciousness of personal distinction can be in time only, as the learning of love. Fullness of love is distinction through the One and the many without consciousness of distinction. Consciousness of distinction as distinction rather than the experience of the distinctiveness of love already involves a measure of separation. Eternity is perfection of life, of love, of spirit. Consciousness of our kind of individuality is in time only, never in eternity. Only the perfected, fulfilled distinction "inherits" eternal life.

Eternity alone is real and what that reality can be we cannot understand. It must yet surely be the reclaiming of the richness of that personal which is love's crowning beyond all individuality. It is the richness of qualitative differentiation which is true love, or love in eternity. In eternity nothing becomes. There can be no addition to eternity. It cannot be quantified or multiplied. Time adds nothing to eternity and yet eternity gives joy and rest, gives peace and love to time. Spirit is eternal; Spirit is One and ever is. *Love is Spirit as Spirit is.* There can be no adding to such love. It is qualitative and full. But such fullness can overflow into time (if we may reach over to incorporate a Neoplatonic metaphor) where love learns, suffers, is denied, is defeated, and is crucified. Erigena well advanced this search through both the Neoplatonic and the Christian. All truth everywhere is now candidate for fulfillment. Love perfected is God returning *through* the finite, but not *as* the finite, into the fullness of love.

God ever is selfsame as Love; the qualitative enrichment of his self-consciousness is no substantive addition to Love, nor is the finite self-awareness, the distinctiveness within love, mathematically or numerically distinct. It is Love seeing totally and through the manysidedness of love which comprises both one Love and distinctiveness within that one Love.

Love is; love lives. Love as Love cannot be born nor can Love die. Man's love can die, but Love never. Love goes out to man, learning love. Man, learning love, adds a dimension of experience to God's life without quantitatively increasing that life. It enriches that life which is ever full in richness. When eternity thus enters time it can work in time and return to eternity but never take time with it. The work in time is for time in order that eternity might be free to be eternity. Such is the purpose of creation. Eternity comes as perfect love, as joy, as victory, as healing, and stands with and for time without being soiled or spoiled by time. The fullness of love means resurrection as return to what is eternal, not to introduce the earthly, which becomes, into what cannot become. The Word can become flesh, but never the flesh, Word. Thus God is rich in and for the finite without sharing its weaknesses, without being of the flesh, and the finite can leave its body of death and, participating in the eternal, enter heaven, as participant of God's life, as the heir of eternity. Creation is real as the learning of love; eternity is real as the living of love. Love lives fully only beyond time, but love can live pedagogically in, with, and for time. Only the experience of love as beyond time even from within time, can make God real for experience and eternal life viable. All these concerns we must discuss at length in the chapter on consummation.

He who has transcended time in ecstasy and has known eternity in time can await that indescribable experience beyond present experience which means the participation in the life of God beyond flesh, the immortal swallowing up and destroying the mortal. The new body of distinction which is insubstantial, that being of the spirit in the Spirit where time stops, individuality that is done to death, and full love as the One in the many, that which ever is and ever shall be—*is* eternal life—what eye has not seen nor ear heard. Love is realized in time and thus learned and appropriated; it cannot be born; it is the acceptance of eternity into time while eternity alone returns to eternity, that time may forever die and eternity forever live.

CHAPTER

III

The Need for Identity

POSSIBLY OUR MOST important task not only for this day but for our entire age is the redoing of the categories of reality. On the whole the West has assumed substance as the category for formulating its total framework of thinking. Lately there has been a protest against substantive thinking, and our intellectual problems have been framed instead in terms of process. Another candidate as a framework for thought, moreover, has been energy, which has been conceived of as a common denominator for interpreting the world in inclusive terms. The East, on the other hand, has been operating in a very large measure with non-being and indeterminate being as basic approaches to understanding in final terms. The East has also thought dynamically in terms of an interdependent and interactive flow or flux, in terms of *maya* as an actuality of process which is nonsubstantial in nature. On this score there is much community of approach on the part of both Western and Eastern rejectors of substance and developers of process. All these candidates for ultimate frameworks need to be examined, to have their truth sifted and garnered, and then to be superseded and fulfilled, if possible, by some fuller approaches to our total understanding.

By substance I mean the understanding that reality consists of subjects that are real in themselves, possessing certain predicates which modify them. These subjects are not to be explained in terms of other entities. They need only themselves in order to exist and are themselves subjects: God, things or persons, that cannot have mutually contradictory predicates. They may be solid and static, or penetrable and dynamic. They may exchange parts and mix, be compounded or redone. But when they are subjects they are self-enclosed entities which persist consistently through change and, as such, may not be explained in terms of anything else. The history of substance is complex and exceedingly varied, even within thinkers, from Aristotle's *Categories* and *Metaphysics* to Austin Farrer's *Finite and Infinite*. The discussion of it by Descartes and Locke, for instance, requires lengthy treatment in detail, and many of these thinkers have seen the objections to substance and tried to guard against them. Both Descartes and Spinoza have recourse to divine substance and to a deterministic wholeness that belies the nominalism of the ultimacy of things or of finite persons. Spinoza's *deus sive natura* requires a most delicate and insightful treatment. But the careful study of the history of the idea of substance will show the prevalence of the general characteristics which we have offered as definition.

By process I mean contrariwise the conception of reality as totally interactive. Nothing can be explained as having separate being but only as totally related. Reality is a process and processes where all things must be understood in the dimension of time. There is no being except as becoming, however much there may be aspects of such becoming that transcend the process in certain respects. Thus in authentic process thinking there is no eminent being in the sense of aseity, or eternal self-sufficiency and ontological unrelatedness. Even God depends on creation as well as creation on him, and in full-fledged process thinking God can be no more than an aspect of and factor in creativity. Relations are both internal and intrinsic to process. The kind of basic Buddhist philosophy where empirical reality is totally interdependent, interactive, and interrelated best illustrates process thinking.

Whitehead is partly a process thinker; but he stressed emphatically to me that he had to have process *and* reality, and that although nothing escapes the ontological principle as explanation in terms of the process of actual entities or later "occasions of experience," such explanation for him, pertains only to the genetic division of experience. Teilhard de Chardin exhibits strong acceptance of process thinking, although he obviously also is more than a process thinker. Bergson is in many respects a strong example, especially in such books as *Creative Evolution* and *Matter and Memory*. Charles Hartshorne's *Man's Vision of God and the Logic of Theism* and *Divine Relativity* also exemplify our definition, especially as he has been interpreted by John Cobb and Schubert Ogden. Ogden's *The Reality of God* with its stress on Eminent Relativity is a prime illustration.

Process thinking is of utmost importance to the genuine understanding of experience, as is substance thinking. I hope to accept all I can from both, but as I develop the categories of spirit and love, along with the personal, I believe that they will establish the conviction that they both correct and fulfill substance and process alike. For our purposes these working definitions will suffice. It is well, however, to heed George Caird's warning in a discussion at Oxford, that substance and process thinking, insofar as they express Western and Eastern thinking, be not equally yoked. The West has used substance honorifically as referring to reality, whereas the East has deeply sought to go beyond process to abiding essentiality. The Western and contemporary treatment of process, however, is, rather, on the level of that of substance thinking.

Substance thinking has afforded us entrance to the question of being, and to be sure, this question is important. What *is?* Entities are. Substances are. Things are. What are they? How can they change? How are they related? Can a substance not be? Does its destruction in one form involve its persistence, possibly in terms of its ingredient powers, in the same or other forms within other entities? What is basic reality? Are there substrates like water, fire, air, or even heavenly forms, supreme beings, or the eminent reality of the one God? What is potentiality for change? Is sheer potentiality ultimately real? Can the most eminent being change? Can there be authentic possibility for change in that which is no matter what, in the really real?

Theology as reality's self-disclosure of what is ultimate and universal offers to answer these questions in terms of its *theos* and its *logos,* the meaning of what really is. The theology of the Universal Word answers in terms of its understanding a multidimensional ultimate. It speaks of God as Spirit, as Love, as Personal. The terms are the ways in the New Testament in which God is basically defined. Christian theology, at its fullest and best, offers to make our total experience meaningful in terms of the Universal Word, the Christ event, Incarnate Love. But these are not the general framework of Western metaphysics, indirectly or explicitly. Christian theology needs to generate its own philosophy; it should not forfeit its own inherent truth by being defined, framed, and exposited with a total framework alien to its own true nature.

When, therefore, Western thought poses the problems of what really is in terms of substance, theologically in terms of Supreme Being, or at least in terms of eminent reality, then Christian theology obviously has two choices. It can either formulate its understanding of reality in terms of revelation, rejecting the alien framework of substance thinking, and formulating for itself a philosophy that accords with and adequately expresses its final understanding. Or it can continue capitulating to philosophy, expressed or unexpressed, formulating Christian theology, as best it can, in terms of the prevailing philosophy. When it does so, however, it not only distorts and does violence to its own understanding of ultimates, but denies in fact its own central revelation. In truth, Christian theology then accepts a new God or commits bigamy. But there cannot be two but only one universal ultimate. Christian theology can, of course, capitulate to some alien philosophy under the excuse that revelation is not philosophy, that religion deals with salvation and not with truth, or that religion deals with truth so high and so ultimate that there is no way of passing from the experience and knowledge of the world to the God of revelation except through the humility of ultimate agnosticism. Those who thus surrender may rationalize their defeat by claiming that natural knowledge lies in the realm of philosophy, which can never deal with the ultimates of theology. After all, they can argue, theology comes from revelation not reason. Even revelation, in this view, may not be considered truth, since even analogy and symbol may be swallowed up in the final mystery of God. We are left, in such a case, with either excessive light on what Bonaventura called *via mentis ad Deum* (the mind's road to God) or with the impenetrable darkness of eternity.

The fact remains, however, that all such evasions deny the claim of Revelation at its center. Either Revelation affords the fullest self-disclosure of reality or it is not Revelation. Revelation with a capital *R* means our final faith stance as to ultimates. Revelation claims that here reality has spoken at its central focus of self-disclosure, affording man a warranted faith. Within the evasive views, however, Revelation becomes undependable and totally irrelevant for man's concrete problems of truth and life. Possibly philosophy can show that God should be, but even here we are left with empty categories, or with mere denials that nothing finite can be infinite, omniscient, or be confined to any such requirements as supposedly belong to the veritable definition of God. The result is that man has been left with some framework of philosophy as the effective ultimate in terms of which to interpret all else, with the content of philosophy as the framework that provides the overall context for thinking, and with philosophy thus as the concrete guide to truth. Thus in reality man's philosophy has become his effective theology! Knowledge has then taken the place of warranted faith. Such procedure, of course, involves, at least implicitly, the dethroning of theology. As far as truth goes, even the truth on ultimates, man has depended on the findings of such Western metaphysics as employ substance thinking.

More than that, the problems of theology, such as the relation of God to the world or the question of whether God can change or suffer, have been framed in terms of the philosophic ultimate. Naturally the solution has been foredoomed inasmuch as the Christian claims, by their very nature, run contrary to those philosophies which make substance ultimate, even though they may perhaps do so in the language of being. Such an impasse is inevitable. If God is perfect substance, or being in this sense, he cannot change or suffer. Theologians have then tried to get out of these problems by calling them "existential" and irrelevant to faith, or paradoxical and therefore of a deeper truth; or some theologians have even said, as in the case of God's relation to the world, that the two kinds of truth are so disparate that they cannot even be discussed.

In the meantime the problems of knowing the ultimate, in classical Western terms, have become intellectually difficult to the point of impossibility. Metaphysics has suffered a fatal stroke, not so much in theory as in the concrete content of its attempts. David Hume and Immanuel Kant, in the field of philosophy, have posed seemingly insuperable problems for ultimate knowledge of any Supreme Being. Not only has "the great chain of being" been broken, link after link, but even the knowledge of it has been severed at its very middle. The Supreme Being and supernaturalism in terms of substance generally have been shown to be unprovable for knowledge. But for the Western traditions these were the ultimates. Therefore the world of philosophy itself has disintegrated and found little to offer except phenomenology, pragmatism, existentialism, and linguistic analysis.

Personalism tried to fill the gap, but it became itself too much formulated in terms of the realities of selves, with external relations known basically through an epistemological dualism, with no recourse to knowledge by mutual immanence or genuine internal relations. Bowne, Brightman, and Bertocci, each in his own way, took over much of the Lotze heritage. The spiritual, in fact, became defined in terms of the personal and the moral rather than vice versa. Self, or spiritual personality, became primary to personal spirit. The category of coinherence as congruence or spirit as identity none of these men developed. Personalism thus, in effect, became partly guilty of the sins and shortcomings of substance thinking. Its God even became designated the Supreme Person or the Cosmic Self; (as a matter of fact, to give away the secret, God was even called Supreme *Being!*) What personalistic philosophy then in effect made ultimate was really a Supreme Being who purposes, who thinks, who loves, but who in effect *is* the Supreme *Being,* in terms of the capacity for an ultimate substrate. God was not a thing; he was a living God, but he became a separate Personality with external relations comparable to the deficiencies of substance philosophy. Personalism is a great, important undertaking, but it has never rid itself of the gangrene of Western metaphysics. With more adequate categories the truth of personalism can also be both corrected and fulfilled.

In the categories of reality we have need, first of all, for identity. For knowledge to be real and dependable there must be some principle and power of sameness. There must be some identity. There must be some continuity. Or can we think a world, a unity of discourse, a universe without any identity at all? Can reality consist of things and persons only different and alike, with some things merely quite similar? Not even two thumbprints or leaves, no, not even two snowflakes are quite similar, or exactly alike; never completely the same in appearance, let alone existence, but with differences ineradicable and often severe—with which we shall deal in our next chapter. Our concern in this context is not even with the problem of universals, how sameness, some principle and power of identity, can constitute some kind of continuity within the group and among its members. Our concern is, rather, with the question of the early Greeks when they asked how we can know anything at all unless there is identity. Is it true that like can know only the like? Again, the question is not now the same as that of idealism. If we know through the mind, idealism put in its special pleading, must not reality *as such* in some sense be mind? Or if we know only as persons, must not reality *in some sense* be throughout personal?

Such posings of the question are, if not of special pleading, then at least of special nature. They make the means of knowing, or the knower, necessarily central to knowledge and determinative of all that is known. That reality contains the knower, of whatever kind, and that it comprises within itself whatever reality the knower has, seems to be an altogether legitimate assumption. If cows could know abstractly, however, or if things could know at all, would they then have to find reality as such to be cowness or thingness rather than the ontological ground of concern and thingness? We surely cannot pass from the part to the whole simply because the part knows. And does any part, for that matter, ever know the whole as such? Even minds and persons require epistemologically only that they be as real in reality as they are. But if they have not always been present in cosmic process, they require for their explanation an adequate ontological ground. No less and no more. The question then comes to be one of the relation of being to non-being and to becoming. Can minds, persons, cows, or things explain the nature of being, becoming, and non-being? These questions are more complicated than the assumption of grounds or counterparts. Cows obviously can know as cows without having all they know to be cows. There is no shortcut from knowing to reality, from epistemology to ontology. We need a far deeper, fuller, and wider category of the reality of sameness, of identity, of continuity. Epistemology must not illicitly turn into ontology. The category of identity must afford maximum universal explanatory adequacy. That and that alone is the final test.

Whatever the category of identity is, furthermore, we cannot become stuck with some Parmenidean sameness that allows for no real change, movement, or non-being in all the creative ways that are needed in order even to approach accounting, at least suggestively, for the nature of the world we know. We know a dynamic world of real becoming. Take then the substance category and try it on for size as to the principle of identity. Substance thinking makes nouns ultimate. There are things, entities, and they are what they are, needing only themselves for explanation. They are subjects with determinate predicates. They are constants in the midst of change. A chair is a chair; a rose is a rose; a mountain is a mountain. A river is water that flows. A fire changes one substance, wood, into other forms of substance like ashes and smoke. A cabbage is a plant with the capacity in it, as substance, to grow. In growing it absorbs and uses other substances like the sun, the soil, and the air. Do we need any other principle of identity than to find out what the substances are, how they can be related and how they can change? We surely do if we are to account for sameness or continuity as they underlie the unity in a universal discourse, the unity beyond the individual and community, and *becoming as real* in the history of process. No static collection of substances can do that, and not even a dynamic set of separate substances. For unity and continuity within cosmic process exhibiting novelty we have to go beyond the separateness of external relations to some common identity throughout the unity of discourse.

Substance thinking, in fact, is commonsense description. We see the world like this. We see things change and we see them grow. We do not explain, only observe and give account. In this view things are ultimate. There may be allowed some ultimate or at least some general pattern for coexistence, some special patterns for growth, and also some predictable possibilities for change within and among things. These may be real, in themselves, as in Plato's ideals or patterns for creation, or real as inwardly directive potentials, forms or entelechies as in Aristotle, or they may subsist in, so to speak, some semireality, or relational reality, as in Whitehead. Even Whitehead teeters on the edge between process and substance. He borrows heavily from Plato, Aristotle, and the Christian faith. As a process thinker he knew his affinity to Buddhism, but, as we have said, he never could arrive at less than process *and* reality. If only he had seen some other ultimate for his reality than obsolete aspects of substance thinking! Substance thinking can go from the primacy of substances or nouns as ultimate to some more revolutionary understanding of reality as one aspect complementary to process.

Western thinkers patch up their position by falling back on Niels Bohr's theory of complementariness, explicitly or implicitly. A vigorous attempt to do so is Herbert W. Richardson's *Toward an American Theology,* where substance thinking par excellence even adds to itself aspects of coinherence or perichoresis! Generally speaking, however, such substance thinking, thick or thin, full strength or diluted, provides no principle of permanent and universal identity at all. It proclaims: Things are, can be related, and can change. But it never explains how or why things are, how they can become in the history of creation, what the nature of nothing can be, what makes change more than an external relation, how parts of one being can become intrinsically part of another as a worm in a fish (and we are not talking biologically but ontologically, if substance be substance), how things can be known or persons know each other, without inner continuity or internal relations based on coinherence; and certainly it never allows for the way all things are actually interrelated and interdependent, yes, interactive, considering that in substance thinking every entity needs only itself in order to exist. Chemistry may deal with compounds and mixtures, but the deeper question of ontological identity as such chemistry does not face nor explain. We have to have, then, a radical, *root-deep* grasp of the reality of identity before we can do justice to the problems of difference.

It may be thought that atomic theory will fill the need. Did not Democritus and Lucretius, scientifically and poetically, explain the world in terms of the accidental and fortuitous combination of the original atoms? As though combinations were explanation at all except for previous observation and subsequent description! What was there in reality that made certain combinations possible and, once made, why did they become active or personal in certain ways? An infinite number of chances? Such a situation is infinitely regressible and may not end up in our way at all. What then of the law of large numbers and the exhaustion of possibilities for aberration, as Margenau uses them in *Open Vistas,* making order at least an achievement capable of at least temporary survival? In such a case we assume a limited universe favoring some *continuity* of order! We have a law of order and an order of survival that are presupposed and not made part of the explanation. Otherwise the next throw of the dice would be basically, if not totally, disruptive of continuity. Given the world in eternal change and given, then, continuity in the world, even long enough for Democritus and Lucretius to live and to write, they would have to rationalize the situation they knew by a most farfetched and fanciful explanation with no logical status at all. Small units in perpetual motion will not account for the identity of world order or the possibility of knowing it. But it is at least a mythical attempt to cope with the problem of the how of becoming. As explanation such reliance on atoms and chance is a faith that partially discovers but never attains adequate explanatory power. We need a far deeper grasp of identity to explain both becoming and continuity. Chance and change can never adequately account for a serial continuity of progressively and organically fulfilling novelties within an accumulative order.

What, then, of modern atomic theory? Granted that we know only this world, the world that we know is as likely as any other world or as no world at all. Why not, then, begin by accepting this world as given and by asking no foolish questions? If, however, we accept any history of development, any evolution, any real history of creation, granting even the steps from the inorganic to the biological, to the psychological, and finally to the symbolic with all its accumulative understanding of man's history, however short, then sheer chance of neutral atoms as directive of ordered change through accumulative becoming into a qualitatively and progressively transmuted order of being begs all questions. Reality cannot be less than what has become nor the order ontologically less than its actual appearance. It can be more but not less, for what has been, has been, and has at least become permanently irreal as the wasness of the past. But we cannot tell what *can be* until we see it become—except, of course, as we discern the direction, the power, and the possibilities of process and predict within a knowledge that must be partly the faith of pointing as well as the knowledge of pointing. Aristotle's grand scheme at least insisted on the priority of what he called actuality over the potential. Modern evolutionism has generally forfeited even this strength. It fails even of descriptive adequacy of ultimate principles and power for identity and for becoming. Even Teilhard assumes a kind of original matter that entails creation as a process of revelation.

Energy as capacity to work, moreover, does not exist as substance and by itself explains nothing. Energy is only a general descriptive formula underlying scientific observations. It is a presupposition, neutral and nondescript. When the nature and concrete coloring of that working takes place we have fields of force, yielding particles and entities, the becoming and working of which, the knowing and nature of which, yes, the purpose and destiny of which, in the total field of their interrelations, are just the questions to be answered. No infinitely layered universe can be more than a myth, a heuristic approach to description of function, and no mere undifferentiated field of force can be more than a positing of some abstraction which can never be located. Talk about locating God! In any case, there can be no reducing substance thinking to utterly minute particles, neutral and interchangeable in nature, that will even approach explaining any of our central and vital problems, as we have described them above. And field theory or energy as the neutral capacity to work are only partial answers which, in fact, destroy substance thinking at its own heart. Substance theory gets its main power from making central our visual world of common sense without any deep and permanent coming to grips with the central problems of identity and difference.

Then what of process thinking? That is a direct, relevant answer to substance thinking. Will not process thinking do justice to the reality and nature of identity? This is the aspect where it is, indeed, the weakest. Its opposite number, substance philosophy, has a complete explanation for identity, until we consider change, becoming and *un*becoming. A thing is what it is and that is all there is to it. But such identity, as we have seen, cannot account ontologically for true transformation into something else, nor for what is genuinely novel. Nor can it account for nonbeing or for the ceasing to be. Nor does such an understanding of identity provide a total continuity of being; it fails to deal adequately with sameness as such. In process thinking, oppositely, there is no permanent identity of any kind. There is no abiding entity either of individual things or of the whole of process. A thing is what it is only in relation to all else and within its total network of interdependence and interaction. It is a locus of occasions. Not only experience, but all of whatever is, comes in drops

which live for a moment and die. Yet actually they are at the same time
involved in the total process in such a way that all that is identical is some
bit of transitory experience or feeling. There can be forms of flux but the
form is not anything except the shape of the flux—unless process thinking
takes recourse to reality besides process. There can thus be loci of experience, confirmations of feelings, continuities of form allegedly without
self-being.

On the scale of the whole, process thinkers have various interpretations.
Some, like Teilhard de Chardin, have an Omega Point toward which or
whom all points; and Whitehead has a limited view of God as the envisager of all possible forms for process in their primordial harmony or purity.
It is with respect to the whole that anything is what it is within a process
where flux and creativity are posited as given or ultimate. At this point
Whitehead especially appreciates Aristotle's analysis of the question. Identity, then, is, with respect to such an ultimate where process itself submits
to reality, relations to a fixed reference for continuity. Sameness somehow
pertains to flux, to creativity as the permanent characteristic of the flux,
and to God as the coordinator of the forms for the flux and the focus for
total satisfaction or goal of the flow. Such a resort to modified process is
at least stronger than to process as such.

Buddhism is the most consistent attempt at process thinking. Nothing
is. *Anatta,* or insubstantiality, characterizes all experiences. Impermanence, interactive and interdependent, characterizes the total flow of
experience. Reality must therefore be *neti neti* or "not at all" of this nature
whether as its total negation or as its total fulfillment beyond all knowledge from within experience. Such is the most consequent philosophic
stress of process thinking. There is no identity in experience for knowledge. Continuity is ultimately unreal; there is no aseity; and yet Buddhism also centers its analysis in the scientific dependability of the law of
karma, the inviolate law of deed and consequence which characterizes the
whole realm of experience. What identity underlies such assumed continuity? Here is a form of the flow, in terms of *skandhas,* or shapes, which
is real in some sense as well as operatively effective. The law of *karma* or
kabba is universal, but not ultimate! It characterizes the empirical world,
but not the real. It is at least psychologically meaningful even though
never ontologically so. Buddhism is obviously also seeking an understanding of moral order, scientifically dependable, and an equally dependable
way to release man from the oppression of life, while affirming negatively
or positively the deeper final identity. What we know, however, is not
identity but rather pure process, a flow of flux. Buddhism is aware both
of the ever-changing nature of experience and of the need for reality
beyond it. Both Hinduism and Buddhism insist on going beyond the
order of experience, for reality, for truth, for salvation. But there is in

any case no real principle or power of identity in such a consequent interpretation of process. On the level of process we are rightly left with *maya,*
a process of experience, a form of flux which lacks real continuity or
identity.

If we ask concerning the nature and status of identity in process thinking, what can be the answer? There are three forms of identity or three
elements: the flux, the form, and the drive. In modified process thinking
we also have some such element as God or the Omega Point. What then is
the flux? Prime material, prime stuff, prime substance, all sound too much
like substance thinking. Do process thinkers in fact presuppose some
dynamic, unbounded, formless stuff? Does this consist of minutest pellets
like infinitesimally small sand, or of some continuous dough? Terms here
are only symbolic, of course, but in either case we have substantive sameness, identity of being beyond process, in fact presupposed by process. If
we get down below protons and neutrons to the most unimaginable entities, are there finally little particles, the minutest substances, or is there
some doughlike mass, dynamic and accessible, on which forms of further
identity are then imposed? What, indeed, is this flux? Does it really say
anything or merely cover a problem under words?

What reality in either case does empty space have within or around?
It is easy to say in Oriental thinking that finally the nature of what we
see as things or as change is ignorance, or *avidya.* It is equally easy in
modern physics to affirm that all our knowledge is phenomenological in
the sense that finally we do not know the nature of things. Minutest particles seem substances; a mass can be converted into the thought of field
force where particles are but matters of geometric locations with no inde-
pendent reality as such. Nothing is, as separate, though distinction of
function or flow can be distinguished. Perhaps some theory of complementariness can accept both the total and the particular as inherently
complementary and interdependent as well as interactive. In that case
identity would be locatable distinction, momentary or enduring, of distinguishable entities and of the total field of interaction, as such, and
through all its constituent operations. Just as substance thinking can be
salvaged by capacities for change, so process philosophy can perhaps be
salvaged by substance capacities for sameness. Somehow we need both
substance and process thinking and no category will do that cannot satisfy
this double need.

What then of the identity of form? We must not call it something, some
substance, but then what is it? If it has no being except in and as the
shape of flux, how can there be continuity? A person never steps in the
same river twice, says Heraclitus, and surely then neither is the person
the same. The form of the flow, the place of the flow, the history of the
flow, the form of the person, the locus of the person, the confirmation of

feelings of the person; are they the same? They all seem to be and not to be so. Let us make the form of the flow representative in a rough and inexact way for the general purposes that obtain in this analysis. The shape of the water that was there at the previous stepping into the river is gone. It went with the flow. If the shape has no being, but only the form of the water, when the water flowed away so did the form also. For that matter the form in the next instance was somewhat different as the context and the contour changed. Then is the form determined by the context and the contour? Not without the water, of course, but with the water flowing or rather with water flowing ever anew in the same situation? Is form merely situational? Suppose there was a stream in the garden using the same water over and over again. Would the stream then not be in some sense more of the same stream than as if the water never returned? Would not the form in some sense be more the same form than other- wise, since it is in a great measure the form of the same water? Not surely as *form!*

What then is identical about the form? The shape as shape? But the shape has no being on this theory apart from the flow itself of which it is the form. In this case we long for Plato's ideal forms laid up in heaven, even for Pythagoras' mystical numbers seen in the perfect movement of the heavenly bodies. How we long to listen to the music of the spheres! *And it is not there.* We long for Aristotle's perfect model attracting all entelechies in the world of change. We understand why Whitehead does not dare to invoke Plato outright, and why he considers the forms to be only semireal, or real only in their interrelation between God's envisage- ment and their use in the consequent nature of God or for the consequent world. Do we say that the form is real only as a possibility, and the same only for the same possibility? If the water flows again at the same depth and speed in the same context and contour, it will fulfill the same pos- sibility. Will it then be the same with it? But what being then has pos- sibility? What is possibility? Why does the same situation produce the same form? And why is flux, which has no substance, more real than form that has no substance?

Process philosophy can help explain change through some theory of mutual immanence and interaction. Things are not merely external to each other as needing only themselves in order to exist but are mutually supportive as interpenetrating and interstructural, whatever then be the reality of such structure. They include each other within the total back- ground of interrelatedness and interreality. But the purer process be- comes, the less flux can *be* substance and the less form can have being. Therefore also the less process thinking can offer any interpretation of adequate depth of identity, continuity, sameness. For that matter pure process thinking makes possibility adjectival to process, not as creatively presuppositional in ontological or theological terms, but as resultative of relations. Thus becoming means mostly change, a new flux of form, or a new form in flux, though strictly speaking both ways of speaking are substantive, precluding true process. With such a view of possibility there can be nothing new and non-being has only a negative function. Our history of creation, on the other hand, in fact, gives a positive place, a presuppositional place to novelty. Without novelty there is no creation; there is nothing genuinely new. Thus process thinking can have change, but no true becoming, even as it can have no genuine understanding of the constituent nature of non-being, even in the sense of *ouk on*. *Ouk on*, of course, means absolute non-being or non-being as such, whereas *me on* means non-being as merely the negation of particulars.

What is far more serious, process thinking has no view of identity that can bridge and account for the relation between being, becoming, and nonbeing. Thinkers like Whitehead and Teilhard de Chardin have added Christian and semisubstance elements like God, unlike the purer development of process thinking in Buddhism, and thus have partly taken care of these lacks but, as we shall see, they need fuller categories of reality yet to account for the total richness of experience. Augustine proposed that God creates both matter and form and that he sustains them in joint-being and activity. Descartes also related his categories of thought and extension, or form and matter, both through the pineal gland in man and supremely through the reality and activity of God. But neither Augustine nor Descartes worked out the deeper why or how of such a relationship.

The New Testament categories of reality, spirit, the personal, and love, beg to be developed for these purposes! They are, we believe and shall try to show, fully adequate for all needed purposes. *Is* there flux and what is it? *Is* there form and what is it? What sameness has either flux or form, what kind of identity, what kind of total self-being? Does not process philosophy, in the final analysis, beg the basic question of identity? Can it ever say what is really the same? Or will it at last have to deny sameness as such? Will it have to claim that nothing is ever the same in any way? Must it not logically claim that all is whirl, and even whirl is never the same whirl or the same *as* whirl? If whirl is king, having destroyed Zeus, or dependable being and purpose, what identity can there be? Can we get along with a total pluralism both all across the board and across time and still speak of any kind of universe, even a universe of discourse? If identity is not substantive and if form has no being except as the concrete shape of flux, as the form of flux, what identity can process thinking possess?

A third aspect of what is universal to process philosophy, moreover, is the drive, be it desire or creativity. In Buddhism the desire is universal but not ultimate. *Dukkha,* or suffering, springs from universal desire, a desire dominantly characteristic of all life. Reality lies beyond desire as well as insubstantiality. In more compromised process thinking, however, creativity can be an ultimate as well as universal. In Whitehead's process thinking creativity is "the category of categories." But in either the case of Buddhism or of Whitehead's "modified Buddhism," what kind of identity can the drive of desire or the drive of creativity have? There are in neither philosophy substances nor beings that have desire. All persons and things are in process and of process. What then are the relata, the principle and process of permanence? Surely the form itself is resultative and has no drive. Platonic and Aristotelian analysis are after all the very essence of what is defined as substantive; *eros* becomes significant in their philosophies. Is the drive of creativity, however, the drive of desire prior to process, logically important as *meaning ontologically real* as well as directive? But meaning for pure process can have no being, no ontology. Is then creativity anything besides or beyond process? Surely desire is not. Is either drive or creativity outside process as an entity? Surely not! Is either of them substance within process? Surely not! Is then the process as such some entity which possesses or exhibits creativity or desire? Surely not, in the sense of macrosubstance or macrobeing! Then, as some dimension of depth? As some power for being? As the abyss of being with no distinct place, substance, or entity? If neither flux nor form is in the sense of identity or continuity, where or what is desire or creativity in the sense of identity or continuity?

If desire is adjectival to no being and has in itself no being, what is it or what reality has it? Is it part of process, in the parts, in the whole, or as the logical presupposition either for the parts or the whole or for both parts and the whole? And what ontological status has a logical presupposition? What identity can such creativity or desire have unless it either is adjectival to being or has being in some sense. The problem of continuous identity will not be done away. Must not process philosophy somewhere tackle the problem of eminent being, of the power to persist through all changes, of genuine identity amid all changes? Can there be being *in* process and *for* process that is not substantive and still does not reduce reality to some nondescript flux or form of flux? Can there be a universal that has a principle or power of identity, of continuity, of sameness in the parts and in the whole, even though the parts and the whole be not separate as substance nor merely interrelated and interactive as process? If so, how is real identity possible? We are convinced that a new approach to our basic intellectual problems will afford us not only a legitimate answer but one that is seminal.

Pure process philosophy would have to seek whatever identity it could in flux, in form, or in some inner drive characterizing process as a whole, apart from some momentary identity of low- or high-grade experience, but all of them would be denied full candidacy because of the insubstantiality and impermanence of their natures. The more identity is made into a universal category in any of these the less we have of the meaning and intention of process philosophy in its rejection of all eminent reality or permanent being. Oriental thought is characterized by indeterminateness; and process thinking should revel in the flux that cannot be caught by thought, where form characterizes merely a constant change of flow and where drive is never real or satisfied. The more flux, form, or drive become ascertainable constants in themselves, or rather in their indeterminate interchange, the more we move toward some interpretation at least akin to substantive thinking or at least toward catering to its main intention.

One such attempt to add reality to process, as in *Process and Reality,* is that of the semi-Christian process thinkers like Whitehead and Teilhard de Chardin who posit some doctrine of God, who is himself half process and half beyond process. They have no substantive, self-sufficient God in terms of being, unrelatable by nature by his very qualitative distinctiveness, but rather only a logical goal of process, or perhaps, as in Teilhard, even a teleological or eschatological goal, which can be realized only by the interaction of the permanent reality with the dynamics of process. Thus Whitehead's view of God is that his primordial nature is beyond the constant change and decay of process, by God's envisagement of the eternal objects or possibilities for realization in process, while his consequent nature is involved, yes, immersed, in the totality of the process itself. Thus God in Whitehead's thought and the Omega Point in Teilhard's are points of permanence, logical and ontological presuppositions for any process at all. Here then is identity, and identity not only in the large but as also present in each part and moment of process.

But in these cases there is also no longer pure process thinking but process thinking *combined* with "reality." We have process *and* reality so that, from one point of view, all things must be referred to and explained in relation to the events or occasions in process, but from the other point of view such an "ontological principle" in Whitehead's philosophy also refers explicitly only to the process analysis and not to the total dealing with the truth of interpretation. Thus we have in Whitehead process thinking only from one side of the problem, so to speak. Whitehead was adamant at this point, refusing to surrender to pure process even while contending with substance thinking. Consequently he struggled continually between Buddhism and the Christian faith whereas Teilhard is more outspoken throughout at the need of both seeing the facts of evolutionary thinking, or of cosmological process, and the full Christian context of God's faithfulness, in terms of which the future of man becomes a decision of faith and obedience along side of, and often in spite of, Teilhard's ringing declaration of the inevitability of the noogenetic advance. *The Phenomenon of Man* needs more than *The Future of Man* to constitute Teilhard's widest context to understanding. *The Divine Milieu* and the *Hymn of the Universe* give the mystic's piercing through to divine identity alongside the scientist's fuller stress on the nature of the evolutionary process.

I shall soon try to advance a view of identity that supplies the answers to the needs that are felt for by both substantive and process thinking. We need a principle and power of identity that remains selfsame while relating all events or processes internally, that is selfsame within all manifestations of distinction, or within all created realms of being, that at the same time will not destroy or diminish the distinctiveness. While preserving the inner identity, such a category must enhance distinctiveness. More than that, the principle and power of identity, while remaining selfsame and thus internally effective as the all-inclusive continuity, must also reinforce and enhance what is distinctive without *in itself* producing separation. Thus identity must be both universal and ultimate, the final manifestation of the universal category of reality in its inclusiveness, while also allowing and abetting the distinctiveness that can create at its maximum the conditions for variation, and, at its highest, not only *of* freedom, but *for* freedom.

Identity, furthermore, must make possible presence and absence at the same time in the same place, in order for there to be a genuinely pedagogical situation and a relation between presence and absence where the fulfilling of presence, even so, makes more real whatever is distinctive. Neither substantive nor process thinking, as we shall see, can minister fully to these requirements for interpretation. The Christian categories of reality: spirit, love, and the personal, understood in their own fullest possibilities for interrelations, both pedagogically and fulfillingly, can perform precisely what is required for our fullest understanding of experience. And yet they have never been worked out to this end. What a task awaits! Before we turn to our constructive task, however, we must discuss also the need for distinction or distinctiveness in our understanding of experience. Reality must be adequately represented both in identity and in distinctiveness. Neither substance nor process frameworks can fill those needs, but we believe the categories generated by the Universal Word can do so. Ontologically, we must develop what a multidimensional ultimate can do to provide categorical adequacy, and epistemologically, we have to produce a contrapletal logic that will be sufficient to cope with the problems of a multidimensional ontology.

The Need for Distinction

IN ORDER for there to be a universe, there must be some kind of continuity, some sameness, some identity. Such identity, however, must not obscure, let alone deny, the distinctiveness which is present to experience. We apprehend sameness and difference. We are aware of continuity and discontinuity. We must not prejudge our interpretation by calling one reality and the other appearance. Those who have called what is permanent for process "reality" seem to have prejudiced the analysis in the same way as those who have selected the process itself as their framework for reality. But words are elastic and mostly suggestive. No harm is done if we are aware of the way we use words in both respects. Distinctions may be derivative from the great Unity or they may qualify intrinsically that Unity. Perhaps the Unity itself, however, may be nothing but a common aspect or function of the many, so that rather than unity, pluralism ultimately obtains, with such unity only as is needed for community and communication to whatever extent we know these to be real, actually and potentially.

Allowing, then, for difference as well as for sameness, whether the difference of distinction or of separation, let us question at the outset the need for the distinction of an ultimate. Why be concerned with some unknown ultimate, or some abstracted substrate, when all we have to do is to observe the world as it is and try honestly to describe its nature? Do we not in fact commit a crime against knowledge when we speculate on some category more ultimate or deeper than the world of experience that we do know? What warrant do we have for such strange and surprising procedures, not strange and surprising historically, but to anyone who simply sets out honestly to try to understand and authentically to interpret the world around us as well as our own experience of it? If mankind had suffered from amnesia and knew nothing of its past, it would, indeed, be futile and frustrating to try to deal with something more or other than we ordinarily experience in the workaday world of human life and knowledge.

We cannot choose amnesia, however much such a state might relieve us from the more difficult task of interpretation. We have the knowledge of history and we have the history of science. Human history goes back to lowly beginnings before the development of speech and any advanced form of civilization; and we have the history of the universe before all human history, with its evolution from the inorganic level to the organic and finally to the psychological and the symbolic. None of the later levels can be reduced retrospectively into what came before. Thus novelty in the history of evolution is basically more than a matter of incomplete predictability because of incomplete knowledge. Novelty is real and finally irreducible. Such discontinuity, moreover, comes within a total context of accumulative continuity—itself a history of the ingression of discontinuity—upon continuity with such an organic predisposition in reality for such ingressions that a new, more complex continuity can arise and accumulate. Some ingressions, indeed, have been so minimal or gradual that stages in between, as for instance the organic and the inorganic, are hard to distinguish. There are ambiguous or borderline phenomena. But when the characteristically new comes, it comes in the form and fact of its own reality. It indicates what the nature of the possible is. Therefore it declares for us the nature of the universe. In this sense the history of evolution is the revelation of the nature of reality.

When such evolution is characterized not only by genuine becoming but also by becomings that are in themselves organically related to each other and fulfilling of each other's natures and which yet also prepare for the fuller ingression of new and newly fulfilling novelties until a series of mutually belonging and completing ingressions of novelties constitute a recognizable, communicable universe, we have nothing less than a history of creation. Evolution is a one-sided word incapable of suggesting the nature and reality of becoming. Such a universe is no chance affair. Whatever its defects, seeming mistakes, wastes and excessive evils, the main fact of the becoming of the universe and of its producing interpreters who can appraise its history and meaning stands strong and straight: The universe bespeaks purposiveness. If the meaning of that purposiveness can be seen most inclusively and adequately in some event that will (1) show us how to cope with our problems, (2) help us understand why we have evil, and (3) prescribe a course of action that fulfillingly can direct human life, then we must distinguish between the total content of the process on the one hand, and on the other hand, that event within it which unlocks its meaning and prescribes its course.

In other words, not all the content in process is then equally important and real, since what has come into process shows increasingly the nature and meaning of the process and indicates what has been behind, within, and ahead of the process from the beginning. If such be the case, *the history of creation*, we stress, *involves the history of revelation*, requiring the distinction of an ultimate. The adequate interpretation of the objective facts call for an ultimate. The final ultimate, to be sure, may not be for human understanding. What we can feel for, and perhaps find, is the kind of ultimate that helps us to interpret and to live most meaningfully within the world we know. Thus no Occam's razor is sharp enough or can be sharpened enough to shave off the question of the ultimate as either unnecessary to or methodologically impossible for human knowledge.

The main distinction, then, is that between the ultimate and the world of our ordinary experience. The ultimate within experience can indeed be conceived of as the dimension of depth. In order to avoid spatialization as a narrow mode of speaking we can say that the ultimate is the height of transcendence, which is the depth of experience. Actually, as we shall see, the ultimate is neither height nor depth; it is neither length nor breadth but a quality of reality which we may best designate as spirit and man's relation to it as spiritward. But when the unconditional Spirit, who can be related without becoming relative only by being Love, "comes" into the world of human history and experience he may perhaps best be conceived of, as Tillich suggested, in terms of the dimension of depth. Whatever persons and things are he is more and other, even though he is fully present and ready for power.

Thus the distinction of the ultimate in the world of the finite is that it is at the same time not the finite and also the very best in and of the finite. Man is himself most fully at the depths of his own being where God is. Thus love and joy and peace come at the depth. The category of the dimension of depth is the category of distinction for the ultimate within the world of experience. Yes, also within the world of nature, for all creation is what it is only by the constant empowering in the present of the God who is the depth of all reality. Things are not merely substances, needing only themselves in order to exist, nor are they merely processes constituted only by their relations. Things are neither merely a changing matrix, some substance capable of change, nor some nexus of change, but are indeed real with regard to a deeper or higher or fuller category than either substance or process can provide.

Within the finite world as such the universals indicate characteristic difference. Each leaf and snowflake, yes, each thumbprint, is different but leaves are leaves and thumbprints, thumbprints because they exhibit common characteristics in comparison to other things. If all we knew were leaves, we would only take leaves for granted, but since there are snowflakes and thumbprints we can distinguish leaves as a class from other classes of things. We can establish by comparative thought the distinction of the ultimate as such from the world of ordinary experience, not that we then compare sense experience with sense experience, as above, but that we compare candidates of interpreted experience with each other with reference to their capacity to give meaning and direction to the totality of what we know and all relevant parts or aspects of it. We thus go beyond bliks of insight or intuitive surmises to investigate the question of explanatory adequacy. The ultimate must be universal, all-comprehensive, relating relevantly and explanatorily to all there is, directly or indirectly. Then there is also the distinction of the ultimate as it is within the finite. The spirit of transcendence becomes the depth of immanence. Incarnation is only immanence at its highest level (or at its deepest depth!) on the part of the fullness of God. Thus distinction comprises several kinds: universals, transcendence, and the immanence of the transcendent.

Universals, if we take our viewpoint from the Universal Word, are real within the creative purpose of God, that is effectively or functionally real in the world of human knowledge. They are not metaphysically real as though they were laid up permanently in heaven. There are no such separable realities. They are only expressively real, or performatively real within the creative Word of God. They are real for human knowledge and for human action. They can be distinguished, classified, and used. They are neither unreal nor irreal inasmuch as they exist within the intention of God and can be known by man. They are part of the process, but not separately real. They are real in and for process, for their "purposes." Even to ask the question as to whether they are real in themselves is to revert to an intolerable substantive thinking. Similarly to inquire whether they have no reality in themselves is to misunderstand the nature of time. They are what they are, not illusion or mere appearance, because they are the expression of God's intention within time as pedagogical process or time as the condition for love. These observations are not arbitrary assertions in the light of our total analysis, for time, as we saw, is not pure or full time in the sense of the realization of the reality of love, but is "mixed time," where love can learn and grow through the indirections of experience where God is both present and absent. Since God is present and absent in different senses, it is obvious that the performative and directive universals of his will differ according to the nature of his will in a particular situation or within varying conditions for learning love. Universals are then functionally or operationally real, conditional to the nature of process.

Universals in nature are less flexible or more persistent than universals in history. The field of psychology, for instance, would exhibit more openness to change than the field of physics in general. The chemistry in a rock would be more fixed than the chemistry in a human body. Anxiety or a will to live would condition the chemistry of the human body. A Bahai writer has suggested that the sympathetic nervous system is affixed on one end to the body and on the other to the spirit! Spatial metaphors can seem gross, but they may suggest what they cannot say. Thus a man can affect his body chemistry either by abusing the body or by having no will to live or by suffering from frustrated pride. Because of the reality of the spirit *in several senses* universals are more permanent on the material level as such than on the biological, and more permanent on the biological than on the psychological. Thus universals are far more fixed in nature than in history. But there is, to be sure, no human history apart from nature. Therefore no clear-cut line can be drawn between nature and history. The more man is in the spirit or the spirit in man the more freedom becomes real and the more flexible life becomes. There is thus distinction between the created realm and spirit as such, between the created realm and the presence of spirit within it, and between the events of creation or among finite entities in terms of universals; or we may start with distinction as universals, and then go on to distinction as the presence of the ultimate in the finite, and the reality of the ultimate in itself.

A false analysis may then conclude that the more persistent universals are the most real. On the very contrary, they are the most remotely and indirectly expressive of the purpose of God. They are the most extrinsic and excarnate. They are the most instrumental and therefore the least real. They are real for what they are, and lengthily express the purpose of God. But reality is spirit characterized by love. Reality as we shall see is personal at its heart. It is Ultimate Concern and Integrity. The reality in creation is highest or most spiritward in the Word. History expresses and contains more reality than nature.

A rock is not more real than a human being because a rock outlasts him! The rock outlasts a human being only at the edges of time, or where time is most thin. As a matter of fact it is a moot question whether the rock is in time at all in the intrinsic sense. Time is learning love. Eternity is fullness of time. Where eternity starts or begets time we cannot tell. Surely on the animal level and possibly on the physical level. There may, however, be a very low grade of spirit and mind in a rock. There has been a suggestive interest in such a theory with regard to evolution from Maupertuis to Whitehead and Teilhard de Chardin. We do not know except that God is there in a most impersonal sense as spirit, creating, continuing, and directing. The more fragile and fugitive the choices of love, the more sensitive and flexible, however, the more real they are, containing more of the nature of time, participating more in the learning of love, and even at times entering into the fullness which is eternity in time.

Is not faithful love, however, also the most unchanging? Is not immature and uncommitted love fickle? Would not God's love be the most unchanging love of all and therefore be the most permanent universal?

The answer is complex. In the first place, we are speaking of time and the conditions of time, not of eternity. Eternal love is full faithfulness and therefore as such the most permanent, the most invariant universal. The distinction between time and eternity in one of its aspects is surely that eternity in its very nature is changeless as the dependability of God's love. But, as we shall see, such changeless love, remaining changeless in itself, changes in history through its ameliorative participation with the world of the finite. It is changeless in the sense of being ever dependable, and changeful in the sense of being superlatively flexible in its capacity to adjust to, or "change" with, every need. In the world the eternal *for-ness* appears as judgment and as fulfillment in ever-new forms depending upon the concrete need of the finite. Such change, nevertheless, is only the pedagogical expression in time of the faithfulness of eternity. Thus even the most selfsame and self-abiding becomes the most flexible universal in human history. Nothing is more open to *change* than *unchangeable* concern.

But what of time? It is clear that the more eternity enters time in human beings the more they also exhibit flexible love. As they participate in the "inner" security and rest of God's Sabbath, even during the workdays of the world, they dare to identify themselves with human need in the workaday world, and thus their attitudes are ever changing with the needs of the concrete world. *The changeless is the most changeful.* Such language is not paradoxical but literal. The logic of such utterances, as we shall see more fully in the next chapter, is contrapletal rather than either contradictory or a matter of logical contrariety. The logic of the analysis is based on a predication according to which several predicates, which on one level or in one dimension of thinking are contradictory, become, rather, supportively and complementarily contrapletal as they relate to the identical subject in different senses, from different levels or in different dimensions of analysis. Process thinking and substantive thinking are incapable of such distinctions and such fuller context for logic. To be sure, Aristotle's logic can handle the analysis once we grant the contrapletal ontology! The contrapletal ontology presupposes a multi-dimensional reality where the same entity in itself, truly itself, can be present and absent at the same time, can be literally there and not there, at once. God, in one dimension, can be truly himself and yet in another dimension participate in what is contrary to himself, because love as spirit can do so in order to further man's freedom and privacy. There is no question of permissive action or inaction at a distance, but of literal multi-dimensional relationships through an aseity, multidimensionally, of co-inherence and literal congruence, of which neither substance nor process thinking is capable. There is here no place for paradox, excluded middle, *totum simul* or *Alles auf einmal*. What we need is a contrapletal ontology or theology expressible only in terms of contrapletal logic.

The more a true parent loves his child, however, the more he can either let him alone or help him according to need; and he can change his strategy as love directs. (But the parent cannot be literally and primarily congruent identity in the child.) Thus the unchanging in nature, like perfectly faithful love, can even from finite centers change in attitude and in relationship. But when the categories of reality are understood on an ever deeper level or in a fuller dimension than even the human, love can be present with its child through the primary spirit even while letting the child alone. Love can keep from threatening the child by its presence in person, allowing the child true privacy and reality of freedom from parental control, even while in prayer it can be present with the child in the total spirit but not in particular spirit, in the total identity, but not specific distinction, offering him help, urging his right use of freedom from within. Man thus becomes participant also in the contrapletal co-subjectness of God. The more contrapletal the relationship, the more real it is, but by that token also the more flexible.

Spirit is the category of freedom. Berdyaev had hold of one of the most important of all truths. He never developed, however, to my knowledge, the category of spirit as also the need for pedagogical bondedness. He failed to use the category as a metaphysical ultimate underlying all else, the category of eternity which alone is full enough for all times and for the remotest conditions for time. He could have used spirit to trace all the needs for pedagogy and to delineate all the consequences in the choices of freedom, but he chose instead to make God finite and thus to limit the final meaning of freedom. The faithfulness of freedom can be only the freedom of faithfulness as both are full in love. Thus spirit becomes a contrapletal category large and deep enough even to include the depths of evil. The eternal "yea" patiently outlasts the long "nay" of human time, which is always, so to speak, under heaven. But enormous is the debt we all owe to that great pioneer of relating spirit and freedom through book after book of interpretation. Nicolas Berdyaev must stand as the great original theologian of "the spirit and its freedom."

But universals as characteristic difference cannot separate. As such they can make only for distinction within the one reality. If separation becomes complete, knowledge dies and process disintegrates. Thus universals in time are real only within the creative purpose of God. Even in eternity they are adjectival only to the love of God, real in him for distinction but in no way divisive or separative. Universals in eternity are directive without being corrective. In time all universals, however far from the center of God's purpose, are part and parcel of pedagogical process. They are largely pedagogical in purpose. As lives become open to eternity, the living of love can transcend and does transcend the merely pedagogical, and thus universals in time can become mostly directive even as eternity enters and fulfills time. Generally, however, universals in time become occasions for separation. A symbol of such separation is the sea. The Biblical claim that "the sea shall be no more" suggests that the nature of the universals shall be directive and not separative or divisive. They shall make for distinction without separation.

There are, then, the distinctiveness of the ultimate, the distinctiveness of the ultimate within the world of the finite as the dimension of depth, and the distinctiveness of classes of difference called universals. We must also discuss the nature of sheer individuality for what this can really mean in a world of communication, but first we must consider that although particular entities belong to many natural classes, they can become members of many more by convention. Thus a leaf belongs to the class of leaves. A leaf serves a certain biological function and can usually be recognized for what it is. But a flower may seem like a leaf or a leaf like a flower. The same leaf or flower, however, is also part of a tree and shares the quality or nature of treeness. But a tree is part of the vegetable kingdom in distinction, shall we say, from the mineral. The distinction may not be absolute, there being borderline cases between the inorganic and the organic, and between the vegetable and animal kingdoms. And surely there are many kinds of continuity between them that may be studied in several subjects in any college curriculum. Nevertheless there is genuine distinction of nature and function between a leaf of a tree and a fin of a fish.

A leaf, moreover, is part of nature rather than of history, although again the beginnings of history in the long line of God's patient evolution of the world may root infinitesimally or most marginally in nature itself. Surely nature wombs and cradles history. In some sense the child always belongs to the womb and the cradle, and the cradle and the womb to the child. Thus each particular entity belongs to many classes, exhibiting many universals. A leaf, too, can be part of a decoration or part of a fertilizing mass, making it belong to some seemingly unnatural classification, except that when history makes use of nature, nature itself becomes functionally transformed. The creatures have the power thus to help change or to multiply the categories of distinction. Universals are both natural and man-made. Or there are even situations where the new function is due to the working of nature, as when a house carried by a flood can become a battering ram to destroy a dam.

No number of particulars, however, can exhaust universals nor can any number of universals finally delimit, for man's knowledge, any particular. They must be experienced in the natural relations to be understood for what they are. Sheer individuality defies description. We know no sheer thatness divorced from all whatness. Nothing can be known apart from any and all universals. To know is in some sense, in some manner, and in some measure, to classify. Knowledge is by nature relational. And yet there is that which is starkly unique in that it refers to one entity alone. No two thumbprints are the same, we keep saying, and therefore even though lines of indentation in the thumb, and similar universals, are used, the particular way those lines and indentations, or unlined areas, come together is characteristic not of a class but of a single event. A person may have a wart on his cheek, but it is a particular wart on a particular cheek of a particular person. How then can it be known? It can be known first of all because knowledge is direct experience. It is apprehension within comprehension and comprehension of apprehension. It is of no use to make one singular and the other plural or vice versa, for comprehension very likely is plural as well as singular, and so surely is apprehension. Nor may we say that we can know only in terms of known universals, for a genuinely new occurrence from another planet or from some new dimension of experience might offer both particulars and universals far beyond any present borders. Obviously there can be no knowledge altogether apart from previously known universals, but there can be such a preponderance of what is new as radically to alter the apperceptive mass itself which is the background of our knowing.

Yet to be known at all, of course, what is known must be known in relation to our present experience and thus not be known as totally other. The totally other is humanly impossible. It is a meaningless assertion, provided there is any continuity at all in experience; and apart from all continuity, in total separation, there could be no knowledge. Thus we must conclude that private distinctiveness is real and can be known even though it can never be known in total isolation, and thus never as it truly is in itself. An isness in itself both is in itself and yet is an isness in some sense for knowledge. To deny such isness is to deny individuality as such. To affirm it as open to knowledge generally, on the other hand, is to deny knowledge in its usual, cooperative sense. The background is inevitably there. And if our categories of reality (which we are now about to develop) are correct, such must be the true nature both of reality and of knowledge in whatever measures and proportions. We can both not know and yet also in some sense know individuality directly and comparatively. Man is such that he knows directly what is, but his direct knowledge is only in relation to what he knows indirectly; he knows the individual but only as the individual is also more than itself.

The same is the case for the self. Each self is both different and distinct. When the word "different" is used we stress what is unlike; we emphasize what separates. The accent is on contrast. When we use the word "distinct" what is always in the background controllingly is what is common, what is like. In both cases we distinguish. We compare. We contrast. But the distinctive is more distinguished than contrasted. The different is a contrasting comparison. Nothing can separate totally, but the distinct may serve merely to enrich the total unity which underlies the one and the many. It may serve the function to deliver sameness from tameness. The total unity is not due to a leveling-down process, to an erasing of difference, but comprises enhancing variation. Or the underlying unity may bring its own potential richness to manifestation. The different may serve the same function more vigorously. The individual entity may stand out as startlingly or at least incomparably different even though part of the same class. This car is different. That girl is different, whereas what is distinctive may more stress the quiet elegance, or the quiet but distinct differentiation. What is loosely called separate can be so, of course, in the functional sense of not being connected. He lived in a separate room from the rest. All these terms have legitimate use in ordinary speech, but in philosophy and theology separate is an unsophisticated word, since nothing can ever be totally separate. We have seen that total separateness cannot even be known.

Yet for effect we say well that men are separated by the oceans, though fuller use of better instruments to use the rich world in which we live is now making even such terms more and more antiquated. With telephone and airplane, with telegraph and television, men are no longer separated in many places of the world. Separation means less and less inaccessibility in the physical sense. But there is still separation of circumstance as a husband away in a war. Especially important is the use of the word "separate" for the kind of inaccessibility that is chosen and supported by the self.

The way this seeming digression in our discussion got started was by our pointing out that the self, too, can be distinct, different, and separate. In eternity there is distinction. There is no love without distinction. Love involves relations. Relations presuppose entities. Whatever the entities are like, they are irreducible as such. God may not be a personality, but he must be selfsame as an entity. The Self must be more than the sum total of selves or the aggregate of selves. And yet, if there is to be both identity and distinction, the Self must be in the selves and the selves in the Self. Distinction and not difference is the word for eternity, because the unity of love is presupposed.

The self becomes most different by self-consciousness and self-choice. A person may insist that he is different and live that difference much to his isolation and loneliness. He thereby violates his self and shrinks his own nature. Or, on the other hand, he may be distinct as a true and authentic member of a community. If he lives in separation, he has failed. If colleges separate students from their ongoing life, they must be judged failures. Man can separate himself by sinning, from God and from man. Freedom for cooperation in faithfulness makes the difference as to whether the person chooses to be distinct or separate. The person who chooses to live in, with, and for the community as his best self becomes distinctive. If he chooses to disregard the community or to work against it, he becomes separated from it. If he decisively accepts the Spirit, he passes beyond both individuality and community into unimunity, a new understanding of society we shall develop in the next chapter and beyond.

At this point we are not to pursue this analysis into its deeper and fuller significance, for that is our next task. We are only suggesting the need for terms that will deal with the one and the many not only in ontological but theological, sociological, and psychological terms. When it comes time to discuss the identity and the distinctiveness of the self, we shall have to pay particular attention to how the case of the self differs from the case of a thing. Entities are not all alike as to identity and distinction. The use intended is for being to connote substance and entity, neutral isness. We must produce a scheme of interpretation that does justice to both identity and distinction, with difference and separation, in the case of being, becoming, and non-being, not only of things but of selves. Thus we must go beyond the facile descriptionism of both substance thinking and process analysis. The term most difficult to control is the term "being," but the context should clarify the usage.

Our concluding topic under the heading of the need for distinctiveness will be on level, direction, and dimension. Paul Tillich attacked level thinking as undemocratic. He claimed that in ancient times there was a hierarchic organization of life that is unacceptable to modern man. There was a descent of authority and opportunity from emperor or king through whatever grades of army officers, professional men or merchants, through farmers and artisans to serfs and slaves, or peasants and servants. Similarly in religion there was descent from pope through cardinals and bishops to priests and laymen. Both secular and religious life was one of domination from above. On top of it all was God, the most undemocratic ruler of all, for all were under him.

But Luther, Tillich averred, by stressing the universal priesthood of all believers changed that whole approach, championing instead democratic understanding of life and religion. Our task, continued Tillich, is to complete for modern man this democratization of religion. (The paper announcing this analysis Tillich read at the Ferré home, and great was the discussion that ensued on the part of the philosophers and theologians present!) Instead of such thinking in terms of direction Tillich suggested thinking through dimensions where there is no level structure, but all functions pass through one point. Thus there can be qualitative distinctions, he proposed, without there being spatial, authoritarian, and level thinking.

What are we to say to such a suggestion? It is catchy and simplistic, I believe, but not interpretatively adequate. Let us at once dismiss the spatial angle. Tillich himself stressed the democracy of the concept. All terms: level, direction, and dimension, of course, are equally spatial! Only the most naïve and unsophisticated would ever fall prey to the idea that dimension, and especially the dimension of depth, has averted the danger of space thinking. "Up there" or "out there" are no more or less spatial than "in there" or "down there." As a matter of fact, with subjectivism a catastrophic temptation, changing the language to inner space can easily lead to the psychologizing and the sociologizing of the faith. Obviously we human beings cannot hope to speak meaningfully if we delete all terms that have space-time associations or suggestions. We can speak of a "superior" student without thinking him elevated spatially above the class and we can talk of a depth thinker without picturing him in a cave. Much of the talk against spatial metaphors is nothing but the outcome of a vague general negativity which appeals to unbelieving man. In the main, it is not the language but the content of the faith that is in question. Language we can find if we know what we believe and why. Such a claim is not naïve or unmindful of the history of language and the role it plays in human thinking. All this we accept and assume. Our fundamental problems of knowledge, however, are not our knowing apart from language and being frustrated because we cannot express and communicate what we know. Rather, our problems root deep into the nature of reality itself and in the depth questions of knowing. Knowing often goes beyond language or deeper than language but when we genuinely know, we can find language at least meaningfully to suggest to *sharers of such experiences* what we intend to convey.

Then why did Tillich opt for dimension rather than direction or level to obviate the difficulties of faith? He did so because with his analysis of reality in terms of the categories of being which were mainly based on substance he could find no room for the living God of the Christian and trans-Christian faith. What a help to him would have been the distinction between being and entity! Nor, naturally, could he have place for the history of creation and the history of revelation. On his presuppositions and in terms of his analysis of such problems, God had to become a finite entity among other finite entities, a supranatural, supreme being that honest and informed man could no longer either accept intellectually or worship. Such a god was to him undemocratic, removed, isolated, or arbitrary and interfering. His will would have to be an unconditional must for man, the expression of his "destiny" that would rob him of his true freedom. But obviously such a god is quite gratuitous. In the third volume of *Systematic Theology*, however, Tillich was on the verge of the use of Spirit as the main category, and of love as the motivating meaning of Spirit. Such a change in him would have altered his whole approach. The great man surely was heading in the right direction.

Granting Tillich's scheme of interpretation, he was right in the brilliant analysis by which he rejected the traditional Christmas view of God and became rightly the legitimate father of the "death of God" theologians. But somehow Tillich wanted to escape from such a negative result and tried to do so by calling God the Ground of Being. As such God was no transcendent being or realm but only the power for being and the meaning for existence. Tillich never fully committed himself, however, as to the explicit ontological nature and status of this power. If it was merely the dimension of depth of each finite entity and of the sum total of finite entities, he faced no problem of ambiguity or inconsistency. But then, too, he forfeited explanatory adequacy. If, on the other hand, this power *was* in any sense more and other than such finite beings and their interrelation, then he *had* some category of transcendence or what supernaturalism has at least intended. So long as he clung to being he had in fact an assumed supernaturalism, which he did not want. Therefore his avid denials! If he had accepted the nonsubstantial Spirit, fulfilling the best in both substance and process thinking while avoiding their respective weaknesses, he could have capped the climax of his system with a revolutionary interpretation.

After many hours of careful analysis in my home Tillich admitted that he did not want to be limited in his analyses to the mere dimension of depth in the world of the finite. In such a case his power for existence and for harmony of existence *was* in fact an entity, had some reality, albeit dynamic rather than static, and surely not objectified in terms of existence. If, then, this power was objectively Ultimate Concern, which Tillich inconsistently both wanted and did not want to grant, Love was for him more than symbolic. It had then somehow to be equated with Being itself (for us Spirit himself). If the Ultimate Concern, however, had no reality beyond the finite, then Tillich indulged in a sheer verbalism and covered up his problems with empty and misleading words. This great spirit and brilliant thinker did, however, point to the problem that requires the abandonment of all theologies of being in favor of theologies of the Spirit. To think in terms of Spirit is indeed, as we shall see, to think dimensionally, since spirit stands for interpenetration, coinherence, *perichoresis*. Any number of entities can, so to speak, occupy the same space in the spirit. If we may use such language, they can be congruent on the same level in the spirit. Spirit is the category of internal relations, however, where finally level and directional thinking both become impossible.

The second and more important reason for Tillich's trying to shift to dimension away from level and directional thinking was that he was caught on the facts of the history of the cosmic process. The history of revelation required an explanatory adequacy in terms of transcendence that Tillich had been denying. If we have to live by faith of whatever kind, caught as we are in cosmic process, the faith with the most adequacy and validity (as becomes apparent in *Faith and Reason* and *Reason in Religion*) and with the most competent and authentic use of both the creative and the critical reason, is faith in the living God, the personal Spirit of Love, the Ultimate Concern who is more than man's concern in right relation to Being itself, who is indeed ontologically the Infinite Compassion whose love in history becomes the Sufferer who understands and whose love in eternity becomes the fulfilling Joy which is the eternal Reality, the Ground and Goal of all creative processes. Tillich tried to avoid this approach from the history of creation, where he was the most vulnerable, by resorting to the distinction between ontological and teleological thinking. But his explicit ontology of the unconditional Being itself was too thin, rather than of Spirit, *plus* Love and the personal; and his dismissal of teleological thinking could be valid only for the *eschaton,* the fullness of time, the living of love rather than the learning of it, and not for the pedagogical process in which level thinking is a fact, yes, the foundational fact of God's cosmic process, the direction of creation.

For that matter, democracy is good as equality of opportunity, but it should never be a leveling process or goal. It should lift all to their fullest development without envy or pride. God himself, for that matter, will always, so to speak, be more real, more true, more powerful, more beautiful and more wise than any created, finite being, even than all finite spirits in eternity. If dimensional thinking aims to democratize God as one of us, the aim is right if it refers to his humility, to his condescending love, to his identification and involvement in our lot and our world. Yes, by all means God is no tyrant, no arbitrary dictator, no authoritarian. But the fact of his love and his humility in no wise precludes his ultimacy and his universality as presuppositional for all creation where he can never be rivaled by man or any other creature. Furthermore, God has created us with unequal ability, sensitivities, and creative powers. We are not all alike and therefore love can become real. To do away with the temptations to pride and bitterness, envy and invidiousness, merely by calling all alike or by the attempt to make all alike is to rebel against God's creation and not to accept the full task of love whatever one's station. An open opportunity for freedom is a far better solution. God did not make justice ultimate, but fullness of development and fulfillment for all in a community of love where all should live the full life of appreciation and joy, not in invidious self-attainment but in the inclusive attainment of all as the care and joy of each, and the attainment of each as the care and joy of all. Such a view of love goes contrary to our unredeemed and unsanctified feelings and causes resistance but is the obvious ABC's of God's love, the very heart of the Universal Word.

If level has its own distinctive use and limited meaning in such a way that to leave it out is to forfeit explanatory adequacy while to use it beyond its proper limit of efficacy is to destroy interpretative reliability, what, however, of our next two terms? What of the choice between direction and dimension?

Let us look at the question this way. Level thinking seems best for the category of being, of substance. It is surely the category for external relations. Level thinking can be block thinking. Directional thinking, moreover, seems more in line with process, with goal-seeking. Directional thinking is dynamic, pointing to change, correction, attainment. Directional thinking is directive thinking. Level thinking is basically preparatory for the fulfillment of process, one level on top of the other, and all of them continuous from the bottom in terms of the whole, but discontinuous from each top in terms of the new. Level thinking is more than the imposition of the new into the old and the old adding to the new. It is the incorporation of the new by the old and the fulfilling of the old by the new; indeed it is the transformation in meaning and function of the old by the new.

Directional thinking is also for fulfillment, for the new, for the discovery to complete what has been delivered. Whereas level thinking as such stands for the truth of being, directional thinking stands for the truth of becoming. There is no becoming apart from being and neither being nor becoming can be understood most deeply and fulfillingly except in terms of spirit. But pedagogically, within the created, objectified world, being and becoming have their proper place; and so do level and directional thinking. Level thinking is basically descriptive whereas directional thinking is prescriptive. Level thinking makes clear where we are; directional thinking where we are going, especially where we should go. Thus directional thinking is soteriological, in terms of salvation. Salvation thinking, obviously, is futuristic, eschatological, goalistic, directive.

Directional thinking is most appropriately adjectival to process philosophy even as level thinking best modifies substance philosophy, the philosophy par excellence of being rather than of becoming. Dimensional thinking, moreover, goes best with either a philosophy of non-being or of process. In a way it fits the mainstream of Eastern rather than Western thought. It can be contextual within some ultimate *nirguna,* some undifferentiated ultimate, some final *nirvana,* some true suchness or agnosticism. But it can equally well be adjectival to the right use of the category of spirit. Spirit is the positive beyondness of *nirguna.* Spirit has all the elasticity and flexibility of non-being while still serving to illumine both being and becoming; it can serve also to relate all the categories, "the unity of unities," to think with Herbert Richardson, as the neutral category of spirit takes on the color and the shape ultimately of love and personal purpose, but approximately whatever shape and color is concretely called for by the situation at hand. In one sense and for some purposes all reality is contained in and created by the spirit. Thus spirit is the womb, the abyss, the ultimate ground of being, becoming, and non-being. All reality roots in and stems from spirit. Here is the ultimate, universal democracy of all-inclusiveness. The color and the shape, the differentiation, is not produced by spirit as such. It can contain all kinds, and all forms, of being, becoming, and non-being without at the same time denying or refusing the ultimate isness of God as a self-entity both omnicompetently present and omnicompetently absent at the same time according to circumstance and need. The next three chapters will try to formulate more precisely how the categories of spirit, love, and personal purpose meet these needs of distinction, as for instance, suggested by such terms as level, direction, and dimension. But here we note the need.

We have, then, studied, at least suggestively, the need for distinction. We have shown the need for distinction of the ultimate as such and of the ultimate in the proximate. We have considered the dimension of depth as one aspect of the distinction of the ultimate, but have gone on from there to discuss the status of universals and their varying functions and degrees of reality. We found universals in history both more flexible and real than the more permanent universals in nature as such. We then considered the interrelation between nature and history and the need to observe what kinds of classes of distinction pertain to the varying degrees of interrelation. After that we considered individuality as such and its meaning both as distinction and as identity. We tried then to suggest differentiations in terms of the terms themselves such as distinction, difference, and separation. Finally, we have ended this chapter by considering how level, direction, and dimension are interrelated and what they characteristically express. Our discussion so far, however, can become fulfilled only as we try positively to produce the categories of reality in terms not of substance nor of process, but of spirit, love, and personal purpose. This undertaking is central to the whole task of this work.

The Categories of Reality: Spirit

THE CHRISTIAN FAITH, we have said, needs to develop its own framework for expressing its universal message. Too long has it been limited by being couched within the thought stance of substance philosophy, while the newer process metaphysics is also unable to do full justice to the universal nature of the Christian faith. Unless the Christian faith is universal in nature, it is not ultimate. If it is not ultimate, it is not true theology. If the Christian name gets in the way of universality, it is better to forsake the Christian name than to forsake the truth. Authentic theology is always not only interfaith but ahead of all concrete religions. Our contention is that the Christian faith centers in the Universal Word wherein all knowledge, religious and secular, finds equal fulfillment and where all knowledge includes *ipso facto* all religions and all branches of secular knowledge. The Universal Word thus outruns all religions. Nothing at all can fall outside the scope, directly or indirectly, of the criterion for interpretation which is the Universal Word.

Analytically the Universal Word has, then, to prove capable of providing categories which illumine all aspects of life and knowledge more adequately than the philosophies of substance or process or any other candidate for the task. As we have seen in the preparatory chapters, the decisive requirement is to obtain categories which can account for identity and distinction within all the gradations of being, becoming, and non-being as well as within their interrelations and interactions. The three categories of the New Testament which fundamentally define God, the Ultimate, are spirit, personal purpose, and love. We turn, therefore, to the examination of these categories as the substrates from which the Christian framework can be formulated without recourse to alien, limiting, and distorting philosophies.

What is presuppositional is nearly impossible to define. It can be understood in no terms other than its own and then only insofar as it most fully illumines or clarifies our world of experience. Some insist that we essay no formal definition of spirit as a category but clarify instead what we mean by spirit by illustrating the way the category lights up experience as nothing else can do and the manner in which it disposes of the persistent philosophical problems that are posed by the philosophies of substance and process. Such power for solution, if it be more than verbal, and therefore also importantly directive for experience, may be the best and perhaps the only way that we can proceed. But as in the case of both substance and process, I feel better if I at least try to share the meaning I give to spirit within the later, more functional analysis. What we are doing is at best mostly making suggestions toward a definition. This much I feel I must do even though to offer one may seem more useless than to explain to water dwellers how an airplane can "swim" in air.

By spirit I mean the capacity for the fullest possible inclusiveness, accepting the maximum of creative differentiation. (Love and not spirit is productive of such differentiation.) Spirit is the power to remain selfsame and yet to participate, as inner identity, in all forms of being, becoming, and non-being. Spirit is that ground of being or power for being which has the power to create what is in some aspects other than itself, and yet to remain within what is created as its inner identity and even, also, as the power for the integrity of the self-being of the created. Spirit is the power for flexibility which by being multidimensional can provide as is needed such presence and such absence with the created distinctions, such participation and such privacy, and such activity and such passivity. Spirit is the reality of perfect identity which yet allows for genuine distinctions of being, doing, and feeling. Spirit is the capacity for congruence that is more than coinherence, and which can yet coinhere as needed. Congruence bespeaks identity, whereas coinherence connotes participation. Spirit is congruent and therefore cannot merely concur. Spirit is and remains the most inclusive reality, the identity before and beyond, *of,* all differentiation whether of being or process. Spirit is the inner unity of all community and communication which is the essence of sameness, with a perfect multidimensional identity which as such can constitute not only the power for all differentiation but the capacity for flexible and conditional relations at the same time and in the same instance but not in the same dimension, of presence and absence, activity and passivity. Spirit most basically is the reality of the kind of identity which as love and personal purpose can create and communicate with what is not itself, albeit spirit remains the inner identity in reality of all there is. These definitions can become meaningful mostly as we work out the three basic categories in their interrelationships and interworkings.

Spirit is the category which exhibits the fullest potential for inclusiveness. Ultimately Spirit is. Spirit is one. Reality, in one of its dimensions, is Spirit. Spirit works through energy. Energy is capacity for work. But

Spirit *is* before Spirit *works.* In this sense the question of what is comes first. It is not enough to say that Spirit works. Spirit is, and as such works. Purpose precedes working; focused or structured energy is logically prior to neutral or random energy. Reality works but working is not reality. This is the reason that Spirit alone, as substrate, is not enough. Spirit is colored by personal Purpose and personal Purpose is motivated by Love. To each of these three ultimates we shall devote a chapter. But first and for our needs now, let us consider Spirit as a category of Reality.

Spirit, then, to proceed, is all-inclusive, because Spirit is prior to all working. I have said that Spirit has, produces, provides energy, but that Spirit is not energy. Nor is energy Spirit. Energy can be neutral; that is why energy can be the carrier of purpose, whether of direct purpose, which is structured and colored, or of indirect purpose, which can be free and open to take on new coloration within itself as well as to be revised or redirected in its flow. Energy can be colored in the form of a cell which itself can be neutral to the point where a cell which starts growth in the body in one direction (a cell of the eye, for instance) can at an early stage become organically reconstituted so as to become a different kind of cell in the body within a new context of growth.

Spirit works in the world that we know at least in one form through energy, but Spirit is also meaning, and meaning works in a different fashion. Meaning has a form of being (isness) in itself, as well as a potential acceptance within personal Purpose, or expression by personal Purpose, which is prior to, other, and more than, the working out of the meaning and the intention. Spirit, in any case, is more than either energy or meaning. Both kinds of working stem from the underlying, inclusive reality of Spirit. Spirit is the sheer, original power to be and to become, or to cease being and becoming, that characterizes the primitive givenness of reality. Spirit is the fount of meaning in a multidimensional reality that focuses and directs energy into such unity as characterizes cosmic process and experience.

Spirit is "everywhere" in the sense that it is the substrate of all there is, not a substrate of substance, but the identity that substrate signifies. The personal is not everywhere; nor is Love everywhere in the direct sense of open or declared Love. Yet spirit is everywhere in some primary form of its reality. Spirit may be present as mostly mere energy, the neutral continuum for growth of the most incipient form. It may be almost entirely passive, ready for the ingestion of purpose of the lowest beginning or for its use by the most developed kind of freedom. Energy is there, but energy is not Spirit. Energy in such a neutral form would be unrelated and unimportant. But energy comes in such capacity for work because of the presence of spirit; such spirit works as the indirect vehicle or carrier of the fuller original meaning or intention.

Thus Spirit is everywhere without ever being limited to anywhere or to anything. Plato groped to fill this need by his use of "the receptacle." We shall discuss this power at length in connection with the Potential Word. Being no thing, Spirit is "nothing and nowhere" in the sense of limitation while still being everywhere in some dimension. All things are in spirit in general. Spirit is the identity of all without being all there is. It is all-inclusive in some sense without being ultimately some undifferentiated ultimate without distinctions of reality. Spirit is never without some qualification, but spirit in general can be purposely passive and neutral. Spirit itself is in *gunas*. It is never *nirguna*. Distinction is of the essence of Spirit, but because of its interreality with love and the personal, Spirit is the perfect identity within and throughout all distinctions. Spirit is quality rather than quantity, the creator of quantified existence. As Jakob Boehme puts the case, "The beginning of all substance is the Logos." Spirit has purpose and intention. Spirit is personal; Spirit is love. Personal Purpose creates; intentions work. Meanings create. In the beginning was the concept, the purpose, the universal Word. It was "with God and was God," for purpose, intention, is with the personal, with Love. And God creates through, and *as,* this Universal Word. Thus Spirit both is and works as, and through, personal Purpose. The reality of the personal Purpose is Love. In New Testament terms, God is Love; God is Father; God is Spirit.

God as ultimate is most inclusively spirit. God can, of course, be defined either as the ultimate in all its aspects: personal and impersonal, positive and passive, direct and indirect; or God can be defined exclusively as the Love that is personal, as whatever is self-aware as Love directly and in relation. Spirit, however, is the most inclusive substrate, which may not be defined except multidimensionally. As a totality spirit is rightly characterized as neutral, for spirit is both spirit and Spirit; it is both the inclusive substrate of reality, the one and only identity, and the colored and structured meaning-intention of reality. Thus spirit multidimensionally is rightly called "it." Not only creation stands out in spirit, as energy and as matter; for us, as cosmic process; but God also stands out distinct as an entity, a focused consciousness, within the multidimensional reality of spirit.

God is not undifferentiated energy or reality of whatever kind. God may be defined in terms of the categories, but God is not merely the categories as such. God is transpersonal and multidimensional but not the categories analytically understood. Nor is God the ultimate *nirguna*. God is inherently love and inherently creative Spirit. Thus both Spirit is and spirit is, for Spirit is one and selfsame, possessing capacity for functional differentiation. Spirit is selfsame in all multiplicity, the identical carrier of all being and the creative capacity that evolves distinction, creating the new and arranging the new. Thus Spirit is also the meaning of non-being, or non-being is an aspect of spirit, a capacity of Spirit. Without such capacity for non-being there could be no genuine creation, nothing authentically new. Spirit, then, as creator within his nature and with capacity for the making of the new, is also the meaning and power of becoming. Being, non-being, and becoming find inclusively their power in spirit.

We shall later observe that the highest meaning of Spirit is Love, but Love is as Spirit and works multidimensionally. Spirit is selfsame, the only and final identity, and is therefore all-inclusive, whereas Love is selfsame but capable of both personal presence and absence. Spirit knows no total absence. Even evil could not be apart from the capacity of spirit inclusively to be present also as power for distorted, partial, and contrary being and working. Spirit can thus never be *ouk on*, only *me on*. Spirit is no thing and no where, but all things and wheres find their meaning and their power to be in spirit. Spirit is no personality, but spirit is personal and all personal beings find their distinctive existence through the reality and power of spirit. Martin Buber, indeed, maintains that those who live in the Spirit address the other as a thou, but such definition does not refer to the all-inclusiveness of the spirit. Spirit, rather, is the all-inclusive category of Reality.

Spirit, then, ultimately is inclusive, but as love and personal purpose Spirit works as meaning and as energy. It is simply wrong to think of meaning as having no ontological status. Meaning outruns existence. Because meaning is, there can be power for meaning. Spirit is as meaning and therefore meaning has power for existence. Meaning is lure for existence. Such meaning can work mostly as attraction or as impact on creation, but the fuller fact is that meaning works because meaning is. Spirit as meaning works from spirit through energy. Energy itself is neutral capacity to work, but receives its direction through meaning. Meaning and attraction *are* as well as *can be*. They have power to be and to call into being. There is no meaning, however, apart from spirit. Wherever meaning is, spirit is prior as the more inclusive reality. Spirit creates meaning as well as carries it. Therefore spirit can both be as meaning: the meaning in and of God, the meaning in, of, and for life; and also have the power to work, even to create new meanings; to purpose creation. Working presupposes being. The reality that works, even of meaning, is spirit. There can be no distinction between the existence of a book as a thing and a book as containing meaning in the sense that one is and the other is not; meaning is and works through its distinctive form of appearance. Spirit *is* and as such precedes all analysis into value and existence. Both value and existence presuppose their power to be; and all forms of being exist within the identity of the one Spirit. Value and existence split apart because Spirit as the only identity of creation allows for the growth of creation

wherein what is meant to be must genuinely come to be. The Analytical
Spirit courts the Historical and fulfills but is also fulfilled by the Potential, as will become clear as we later pass from creation to consummation.
Spirit also constitutes the power to be in the case of intention. Meaning,
we have seen, both is and can become an aspect of the ultimate. Meaning
has its own power to be from Spirit, as distinction, to be sure, not as
identity as such. The life of God, of course, is meaningful as love apart
from all creating. Love is no mere means to creativity! Creating enriches
meaning. The world means more. The creation of new meaning comes
from spirit which simply is. Thus meaning both is and can become within
and for spirit. But meaning, moreover, can intend its extension, its cultivation, its enrichment, and its culmination. Such use of meaning by spirit
is possible only from within the fullness of reality. Indeed, such inten-
tional use of meaning by spirit is no mere possibility *ab origine;* it presupposes the potentiality, as we shall see later at length, which modifies
the order of actuality. Spirit through intention informs being with meaning. But being is not everywhere as Spirit is, in some form; nor need meaning become totally objectified, although naturally it keeps becoming
objectified.

There is identity in Spirit both *of* and *for* meaning, regardless of its
objectification. Intention adds no new reality to the identity of spirit.
Spirit underlies all reality whether of being, non-being, or becoming. Intention is a form of being for becoming, often by non-being, in and of the
spirit. Spirit is in the form both of meaning and intention while spirit
also becomes present in all objectification. The identity in both being and
becoming is always one and the same. *In this sense* there can be no potential in God as though actualization added to the identity and reality of
Spirit. In this sense *ex nihilo nihil stat* is true. Thomism in one respect
guards an important truth. The potential in God is on a different level, in
a different dimension. The potential in God is not a question of ultimate
reality, as we shall see in Part Three, but rather expresses the creative
nature and power of Spirit.

Where are we, then? Spirit is the inclusive ultimate, the category of
identity in reality. Love's dimension of meaning is never apart from meaning. Love is never meaningless. Such meaning, however, is also ultimately
as Spirit. Spirit is then as meaning. For objective function, moreover, Spirit
is as intention. From the side of actualization, or from the side of creation,
spirit is potential. But the potential itself has its reality in and of Spirit.
We said initially that spirit not only is but spirit works. Spirit in creating
never *becomes,* nor is spirit *non-being,* but spirit is the meaning and the
power in becoming and thus the only ground of non-being. Spirit constitutes the identity in the meaning, the intention and the function of non-
being. Love is creative, but is creative as Spirit, and non-being is presup-

positional to creative spirit, the intending spirit, the potential spirit, the spirit of becoming. Thus becoming is within the spirit; creation is within the spirit; distinctions become because of the spirit of becoming, but Spirit as such never becomes; the depth formula is always simply: *spirit is.*

Thus spirit as a category is ever selfsame; and yet it gives rise to dimensions of distinction. It is the ground of the neutral substrate of energy as such; it is also the ground of inorganic matter or the inorganic world; it underlies the organic and the power for growth; it forms an intrinsic aspect of the reality of personal relations; and it finds its truest fulfillment in the relations of mature love which is its own highest inherent nature. Through all these forms of existence and experience spirit is. It is the power of selfsameness underlying all, the final inclusive reality. But Spirit also gives rise to, *produces,* ever-enriching distinctiveness because not only is its nature to *do* so but its nature is also to *be* so. The reality of distinctions within spirit inherently and eternally becomes more than reflected in creation; it becomes enacted in creation. Spirit produces distinctiveness because spirit possesses distinctiveness. This is what I mean by claiming that spirit as such, the inclusive ultimate, the final identity, is never *nirguna.* Spirit is not only selfsame but selfsame within its eternal richness of distinctions. Spirit is one and is distinctions. Spirit is one and many. Reality is as much pluralism as monism.

The level of the most neutral energy expresses the most indirect presence of God. Spirit is there, for such energy is in spirit; it is a way spirit works. Such energy is, indeed, capacity for work open to the greatest range of possibilities. It is ready for coloring or for entering into some more conditioned situation. Its neutrality lies in its capacity for distinction. Spirit is not intrinsically neutral. Spirit intrinsically is Love, personal, purposive. But Spirit that is thus intrinsically colored or structured is capable of providing capacity to work, open to unnumbered possibilities for use. It has capacity to become neutrally passive. The absence of existential "coloration" and structure is the kind of non-being that becoming presupposes. It is prerequisite for creation. Thus non-being is not only *ouk on,* some general nothingness, some so to speak neutral nothingness, but specifically and significantly also *me on,* spirit's purposed potential openness to new coloration or structure. Some new way of functioning may be in store for the neutral capacity to work, not only in general, but with regard to specific options in nature or history.

Thus spirit is and spirit works. Spirit and energy are of the same reality, but are not the same reality. Spirit is, but with the capacity to create; or is by nature creative. And creation is not only some brand new production. Even though the new must in some sense be new, *ex nihilo,* or there would be no genuine newness at all, creation is also a fashioning and a coloring. The most neutral dimension of the spirit's working is with respect to the most neutral nature of energy, shall we say energy as such. Energy as such is not only an analytical abstraction, but a logical-onto-logical characterization of the passivity and permissiveness of nature as exemplified in its minutest units of capacity to work and in its lowest level of biological development.

In between seem to lie levels of so-called solid substances which seem mostly determined, or well structured and thoroughly colored for long-range purposes. The flow of flux exhibits a form of flux that functions as solidity. In such cases there seems to be such regularity of relation as to amount to almost complete prediction of function or a mechanically de-termined relationship. It is with respect to such relationships that the occasion arises to turn science into scientism or to extend measurable relationships in a functionally predictable sense to the world of experi-ence as a whole, thus going beyond the proper limits of methodological efficacy. Take a rock or a mountain for an example. How stable and last-ing it seems! But rocks can be crushed and mountains reduced to dust. The energy itself within them in its constant whirl and its rate of flux is colored or structured only by a situational necessity. Energy can be re-leased, redirected, and appear under new conditions. Form with regard to such arrangement of matter as rocks is less flexible than form in a pile of sand, but the energy itself has only taken on color and structure as it becomes part of a certain kind of function.

Behind the nature of the structure or the pattern and intensity of the flow of energy lies a lengthily enduring purpose, to provide a certain kind of stable environment for the pedagogical process. Thus Spirit is and spirit works. The entire pedagogical process is in spirit; it becomes dis-tinct within spirit; it can be changed within spirit; it can cease to be within spirit. Spirit is, but works through flux and form in their inter-relationships. Purpose imposes form on flux. The more passive or less subject to change the nature of the objects, the more indirectly related they are to the personal purpose, the ultimate Love. And Spirit is intrin-sically adaptable, is capable of appearing in and with all forms of energy.

But Spirit is there, for all is in spirit. Spirit interpenetrates and sustains all being, giving meaning also to all becoming and non-being. Spirit creates lengthily enduring forms, solid substances of varying degrees of solidity as the continuum, the container for life. Life is characterized by irritability, that is, by capacity to respond. Thus here we have a less merely indirect or neutral relationship. The biological cell has genuine capacity for neutrality for its purposes. Its change of function can come about through change of organic environment. Cytology becomes an ever more complex subject. But the more life rises to higher levels of response the less neutral becomes the total functioning of energy, the capacity to work. Higher animals change the environment itself in their favor. They build nests as well as adapt to the ecological situation. Spirit is there;

spirit works there; but instead of merely continuing chains of causation, or structured forms of energy, there is now more of a passivity of spirit and less of passivity of the event. Life uses, directs, purposes.

In man, too, of course, spirit is both present and works. But spirit is most passive since man is most active as a purposing or directing creature. Man is given responsible freedom for self-determination within degrees of conditioning circumstances. Thus spirit is present and works in man passively where man truly decides, even though man is also conditioned by and encounters structures which are more durably colored and more firmly structured. Freedom is always within a network of continuing causes. The freedom of man, however, allows the flexibility for growth, through responsible choice, because spirit is present to make man, his environment, and his choices possible through the passivity and permissiveness of the ultimate. Freedom is mostly an aspect of distinction and not of identity. In one sense, then, passivity of spirit is the precondition for activity of finite selves, but the spirit must nevertheless be there in the sense of maintaining the reality of the continuum and empowering the capacity to work.

Man can also, furthermore, open up to the meaning and reality of Spirit. Man can respond to personal purpose. Man can learn love. Therefore, Spirit can be present to man not only passively and maintainingly, but also in active encounter or in direct community and communication. In the case of man spirit is always present, to be sure, as the maintainer of his self and of his environment. This presence is a dimension that is mostly indirect and passive. The spirit can also be present in an intermediate manner as moral prompter. The operation of spirit precedes the cooperation of Spirit. Then the Spirit can work in, through, and as the coloration of conscience in its responding to the image of God. Such presence is halfway indirect and direct, or halfway passive and active. Spirit works but not as the full meaning and reality of Love. In *The Christian Understanding of God* I have called this kind of presence and activity the Spirit of God rather than the Holy Spirit. It is neither merely an "I" nor an "it," but a combination of the I-it, of the personal and the impersonal.

The coloration of Spirit is neither seen nor working at its fullest, either in the world of nature or in the moral nature of man. The Spirit is in these instances not personally present, or present as Love, in the full sense. Where love is, the Spirit is present in both the most passive and the most active sense. The Spirit in love guards and enhances the freedom of the finite and therefore as such is and works passively, but the passivity is under the constraint or direction of a direct presence, a purposing, which is also supplemented by an interpenetration of understood and accepted Presence. Thus the direct fulfills the indirect. The indirect relation brings into the personal confrontation or community the whole accumulative history of the person who right then is his own history. The indirect relation also includes the functioning of the natural body and mind which carry the self. But beyond and fulfilling such indirection and passivity is the direct relation of accepted, understood, even loved Presence.

What is important about the spirit as the most inclusive category is that spirit can be present and absent at the same time. We are dealing with contrapletal logic, not the logic of contradiction, or even of contrariety. Ascriptions to God which on one level are contradictory can yet be ascribed to him on the higher level where they become contrapletal. Contrapletal logic, which we began to discuss in the previous chapter, is not a neologism of my own making. It has long been in the philosophical dictionary. It was first called to my attention by a professor of philosophy who formerly taught in China, Dr. Roderick Scott. The key to it is its multidimensional nature. Contrapletal logic characterizes a multidimensional ontology and has no need or meaning apart from such an understanding of reality.

A general use of contrapletal logic, to be sure, is to include the large phenomena of complementariness or polarity. A prime example has been the Chinese use of *yin* and *yang*. Two realities like day and night or light and darkness are contradictory in one dimension and yet fulfilling of each other within their place in nature and man's experience. Some scholars like my perceptive former colleague, Professor Robert Brank Fulton, have been anxious and almost insistent that contrapletal logic should be limited to such uses and not employed to sanction contradictions within rational discourse. I found this attitude at first among some scholars at Oxford University. But both Dr. Fulton and these Oxford scholars, I believe, came to see that the fuller and more needed use for contrapletal logic is that of accepting contradictions on one level or in one dimension as not contradictions on another level or in another dimension.

This fuller use, which safeguards the critical use of reason by its creative extension to express the truths of a multidimensional ontology, depends completely upon the reality of this kind of ontology. If God is transpersonal and not only personal, for instance, that is, if he is not personal in all respects but is himself also the spirit present in the impersonal impersonally or semipersonally in man's moral urges and the workings of conscience, then he can be present and absent in the same man at the same time, or present and not present, according to need and will, without any contradiction in terms. In other words, predicates which can only be mutually contradictory in one dimension become contrapletal within the multidimensional ontology. A multidimensional ontology, in truth, requires a multidimensional logic. At our discussions in Oxford, the Chairman of the Board of the Faculty of Theology of the University, Principal John Marsh, eloquently explained the derivation of the term "contrapletal" from "contraplex," and its history from the way communication, particularly in the case of the telegraph, depended upon contrapletal interpretation. Long before the telegraph, however, Ramanuja in one of the most profound treatises in human literature, *Vedarthasamgraha*, worked out the meanings of contrapletal logic in his fierce dispute with Sankara as to whether or not God could be an entity, especially an entity with personal characteristics. By going beyond substantive thinking of personality and in effect considering God a personal Spirit, Ramanuja brilliantly and profoundly answered Sankara, and in so doing worked out in the *Vedarthasamgraha* the needed nuances of contrapletal logic. Western thinking, if it is to outdistance substantive thinking, has much to learn along these lines.

Within contrapletal logic God is present and absent with his creation in different senses, but at the same time, even while God in himself is ever one and selfsame. As spirit in general, as passive spirit merely maintaining the created order or continuing the chains of causation in their ordinary working, God can be present, as Spirit is in itself in that dimension, without being personally present, or present as declared, understood, and accepted Love.

God can also endow, and does endow, the created order with certain types of working that can further his control indirectly and lead toward his being understood and accepted. Not only is the neutral order necessary that allows some freedom for responsible human decisions and growth, and not only is the environment necessary, which man can count on as the medium for his decisions and learning, but also necessary is the realm of human community that can be the continuum for growth in love, and God's direct presence to the believer as Love. All these belong to the full situation which, pedagogically speaking, is usually far from full. Thus God can absent himself in the personal sense in order to make room for freedom and for privacy, for growth and for learning; but he can also make himself personally present as the companion who understands and shares man's inner experience and his outer community.

No two objects can occupy the same space at the same time, but spirit and object can do so. No two personalities can occupy the same place at the same time either in physical or in psychic space. Personalities are distinct and consciousness does separate. But in spirit two persons can be one, and spirit and a person can be one. All identity in spirit is. There simply cannot be division in spirit. Is Christ divided? Certainly not insofar as "the Lord is the Spirit." We are all one person in Christ in this sense. The universal Word owes its universality to the nature of spirit. The unity of the spirit is. Where there is no unity, there the distinctiveness has never become consummated or has become falsified. Relations can be wrong to the spirit and among the spirits insofar as they are personal. But there can be no inherent division in the spirit as such. Spirit is the identity of Reality. Spirit is always present in some sense, and all objectified beings can be freely related and communicated only because of the inner identity and reality of the Spirit.

Community has its dimension of depth in spirit. There can be and are communities on the level of objectification. But no community becomes fully right and real except it be right and real in the spirit, unless it become "unimunity." What I call Unimunity goes beyond both unity and community, the two terms which first suggested to me the profound meaning of unimunity. Unimunity has full and perfect identity in spirit and is the principle and power for the fullest and richest differentiation because spirit at its highest is Love. In the chapter on love I shall develop this concept more fully.

Spirit, in any case, allows freedom because of the passivity it provides on its preparatory pedagogical level. In such communities there can be and are disharmonies, ignorance, tensions, conflict, as well as degrees of the opposite values and virtues, but on the level of the full meaning and reality of Spirit, the Spirit of personal purpose, of Love, there can be only harmony and creative togetherness. The deepest identity of maturing community is always Spirit, the unity of the Spirit in the bond of Love. When the nature of Spirit becomes not only understood but also incarnated within a unity rich with diversity, individuality and community pass over into their fulfilling reality: unimunity. This concept is one of the most important findings of this work because, as we shall see, it shows the implications and implementations of spirit as a category.

There can also be depth communication within the reality of the Spirit. Ideas and moral admonitions are communication from selves to selves. They pass from ego to ego. They are mostly on the level of ideas, feeling, or willing. They motivate largely through fear or desire, although ideas as such have also attraction. They move, however, mostly through attraction or repulsion on the part of the ego or the group. But such communication is also superficial in comparison to the communication of spirit to spirit, *de profundis*. Spirit is reality and true meaning. Man is made for the goals envisioned and pursued, yes, promoted by the Spirit. Therefore man becomes himself only as he understands and finds himself in the Spirit in which he most deeply is. Communication here reaches the dimension of man's ultimate being and meaning. In the most profound sense communication becomes natural. Spirit speaks to spirit. Therefore there is a power of communication beyond mere ideas or exhortations. There is the quiet confrontation of Reality. Motivation here is of an order which can be rejected, but not merely dismissed as the ideas of persuasion of other selves. Man knows himself addressed on the level of the deepest reality. Thus meaning and motivation can marry in reality and bear the children of truth, peace, and concern. Where Spirit is understood and accepted, Love is always the fundamental reality. The personal is enhanced and the Holy Spirit "pours love" into the hearts of those who listen, understand, and accept.

I have done my best to hold off the discussion of the categories of the personal and of love, but such separation is artificial and finally impossible. Spirit cannot be understood apart from and except as in some dimension personal and love. Thus complete suppression of aspects which are integrally defining of spirit is misleading. Yet for the sake of the best possible communication I have tried at least to stress most intensely and devote most attention to the topic under discussion. The definitions of spirit cannot become clear and full in this chapter, but they should contain emphasis on spirit as capable of coinherence and congruence, as substance is not, and on multidimensionality and contrapletal logic which cannot characterize substance. I have also stressed that spirit possesses an identity of total inclusiveness which goes beyond the energy that spirit uses. Spirit too is finally focused and directive. Such discussion should begin to make it clear how God can be both an entity or a focused isness ultimately and still be universally present in some sense.

I have not shown in this chapter how spirit can fulfill process thinking by solving the problems of eminent being. Entity and being have, to be sure, the same root, but for our purposes entity means simply distinct isness, whereas being has become connected with substance thinking. The next chapter will set forth how God, in this sense, can be an entity, the supreme Spirit without being the supreme Being. The discussion of the personal at some length in terms of personal Spirit rather than spiritual Personality is a prime need for our day. Then we can go on in the succeeding chapter to the discussion of the category of love without which spirit cannot begin to be understood and which also holds the key to the category of the personal. The order of the categories is purposefully climactic. In each instance I shall have to bring in all the categories, but the strongest stress will still be on the category under discussion.

Early in this chapter I stated that spirit is and works as energy, visible or invisible, in objectified or unobjectified form. Spirit becomes creative through meaning and intention. Spirit is the reality of identity, the scope of universality, whether of being, becoming, or non-being; spirit is the total extent of inclusiveness. All things are in spirit, but spirit is more and other than all things. Existence is the created order, not the primary order of reality. Spirit is wider and intrinsically more structural than energy. Energy is capacity for work and spirit is wherever anything works, but energy is not spirit. Working presupposes reality, what is. Thus spirit alone is universal, all-inclusive, as well as ultimate, the only and final reality of identity. Energy as such cannot explain our cosmological process and our complex experience. Spirit as focused and directive multidimensional reality can do so as we shall increasingly find.

Spirit, moreover, is also the power of permanence. Spirit always is.

Spirit is given as the stuff of reality. We have even dared to suggest its being likened to a substrate! It takes the place of *materia prima*. Energy may be constant within the created universe, but Spirit is the eternal Source and Directiveness of energy beyond all creations. Universes may arise and die. In some sense the personal God, as we shall suggest later, may be born and die. The personal God is the Spirit in awareness of the created world and in the makings of creative purposings. Such a God creates choices. He makes cosmologies. He is himself, nevertheless, distinction within Spirit. But permanently? We shall soon see that such personal awareness, choices, and creations involve finitude. God is not everywhere personally present and his personal awareness is conditioned by his world of experience. Thus Lao-tzu's famous saying, "I do not know whose Son it is, the image of what existed before God," has real meaning. So does talk about the death of God. But the Spirit cannot die. Nor can the meaning and reality of eternal Love as such die. Love and Spirit may create the personal gods of epochs and universes. But Spirit has the power of permanence. Spirit is eternal.

The fact that spirit gives rise to a contrapletal logic in that spirit can be absent and present at the same time does not make the spirit as spirit finite, for finally spirit is multidimensionally and eternally all-inclusive. When the spirit is not present with creation in some sense, absence does not involve limitation. In whatever sense is necessary the spirit is always present. Finitude, moreover, must itself be defined in terms of true ultimates. When God as spirit limits his personal presence for the sake of man's privacy, he never limits his love. His love is still present as spirit passively. Love then provides the needed medium, the pedagogical process. God as spirit is everywhere as needed. Limitation is not defined substantively or mathematically but in terms of ultimate reality and purpose. Thus spirit is universal in the ultimate sense precisely because spirit is present everywhere in the proper sense according to the dictates of Love. All things are in spirit; all persons are in spirit. But the personal Spirit of Love purposes passivity as the infinite expression of Love, or of God's very being. In the same way the absence of spirit in some sense does not mean that the spirit as Spirit is not eternal. It means only that eternity as God's time is both active and passive, containing both the direct and the indirect modes. The fullness of time is the fullness of Love, and the reality and meaning of the Spirit in this sense is both universal and permanent. Spirit, in fact, is the ultimate identity which must as such be both universal and permanent.

Methodologically we have now shared something of what we see in spirit as one dimension of the ultimate. In previous chapters we have tried to indicate deficiencies in other candidates for ultimate categories and to give criteria for acceptance in terms of need. This chapter should enunciate (the ultimate order can do no other than to offer us the vision of needs met) final presuppositions for a coherent interpretation of the totality of our experienced world. In this volume, however, I shall have no chance to enunciate nor even to enumerate the manifold aspects of the vision. I can barely mention for later work or for other workers the way the understanding of the spirit does away with the conflict between supernaturalism and naturalism. The spirit being identical throughout and yet, as we shall see in the next chapter, though no being, a distinct entity, the problems of supernaturalism posed by substance thinking are done away. There is not even a question of *a* God separate from creation. And yet since the Spirit that transcends is the same identity as the identity in nature and history, we can have a strong naturalism without reductionism. The problems are not oversimplified, moreover, because they become far more complex but also far more adequately answered. In the same way pantheism is fulfilled. In one dimension all is one spirit. There is only one final identity. Yet since love, as we soon shall see, by its very nature works to create, maintain, and enhance distinctions, panentheism becomes viable. The theism of substance and the panentheism of being, let alone pantheism as such, will not do. The categories of spirit, love, and personal purpose, however, propose proper solutions.

Symbolism also becomes clarified. With spirit the only identity, but an identity capable of producing genuine and rich variation, symbols do necessarily participate in what they symbolize, and not only in terms of ultimate identity but also in terms of the ultimate multidimensionality which underlies creative differentiation in nature and history. Substance thinking shuffles between sign thinking and agnosticism as to the knowledge of the ultimate. To avoid the extremes of anthropomorphism or agnosticism, substance thinking resorts to analogy of many kinds. But symbols as event-meaning and myth as event-happenings can reliably become channels to understand transcendence when the full meaning of the multidimensional identity of spirit is understood and when love's creative distinctions stand out as real—although never as separable from the ultimate identity. Even the question of analogy becomes revolutionized by the new ultimates. Some of these questions will at least be broached in this work, especially in the final section, and some have already been written under the title, *The Explanatory Word,* to be published later, but most of the work along these lines must be done by vigorous thinkers with interest to explore trails I have hardly begun to blaze.

Beyond that, enunciation should rise through analysis to poetry and descend from poetry to prophecy. The poetry and prophecy remain to be written; I can only offer as best I can, the vision I have of the adequacy of spirit as one dimension of reality and what that entails. Spirit as a category cannot be grasped even suggestively, however, except in a completely symbiotic relation to personal Purpose and Love.

CHAPTER

VI

The Categories of Reality:
The Personal

THE PERSONAL is one of the categories of reality; personality is not.
God is not a spiritual Personality who is Love, but Love who is a
personal Spirit. The New Testament rightly defines God as Love, not as
loving, for God is not a personality. Personality is no ultimate category,
but belongs to a limited class of finite beings. God is not a personality but
creates and deals with personalities. What is, then, the distinction between God's being a personal Spirit and his being a spiritual Personality?

Qualitatively, so to speak, God is Love; in terms of universality or total
inclusiveness he is Spirit. Spirit is the universal substrate; in some sense
spirit is everywhere; the personal is not everywhere, nor is love. Everywhere the Personal purposes, plans, imagines, controls, directs; everywhere Love acts in all ways, but is openly or directly present only in some
way and in some senses. Love reaches everywhere but is often present only
as meaning, intention, or condition for learning love. Only spirit is
everywhere and nowhere, the ultimate category underlying being, becoming, and non-being. Spirit works everywhere at the behest of purpose and
in the interest of Love. But spirit works through energy because it is
everywhere. The language we have used, to be sure, is spatial. Quantification such as inclusivness is characteristic of the spatial order, but once
and for all we must stress that such quantification is symbolic. If God cannot be spatialized; if God is "nowhere and nothing"; if God does not
exist in the finite sense because he is the living God before and beyond
existence, we can hardly speak of God being everywhere in some limiting
spatial sense.

All things and "wheres" are, rather, in God who is the womb or abyss
of all things. And yet with relation to the world we know and in which
we can speak meaningfully we must say that spirit is present everywhere,
that is inclusively or universally, without God being personally present
everywhere. Such omnipresence is no limitation by quantification. God is

present as spirit, carrying, interpenetrating all things, even though at his discretion he can be personally absent, and absent as directly acting or encountering Love. God can be Love even where he is not loving! We speak, then, of quantification in this sense in order to make sure that God allows for privacy and freedom in the created world, especially of human history, in order to let persons become real as finite spirits through authenticity of experience.

To affirm that God is not a personality means that he is not like a thing. God is not a substance; God is not even a thinking and acting substance; God is not even a loving, separate thing, substance, event, entity. In these senses God is no supreme Being. We use all these words almost irritatingly to rub in, to drive home, to nail fast the truth that God is not a personality with external relations. God is first of all spirit who is with, in, and under, who is the carrier of, who is the womb of, all there is. There is nowhere that God is not, as spirit. Therefore God cannot be limited to external relations. External relations are only a matter of pedagogical moment in God's life, basically limiting creation and not God. God is not a being among other beings in this limiting sense of personality. Personality is always one among others. God is not the Cosmic Self, the Macroscopic Self, the Supreme Being in the traditional use of the words. God is spirit who is everywhere, and plastic, flexible to all there is. God interpenetrates and thus is present far more easily than any process of osmosis. God is intrinsically one, identical, and universal as Spirit. Therefore the ultimate to go with Spirit cannot be personality, but it can only be the personal, the quality of Spirit as Love to be self-aware and concernedly, creatively purposive. The reason that we hesitate to capitalize personal as a category is that the personal is adjectival to Spirit, but intrinsically, eternally, permanently, inherently adjectival, a "hypostatic" union if we were to talk substance language. The ultimate is definitively, normatively, determinatively personal, but not everywhere or for all purposes.

God is no personality, no being, even the Supreme Being, who can be thought of in terms of substance, either statically or dynamically. And yet the ultimate category is personal, as the self-conscious, nonspatial purpose that characterizes spirit at its heart. Spirit is no mere reality back of the energy that works. Spirit is no unfocused *materia prima*. Spirit is no being or substance unimaginably light or thin, invisible for us, permeating all things. Spirit is the reality of identity, the power of permanence, the universality of reality, the capacity for creative distinction for persons and things, for community and communication. The personal is the seat of awareness, so to speak, of self-awareness and of what is non-self. It is awareness of what is and of what may be. The personal is recognition and the seat of knowledge. The personal is capacity for purpose and for initiating purposings. The personal is, therefore, the meaning and reality of spirit at its heart. It is the inner self-experience and directing reality of spirit.

The spirit is also moral. The spirit is holy. The spirit is the seat of integrity, of pureness, of wholeness. The spirit is the inner reality of authenticity. The spirit is "true suchness," to use a Buddhist conception of *nirvana*. Thus the moral is the real. The moral is not only the holy in the ceremonial sense, nor in the legal sense, nor yet in the sense of the sacred. The moral, to be sure, is the source of right conduct and dwells in such conduct. The moral can be experienced in the ceremonial and in the grandeur of law. The moral can be sensed in what is mysteriously grand and important. The moral can refer to the inner command for rightness and its outer enactment. But the sense of the moral is in true rightness, true suchness, in the holiness of integrity, in the ultimacy of right spirit, even beyond right being and right doing. The moral can comprise aspects of right thinking and right feeling, but the full meaning of the moral is rightness within the meaning and mystery of what is ultimate. Morality is being in right relations unconditionally and ultimately. But such moral qualification of spirit comes not in spirit as such, not in spirit in general, but in spirit as personal purpose, in spirit as inner consciousness and as intending eternally for creation.

This means that spirit is focused and thus an entity. Is spirit then a separate entity, after all, at least insofar as it is personal? No, the personal is not personality. The personal is no lump, so to speak, in the invisible ubiquity of spirit. The personal is not local in the meaning of space. The personal is no thinghood within spirit. The personal is not merely spirit. The spirit is transpersonal. There are aspects of reality where the personal is not. God can be personally absent even when he is present as spirit. The personal constitutes Spirit a distinctiveness of entity so that Spirit is no other things or other personalities. Spirit is not even other spirits. Because Spirit at its heart, its center, is personal Spirit, Spirit can be selfsame and other while also selfsame and the same as all others. Spirit can be the one ultimate identity and yet also the full power of genuine distinction. Spirit can be an entity without being either a separate entity or merely the sum total of all entities in their deepest meaning and purpose. The personal constitutes the spirit an entity that is distinct but not separate, that is total identity and yet also distinct as total.

That Spirit is personal means that it is focused. The heart and center of spirit is, of course, not spatial, but qualitative. But a nonspatial consciousness can be focused, have a center of meaning, a scale for appraisal, a basis for directives. We could say that Spirit is inner reality, nonobjectified, but all aspects of spirit are fully real and fully eternal. Spirit, then, is no vague, general substrate, but, to use a figure, a focused field, the final all-fields-encompassing field, to think with Jaspers. It is no mere power for being but a purposing power for being. Spirit is no mere capacity for creativity but is rather the envisaging capacity for creativity. The meaning and reality of Spirit is that it is personal in nature, even when it is more than personal, in one sense, and less than personal, in another. It is more than personal in the sense of universality and less than personal in its impersonal manifestations and activities. Spirit is a wider category than the personal, so to speak, and also a qualitatively less high category. Nevertheless both are selfsame. Both are the identical reality of the selfsame Spirit. Spirit adds no personal dimension in some place. Spirit is not shut out as spirit by some where, by some thing, by some other entity. Spirit is not limited from being fully Spirit because it is not everywhere personal, nor in another sense is it limited from being fully personal because it is not personal in every sense or everywhere. Spirit is full identity and full power for permanence.

Spirit, to be emphatic to the point of redundancy, is ubiquitous universality. The personal is the focusing of Spirit by personal purpose, by Love. This personal focusing constitutes Spirit a distinct entity even though also all-inclusive or the ground of all. Spirit is moral throughout but not in all senses personally moral, or the carrier of personal holiness. What then does it mean that Spirit is personal while Spirit remains ever selfsame? What does it mean that personal Spirit can be distinct as the Ultimate, the Eternal Spirit, and yet be always and everywhere, so to speak, the same? What does it mean that the Spirit as personal can have external relations and yet be at the same time and equally capable of having internal relations? We must explore this contrapletal logic more fully.

The personal means self-awareness as an entity. Self-knowledge makes distinct. Self-focused spirit characterizes Spirit as such as a distinction of the whole, distinguishable from all finite occurrence. Such a self-awareness is focused in such a way that it is subject having objects, even while these objects are also included congruently in the self-awareness. It is no mere matter of subject-object relation, but of Subject-subjectobject and Subject subjectobject relations, in one dimension identical and in the other distinct. It is simply wrong to say that God is a distinct entity if he is merely Subject or totally beyond all subject-object distinctions. Such an ultimate is without qualifications. Such an ultimate cannot constitute an entity, even a distinct entity. Yes, God as self-conscious Spirit is distinct to the point that he is authentically capable of having external relations. In this basic sense God is Self, but the comparison of Self to selves does not extend to the limitations of external relations in the human sense. God is Self, without being cosmic Self, and without being eternal Personality. How can we make such a claim? Upon our answer to this question hangs our whole distinction between God's being not a spiritual Personality but a personal Spirit. The meaning and nature of personality with its selective, limiting relations, its power of exclusion, is not ultimate, but rather the nature and meaning of spirit.

The personal as an ultimate category is focused Spirit and as such a distinct entity. Spirit is. Spirit works. Spirit is and works but not from an indiscriminate void that would afford no explanatory adequacy but from a purposing focus that constitutes the identity of wholeness. Self-consciousness is, however, no thing; self-awareness is no substance; self-knowledge is no personality with limiting relations as such. The selective nature of consciousness in God is the power for discrimination without the need for limitation. The wholeness of Spirit is intact. The wholeness of Spirit is focused without there being a hard lump, some separate thing, some excluding personality. Spirit has the reality of the personal in such a way that Spirit can be radically present and absent at the same time to the finite without destruction of inner identity. The coinherence of Spirit is such that God can be present in himself totally in the inner heart of Spirit while also absent from the finite decider for the sake of privacy and freedom.

God's own self-awareness everywhere does not involve his total offering of the personal aspect of Spirit everywhere. God's thus not offering himself as personal where he needs to be personally absent is no diminution of his full personal identity always and everywhere. His self-consciousness and his full knowledge of all things within that self-consciousness do not involve his offering of that personal self-consciousness everywhere and at all times. Thus Spirit is always metaphysically one and identical; ever selfsame and integral; and yet also operationally capable of being personally absent. God's withholding of the personal presence from the finite in no way involves its diminution or subtraction within the eternal identity of Spirit. External relations *in this sense* are a reality we must consider further.

Spirit is; Spirit is identical; Spirit continually enacts distinctions; Spirit is selfsame and as such distinct; Spirit is an entity while also being the inner reality of all there is. Spirit is the distinct entity of Wholeness while yet not being a monolithic whole. Spirit is the identity of wholeness and the distinctiveness of wholeness. The identity of all there is, is Spirit; the identity of all that works is energy; Spirit generates energy, but Spirit is not energy. All creation is from and in Spirit, but Spirit is not what is created. One aspect of the distinctiveness of Spirit is self-consciousness, self-awareness, self-knowledge. But such awareness is no added thing; it is no substance; it does not constitute a separate personality. Rather, the personal becomes distinct as the focused Spirit who always is and always works. God is not before all creation but with all creation. He is not before all finite spirits, but eternally with all finite spirits. Chronology as learning love does not concern finally eternity as the living Love and the living of love. We say that God is with creation. But withness is no quantity, no thingness, no substance. Withness is a qualitative distinction of focused consciousness. Withness means not the same in the qualitative sense of consciousness as it does in a quantitative, substantive sense. *Qualitative* withness is spaceless meaning, a quality of Spirit. Thus Spirit is no extremely thin substance, but no substance at all. Coinherence can never characterize substance, but it is integral to Spirit. *Perichoresis* is always a contrapletal reality.

Thus Spirit, although personally focused, is yet everywhere as spirit. Spirit is; Spirit is the only ultimate identity; Spirit is the ultimate, universal reality of all there is, infinite and finite. The Spirit both is the same as and other than, but spirit as interpenetrating is selfsame in all things, while as personally self-conscious, it is itself distinct. There is ultimate identity, as indeed there has to be, with distinctiveness on the part of both the ultimate and the created, on the part of both the infinite and the finite. Thus the category of the personal is the category of distinction, in this one aspect that we have mentioned, ultimately, as an integral, indispensable aspect of reality. The personal, however, cannot ultimately be separated from Spirit as though there were another Spirit that is not personal or as though there was any aspect of the Spirit that is not ultimately personal. The Spirit is and is personal; but the Spirit is not personal wherever it operates impersonally; there it is impersonal, the activity of spirit apart from the fullness of the Spirit as such.

This way of speaking may sound like double-talk. It seems logically contradictory. But the contrapletal truth characteristic of the ultimate is that Spirit as Spirit is integrally Spirit always and everywhere and can yet allow for the distinctiveness of secondary spirits and created being where Spirit both fully is and is not; or where the Spirit is both personally present and personally absent. The presence and absence of Spirit, then, is operationally effective not as diminution of self-reality or as a limitation of self-consciousness but as the capacity for providing the absence of Spirit in the sense of its distinctiveness that affords the reality for pedagogical purposes of finite distinctiveness. Thus God is present and absent at the same time contrapletally. Such absence means that Spirit is Spirit integrally with the inherent capacity for distinctiveness. We shall see later that man's distinctiveness as personal spirit is analogous to God's, but here in the discussion of the categories it is well to mark and inwardly to digest the fact that Spirit can be spirit in the general sense of the identity of internal relations and there, so to speak, be universally present, while also personally Spirit, in the total and integral sense, without need to be present everywhere in the distinctive nature of the meaning and reality of Spirit. One of these meanings is self-consciousness which

is the reality of focused Spirit, capable of external relations in the sense
of integrity of self-identity as distinctive while yet remaining the universal
Spirit that participates in the inner reality and relations of all finite distinctiveness without diminution or destruction of either distinctiveness.

Notice, however, that we have stressed self-consciousness, not consciousness as such. Consciousness adds no thing, no substance, to spirit. Self-
consciousness is equally free of making any addition to spirit. Spirit is.
Consciousness is rather the quality of awareness on the part of Spirit.
Such awareness can make for distinction of entities without separation of
substance. Thus consciousness as such is no barrier to free internal relations, or to a perfectly ubiquitous coinherence, perichoresis, or interpenetration. There is no necessary separation either within or on the part
of the world of which consciousness is aware. Two consciousnesses can be
aware of the same realities without subtracting or detracting from them,
yes, and without adding to them or altering them as they truly are. Thus
contents of consciousness can overlap without rivalry. Consciousness can
thus color spirit without altering the world or separating spirit from the
world. Consciousness can structure spirit without changing the world or
spirit. Or consciousness can focus spirit without making a cleft between
spirit and the world. Nicolai von Hartmann surely made a mistake when
he said simply that consciousness separates, whereas spirit unites. Consciousness *can* be the occasion for separation by self, but *need not* separate
in itself. Consciousness necessarily distinguishes, but can distinguish without causing separation. In this sense consciousness can be a purely phenomenological or descriptive act. Husserl was surely feeling for some of
this truth, and Abellio in *La Structure Absolue* likewise speaks of the
absolute structure of consciousness which is beyond the psychological and
the empirical. Both perhaps had experienced some influence from Bud-
dhistic true suchness, which means authentic identification with the experienced world rather than its distortion or separation by and from the
self.

It is the limiting, not limited, self that separates. Therefore it is not
consciousness, but such self-consciousness that separates. Some claim to
have experienced vividly this distinction while under the clarifying, or
consciousness-lowering, power of drugs. Consciousness as such distinguishes but does not by itself separate. Consciousness reports; the self
interprets and uses consciousness, and in so doing generally abuses it.
Whitehead rightly affirms that the immediate experience is infallible
whereas interpreted experience becomes fallible. The world is as it is;
consciousness is as it is; but the reading and directing of consciousness
of the human fallible, limiting self needs interpretation in terms of its
total history of experience and interpreted experience. We may want to
experience the world in a way prejudicial to us or protective of our wants

and wishes and therefore we read our experience selectively or distortedly in accordance with our wants and wishes.

But the faults and lacks of finite consciousness within imperfect and sinful men cannot be the standard for Spirit as Spirit. Spirit experiences and interprets what is perfectly; therefore Spirit can be distinguished as an entity, as self-consciousness, as self-knowledge, as self-awareness, without causing a false cleft between consciousness and what is experienced. Thus Spirit can be a distinct entity through self-consciousness without being separated from what is in consciousness. Thus Spirit can have unimpeded internal relations; be truly present with and identical with Spirit everywhere; be the power of permanence; and yet also be focused, be an entity, have external relations as personally distinct. Spirit can be present and absent in this manner at the same time; Spirit must thus be understood through contrapletal and not through contrarietal or contradictory logic.

Perfect self-consciousness on the part of Spirit, ubiquitously and eternally, thus focuses Spirit. Spirit is centered in purpose, in initiative, in compassion, or whatever we find to be the characteristics of Spirit, and thus the Self-consciousness, or Spirit as Spirit, is an entity, an experiencing reality, a focused center of all perspectives, without being a personality in the sense of separateness. All finite persons are generally, in some sense and measure, separate as well as distinct. In the Spirit some personal spirits even during their temporal pedagogy can occasionally become one beyond separation while still maintaining distinctiveness; but overwhelmingly, to be finite is to be more person than spirit, more self than socius, more divided from the world than distinct from it. Tillich used to bemoan the fact that few people ever experienced or understood his "ecstatic reason," the eschatological, mystical experience of being grasped by the unconditional! Personality, in any case, is more separate than distinct. Personality makes a self like a thing divided off from the world. The basic perennial wisdom of man affirms that one must lose one's life to find it. Jesus knew this and taught it. Buddhism almost centers in the fact that to find freedom from the false, fear-driven, suffering self, a person must cease being a personality, a self that considers himself first of all an individual, and come to know himself as false and feverish as long as he clings to his fundamental illusions.

The whole point of life is to become personality in order to gain the reality of self-being through the conscious choices of a self that is mostly an individual, in order, furthermore, to pass beyond such falsehood of life by scaling the walls that separate man from the rest of the world. Then, and only then, can man pass from being a spiritual personality to becoming a personal spirit. Then, and only then, shall man indeed accept the image of God in him. The meaning of life is neither to isolate man within the walls of self, the very hallmark of Western individualism, nor to lose onself in the all, or in the void, which is the opposite abuse of Eastern religions, but rather to become a distinct center of experience and appreciation, of creativity and satisfaction, beyond the walls of the separate self, or apart from the walls for the individual.

Thus even self-consciousness can give distinctiveness of experience without separation. The self as such separates the individual from the world, but self-consciousness can become so real *in Spirit* that as the self-consciousness of Spirit there can arise a distinct entity that is not a separate thing or a discrete personality. The perfect consciousness would experience all things, all relations, all happenings and events, and all consciousnesses insofar as they constitute the general feeling tone of the experienced and experiencing world. To the perfectly sensitive spirit, feelings are public as well as private in the sense that the feeling tone, the music, the color of the experienced is accessible to other consciousnesses. Zen Buddhism's perfect identification in *satori* becomes intelligible through this interpretation. All are one in Spirit. Spirit is. Spirit is everywhere or in everything; and all are in Spirit. Spirit interpenetrates all the fields of reality perfectly and unexceptionally. Only Spirit *is* in the sense of identity.

Therefore all conscious experience is ultimately dependent upon Spirit and is in Spirit. The more Spirit interpenetrates, the more all things are experienced. Spirit does so perfectly as such. But when the finite self is in the Spirit, the more the finite is open to and can transparently become interpenetrated by Spirit, the more sensitive that self becomes to the feeling continuum of the world. Openness to Spirit becomes openness to the world. Openness to Spirit becomes sensitivity to the world, not only to the objective world but especially to the subjective world, and that not merely externally through sensitivity of concern which works through analogy and inference, but rather through the direct empathy, sympathy, compassion with others, the entertaining of the inner "music of the world."

Such sensitivity, however, never destroys or reduces the distinctiveness of self-consciousness. Self-awareness thereby becomes only more real and more distinct. The self becomes more focused and an entity without becoming separated from its world. Thus in the perfect Spirit, in the eternal Spirit, in the original Fount of Spirit, in the Source of Significance, there is no false separation—no separated Self as a thing rather than an entity, no Personality rather than the personally colored and directive Spirit—to prevent external and internal relations from being maintained with regard to the same world in such a manner that God can be both absent and present at the same time. Or God's personal presence can be both absent and present at the same time. Or God's personal presence can be withheld or withdrawn so that even while he is present as spirit in one dimension, he is not actually present himself as the whole integrity of personal Spirit, the personal Spirit who is Love.

The personal Spirit can and does withhold attention in the sense of personal observation and companionship, for the sake of the privacy and freedom of the finite person, in order to allow him the opportunity to develop or mature from a spiritual personality to a personal spirit by means of his own choices and growth. In this sense God is transpersonal. Everywhere in himself he is personal Spirit, he is Love, in the full integrity and integralness of the term. But that same personal Spirit can choose a relation of passive rather than active experience. Love does choose to absent itself personally in the operative sense. By so acting Love fulfills its own self, its own purpose, its own genuineness of creation for maturation in freedom and love. If this presence-and-absence is regarded substantively we have a vicious excluded middle, a wanton double-talk in theology; but if self-consciousness rather than consciousness, constitutes the meaning of the personal and if such self-consciousness adds or detracts nothing from Spirit as Spirit substantively, God's transpersonal functioning neither detracts from the fullness of Spirit nor makes unreal its effective absence for the sake of human freedom and responsibility.

Spirit is; Spirit works through energy, immaterial and material. But Spirit is focused; self-aware; self-conscious. Spirit is, needing only Spirit; Spirit is ultimate; Spirit is identity and universality unconditionally; in some sense Spirit is nowhere and nothing, no substance, no thing, not placeable, yet in another sense Spirit is everywhere and all wheres are in Spirit; all that works comes from Spirit; Spirit generates energy, provides capacity to work; Spirit creates, providing energy for the new and directing the energy according to purpose. Purpose is thus everywhere, directly or indirectly, but not as *personal* purpose. Spirit as purposeful provides the neutral energy, neutrality in biology, chance for change of function in physiology, chance for creative freedom for persons within a flexible environment where responsibility counts. Energy does not flow merely according to chance; flux has or takes on form; the flow has direction and boundaries; organisms seek growth as goal; people live to mature. Spirit is thus structured by Self, the eternal self-consistency of Spirit; Spirit is, indeed, structured by personal purpose, the envisaging some good and the providing appropriate processes to attain it. Spirit as purpose creates and effects goals, sometimes more directly or "mechanically"; sometimes more indirectly, through organic growth or through the creation of secondary purposers or finite persons. The Spirit lives richly, daringly, excitingly, enrichingly within and with finite purposers.

Spirit is; Spirit purposes. Eternal purpose is quality of differentiation. The process of becoming and even the process of change should never be viewed as mere organism. Organism, to be sure, is exceedingly purposeful. Sherrington's *Man on His Nature* gives astonishing accounts of the interconnectedness and interdependent interworkings of the cells of the brain, far, far more complex than the London telephone exchange in its total functioning, and Sinnott in *The Biology of the Spirit* has described how even a sponge, when cut asunder in small pieces and scattered on the waves of the ocean, will reassemble purposefully for larger units of organic interaction. Purpose is fierce in nature; and organism could be a model for it, but organism is neither high enough nor rich enough to account for Spirit as purpose; neither is cosmology. The interworking of the starry sphere astonished the great Immanuel Kant, and anyone who has worked as even a lowly assistant in an astronomy department can marvel at the ever-richer understanding of the galaxies and the universes upon universes. The distinguished astronomer, Professor Harlow Shapley, of Harvard, once confided in a private discussion his belief that we have not even touched the smallest corner of that mysterious infinitude of reality to which the astronomical findings so far contribute their minute suggestions. But cosmology cannot define the fullness or the finest of ultimate purpose. Only the richest personal purpose, the costliest and most fruitful love, the most creative mind moved by Ultimate Concern can point toward it with some straightness. Purpose should, then, be defined neither by organism nor by cosmology but by Love. *Purpose is Personal.*

Personal purpose best suggests the outgoing nature and activity of Spirit; later we shall see further how personal purpose is best understood in terms of love. Personal purpose creates relations. It is creative. It initiates new series of activity while redirecting others, even while personal purpose for the most part mostly keeps sustaining the ongoing workings of the world. But if Self-consciousness involves the focusing of Spirit as consciousness (not of consciousness as such which is focused by purpose) how can there be self-consciousness of Spirit without there being limiting relations? Personality is obviously a matter of selective limitations; how can we escape the problems of personality by calling God personal Spirit rather than spiritual Personality?

Consciousness as such is no limitation, we have already found; consciousness as such in its perfection adds no thing, no hard lump, no exclusive relations to Spirit. Spirit is, and is everywhere conscious in some sense, but Spirit is not everywhere Self-conscious. By withdrawing from personal relations as needed, Spirit is yet present as sustaining activity, and possibly as total consciousness, while still absent as attention in the selective sense of what the self consciously entertains within its self-awareness. One can be conscious of a field of vision without knowing that one is conscious of it. The functioning of the heart is ever part of human consciousness even though one is seldom aware of it. For special reasons one can become conscious of the beating of the heart. And human consciousness is, of course, gross and turbid. Thus in one sense God knows everything perfectly, and not only on a secondary level. In another sense, however, God pays no direct attention to areas which he should know only indirectly. He knows them all perfectly in the operational sense of coinherence; he does not know them personally in the sense of attention. God withdraws personally. God provides privacy and freedom, not from himself in some dimension nor from his order, but from his personal presence. Thus God is perfectly present as consciousness while truly absent as personal participant. Or God may be present as impersonal Spirit in the sense of concurring as directive power. Full presence is no limitation especially when Spirit is the inner identity and thus congruent reality of all there is. Personal presence may be characterized by a *decrease* of control in a scale where the fullest maturity of the finite person involves the maximum decrease of control. But does not absence involve a limitation of some kind; of power of control? How else could there be a freedom and privacy of the part of personal spirits? What, then, does such limitation in God mean and involve?

In the sense of inner identity God is infinite Spirit. Spirit is universal presence as well as the inner power for all permanence. Continuity is more than genetic; it is more than derivative; continuity is based on the reality of Spirit. But distinctions are real both in the total identity and in its parts. The whole is fully in the parts and the parts in the whole. Spirit is, but Spirit is distinction as well as identity; and Spirit generates distinctions. Spirit is distinct as Self-awareness and as Purpose; Spirit creates. Self-consciousness, however, involves finitude where it purposes absence of control, and therefore God is finite or limited in his self-consciousness as it relates to creation. Selective attention means selective presence in the personal sense; hence creation and human freedom are both real. But it means also surrender of psychic and spiritual "space." Finite distinctions are real, especially with respect to human or other selves choosing genuine self-being, and against God and others, in order to become real. Such genuine self-being erects external relations, builds walls for privacy, creates individual separateness for freedom. In such a case Spirit is both authentic identity and yet capable of genuine personal absence or withdrawal of attention and control.

Thus Spirit is infinite and the personal is in some respects finite; how, then, can they "coexist," if we may or must use such terms? The personal selection of attention, of personal presence on the part of Spirit, limits the personal aspect of Spirit without limiting Spirit. Spirit is, and is the inner ubiquitous identity; and as such is never limited (as we shall explain in the next chapter). The Spirit is the inner reality and generator of all workings, the source of all energy as well as of significance, of the meaning and purpose of what is created. Hence Spirit is paradigmal. It is primary reality. It is no prime stuff to be excluded anywhere, but is everywhere for being nothing and nowhere. The ground of all cannot be limited or expressed in terms of things and wheres. It is fount and reality of all. It is indeed infinite.

Spirit is; Spirit purposes; Spirit is conscious; Spirit or Love is personal. But consciousness on the part of Spirit adds nothing to the world of space. The created world for the most part is not conscious. It is within the consciousness of Spirit as ubiquitous consciousness is infinite and infallible. Spirit as Self-consciousness in relation to pedagogical process, however, we found to be selective, exclusive of certain relations and finite. Such finitude, however, in no sense limits the universal presence and power of the Spirit in the sense of self-being or of creative concurrence, even as the inner identity of concurrence. Concurrence is not only running *with,* but running *in* and *as* all things, without denial of their own several distinctivenesses. Pedagogical concurrence itself is "based on" co-inherence, or congruence of spirit. Personal absence means the purposed absence of Spirit's self-consciousness, possibly not of its consciousness, and surely not of its inner identity. Infinite Love expresses itself as perfect Spirit by limiting its personal presence and power according to the needs of creation. What is limited, then, is, in some respects, the personal in Spirit, *not* Spirit.

If the nature and meaning of Spirit as personal is Love, however, then the limitation of Presence in the personal sense is merely the affirmation, we repeat, of the genuineness of creation and human freedom. Therefore the nature and purpose of God are not limited by absence, but indeed expressed by them. The pedagogical process is the expression of Spirit, not the limitation of Spirit. There is neither limitation of substance, for consciousness is no substance, nor of love, for love is expressed by having relations. Thus perfect Spirit and perfect Love are, and are expressed by the self-willed limitations of *personal* presence and secondary power on the part of the Spirit of Love who God is. All the categories must increasingly be understood as intrinsically illuminating the rest *coinherently.* We turn therefore to the meaning of Love further to illuminate the meaning and purpose of Spirit.

The Categories of Reality: Love

THE THREE CATEGORIES of reality we have taken to be spirit, the personal, and love. But the greatest of these is love! Love defines the very nature of being, not as substance, but as Spirit at its own most real and its own most high. Love defines the inmost nature of becoming, not as a process of change, but as the creativity of the highest purpose. Love defines the deepest meaning of non-being, not as mere absence, nor as opposition or contradiction, but as the positive presupposition for creation, the counterpart of creative Spirit. Love, then, is the meaning of Spirit and the purpose of the Personal. We need to take seriously as truth the New Testament categories, its definitions of God. God is Love; Spirit; and "our Father." The universal Ultimate, the power of Permanence, the reality of creative Spirit, the One in and for the many, and the many in and for the One, the heart of the categories of Reality: this is Love.

Inmost to reality is Love. Love is the nature of what is ultimate. To be sure, the Spirit also is, but the Spirit is colored and focused as Love. Love not only is, but works, but the "isness" that works is at its depth and height Love. Love, not substance or process, is the nature of ultimate being; it is not being that is; such a statement means either that isness is, which is redundant, or that being stands for something else than being. When that something else is other than Love, or the Spirit of Love, then that "something else" is wrong, for Love is, as Spirit and as personal Purpose. Love is self-sufficient. It is no final substance or substrate. Love is the living Spirit who is and purposes, who is and creates, who is and works toward consummation. There is no self-sufficient being, no being itself; only love is ultimate as the nature of Spirit and the meaning of the personal. Therefore only love is self-sufficient; there is finally only the self-sufficiency of Love. As Ernst Fuchs keeps contending: when one asks for the reason for the being of love, there is no other reason than love to assure its reality and ensure its nature. Love is ultimate and can be reduced to no other terms. Love gives final meaning, but there can be no final meaning for love.

What then is love? Love is joy in the other. Love is satisfaction in the other. Love is freedom for the other. Love is creative concern for the other. Love experiences joy and satisfaction *in* the other and has freedom and creative concern *for* the other. Love is not merely outgoing; love is within an intrinsic relation of joy and satisfaction. Such joy and satisfaction eternally are in and of Love. The lover does not create the joy nor obtain the satisfaction. The experience is neither mere obtaining of joy and satisfaction nor of giving joy and satisfaction. The experience is before it can either find or give. Love is. Spirit is. The New Testament put down a firm foundation in this respect: God is Love before he loves or before he is loving. Love does not depend upon the object of love as though the object of love or the goal of love were more real and more high than love itself. And Love is more than any Lover, eternal or in time. Personalities are not more real than Love. Love is personal Spirit. Ultimate is self-sufficient love, needing only love for explanation. There is no apologetic appropriate to love. Love is its own and only reason for being. *Love is.* No experience is higher or more ultimate. No experience is finally more explanatory. But love explains and as such is more real than what is explained by love. Love is and purposes. Love is and gives, but love is the highest meaning and nature of Spirit.

How can love be, however, except as the experience of a lover? How can love be except as experience? Then are not lover and experience more real, even more ultimate and eternal than love? No, love explains the personal, the nature and meaning of true experience. The personal and experience are not *ipso facto* love. The personal and experience in the ultimate universal are love; they are, and express love; they are, and work to give love. They are, and try to create the conditions of love. Love generates experience, not experience love. Love is conscious; consciousness is not all of love, but all ultimate consciousness is Love. Spirit is everywhere in the service of Love, not merely as personal confrontation and not merely as personal purpose, but also as the for-ness of the impersonal spirit as the means of Love. Love is everywhere and works everywhere, expressed or in condescension; the nature and meaning of Spirit is love. Love can thus be in both absence and presence. Where personally present God is Love; where personally absent God is love. The wrath of God is love punishing to reform; the indifference of God is the passivity of God humbly offered in order for freedom to be real. Thus in presence and in absence God is love; directly and indirectly God is love. Being or working, God is love.

Love is more than the self-awareness of reality; Love is both the self-awareness and that of which and of whom it is aware, forsooth, the total relation of awareness. In such terms Augustine understood the Holy Trinity: the lover, the beloved, and the relation of love, not triple but ternary. Love is never a discrete individual; God is not Love in this sense; he is only Father as distinct; love is identity and distinction. Love is the personally distinct, the identity of the one personal Spirit, the eternal Spirit, the home of all finite spirits. Love covers all, being in and of all, and being also creatively for all. But being is primary to doing; doing is no forced situation. Doing is in freedom. Doing is by choice. Doing is balanced by not doing, by being, becoming, and non-being. Love is, and basic to all. Being, non-being, becoming, doing, and not doing—Love is and remains self-sufficient. Love is unconditionally. Love is not only unconditionally faithful but also excess of creative power. Love never becomes exhausted. But love is unconditional before it remains true or creative in any relational, secondary sense. Love is an eternal being in relation. God is being in love. Love in Spirit is God. Love and Love alone is self-sufficient being, or isness, but Love is self-sufficient in more senses than that of being. Love is; Spirit is; the personal is, but the meaning of the three is Love.

Love is and has relations; love is and creates relations, but that love is relations is a deeper truth than that love has or creates relations. All of reality is colored by love. Reality consists of personal Spirit; nothing less. God as personal Spirit rather than as spiritual Personality is personal consciousness in relations, identity and distinctiveness, that both has and creates relations; but Love is relational intrinsically, for Love is Spirit, not substance, nor Personality. Love is; Spirit is; ultimate is the personal Spirit of Love. At its highest Love is personal; it is a conscious self-awareness of joy, of satisfaction, of piercing Reality. Only ecstasy can glimpse its truth. The final truth cannot be written; it cannot be spoken; it cannot be sung; it cannot be sculptured; it cannot be painted; truth is a human reliable understanding of what is and how reality relates; but Truth towers beyond all human approaches, the mountains are inaccessible beyond the foothills. Love is; Love is Truth; Love is Reality. For human beings, love is a tempting experience to have; to increase: to be in love; to grow in love. But eternal Love is joy only grasped by human beings in anticipation in the experience of ecstasy where one moment outweighs the rest of life; where one experience of reality is far more real than all else. What can that Truth, that Reality, that Love *be?*

Love is; Love is personal in personal relations. Love never is full in personality. Love is never individual. Love is never plural. Love is neither one nor many. Love is unimunity. Love is never a matter of feelings between two or more personalities. Love is the one and the many in all their relations. The total quality; the total relationship; the total being, becoming, and non-being of reality (not of actuality!) is Love. Ultimately there are no separate personalities; ultimately there are—and is—one God; ultimately there is no order of being; ultimately there is no process of change or becoming; ultimately there is no power for creativity; ultimate is Love alone, Love as personal Spirit; and all else find their proper and full meaning only within Love. Love is no matter of relata or relations; Love is in relations and relata; in identity and distinction; in sameness and difference; in sameness and diversity.

Love is; Spirit is; the personal is. The Spirit is selfsame and entire; the Spirit is personal with distinctions within Spirit. Love is neither one nor communal, but one in the communal and communal in the one. Call the ultimate Trinity; that is a human estimate of a historic religion; such an affirmation is far better than either tri-theism or the undifferentiated One. Perfect coinherence among the persons? Of course! Shared consciousness and perfect unity of the ultimate? Of course! Richness of distinction within consciousness, limited to no one self-awareness exclusive of selective self-awareness within Love? Of course! Love is one and Love is many without being one over against the many or to the exclusion of the many. The one is and is one in the many; the many are and are also one. Love is neither a congregate of individuals nor an individual-less collectivity. Love is unimunity. Love is relations and more than relations; Love is, and in relations intrinsically, beyond exclusiveness of the personal in the sense of personality, beyond the poverty of the undifferentiated that lacks self-awareness and, so to speak, beyond fields of enriching self-awareness.

Thus Love is relations and not exhausted by relations: Love is; Love is and *is* in relations. Love is and *has* relations. Love creates; Love shares; Love gives; Love produces; Love makes. Love is and is totally *for;* Love is and is no mere for-ness, even though it is total for-ness; Love is and is relations before it creates and has relations. Ultimately Love has only internal relations. The Self-awareness of Love is as one, and is as one in all distinctions of ultimate nature. Love is total in the whole, and more than total, for it is equally in its distinctions; Love is total in the distinctions and more than total for the whole is there also. Love is the infinite richness of the one in the many and the many in the one in perfect coinherence, perichoresis of Spirit; personal purpose is no barrier in the Ultimate.

Love is; Spirit is; the personal is. And all are one and the one is in relations as the many. Love is qualified by its nature as Spirit and as personal; and is further qualified through distinctions in self-awareness. But Love also has relations. These relations need genuineness, authentic existence. The identity of love is truly there; only reality is ultimately, in the primary sustaining sense, but Love has relations where the personal is absent which allow for the genuineness of nature as nature and of human beings as human beings; or of life as life. Thus Love is and is in relation ultimately, but with all internal relations; yet Love also is and has relations, proximately, but now with both internal and external relations. Love is; Spirit is; the personal is; and all are one and the one is in its qualifications. Love is no substance, no personality, no spiritual personality having Love, but personal Spirit totally being Love. Yet such Love has relations which are no limitation to Spirit as Spirit and no boundary to Love as Love, but which do limit the personal, making God absent and present at the same time for the sake of the genuineness and the privacy of creation and human history. The limitations of personal presence and the personal exercise of power express perfectly the nature and purpose of Love through the nature and meaning of Spirit. I hope that in these interweaving paragraphs I have somehow succeeded in suggesting the interpenetration of the three chapters.

Love is thus alone self-sufficient, being Spirit and being personal. Only Love is self-sufficient, although Spirit and the personal are also ultimate categories of reality. Love is thus the meaning of being; in its most neutral, general sense being is no substance; being is no process; being is no personality; being is no mere isness. There are secondary forms of being, all important in their place and function. But only Love is as Spirit and as personal. Thus creatures are beings learning love and at best are beings in love. They are beings in love when they become personal spirits maturely; then they become beings in love because they are spirits in love, and spirits in love have their identity in Love as Spirit with their distinction as personal realities, being and having purpose, but above all being in Love. God is Love in being, Love as Spirit; Love is, and being, or what is, must ultimately be defined by Love.

That God as Spirit, or that the Ultimate Universal, or that Love as such has relations introduces the topic that Love defines not only being but also becoming. Love *has* relations, not only *is* internal relations perfectly, because Love creates. Creation is the meaning and the realm of becoming. Creation is because Love is. Love is and lives within eternal distinctions and within eternal unity. Therefore Love has no external or internal need to create in terms of deficiency or mere efficiency. We shall defer treatment of this question, however, until the final section.

Only free spirits are distinct from Spirit in the sense that they can be over against Spirit in terms of genuine self-being. Nature is real as creation in the sense that God is absent from it in the personal sense, but he is not shut out by it. Spirit energizes a patterned flow of cosmic process, sustaining, maintaining, even increasing the several processes within this total cosmic process. But in relation to the process and the processes there are no external relations in the kind of distinctiveness that obtains with regard to personal Spirit. Spirit is and interpenetrates all creations that are passive to the indirect purpose of Love and therefore mostly passive to man and only indirectly related to Spirit. Such indirection provides the conditions for freedom to be born and to grow; and only freedom can make for genuine self-being and for external relations to the ultimate category of the personal. Spirit is everywhere in some sense, since Spirit creates every "where" and all wheres are in Spirit, but God is personally absent; or the personal presence is missing where finite freedom obtains and does not invite in or entertain personal relations with the Ultimate.

At this point we should properly take up once again the question of unimunity. The term, we may recall, is a combination of "unity" and "community." Unimunity is the relation among men where the Spirit as Love has full sway. The spirit is the only identity and therefore, in one dimension of being, all are one. The Old Testament knew something about the nation considered as a corporate personality. In fact, however, in one dimension *all* creatures are one. They have their perfect identity in the One. We are even told that there is such total interrelatedness and interactivity that with the proper magnification we could hear an insect cough on Venus—if such there be! In one dimension the volume of every atom is the universe. The identity of spirit goes beyond every unity, sustaining all community and communication. Thus in unimunity, the source of our being, personally and communally, all are one by creation and made to become one in spirit of understanding and togetherness. The unity of spirit, in perfect identity, awaits its further creation by personal purpose in love where the drive is for the fullest and richest possible differentiation. Love furthers all possible self-being and group being. Love works to make selves and communities real and rich.

Unimunity thus goes beyond individualism and collectivism. It goes beyond self-love and other-love. It leaves behind the conflict between selfishness and selflessness. The individual is by creation one with all and one with any community to which he belongs, but in such a manner as to need also to become one. Unimunity works to make each person and group real and rich, not over against anyone or any group, but within each group and for all. Differentiation becomes diversity without division. Variation becomes cooperative, not conflicting. Unimunity by its very nature as one at the source of all and every being requires universal and concrete for-ness. Self-love can be no less than other-love, for the self and all others are inescapably one. Nor can other-love be real at the expense of self-love. Erich Fromm is right that the world suffers from lack of proper self-love. Unimunity proclaims this truth by going beyond both selfishness, which is pushing the self, and selflessness, which is running away from the self. Instead, unimunity is selfful. The self is always fully included but never at the expense of the other; rather, in such a way and in such a spirit that the better each self becomes, the more it contributes to both the concrete and the relevant good of each group and of all.

Unimunity holds that all are equally real in the spirit and equally loved in the spirit. Unimunity is total for-ness in the spirit, but according to the realism of relevance. Finite beings cannot play the role of God nor take the place of the universal spirit. They can be more or less universal in their outlook and outreach, but always only partially so. They must rather be real and develop as concrete selves and as practicable societies as possible. Thus no one can take the place of anyone else, think for him, love for him, live for him, even take a bath for him! Each person contributes the most to his group and his world by becoming the most authentic self and the most mature and creative self possible; similarly no other group can take the place of that group and the best contribution that group can make is to carry out its own concerns as effectively as possible. There is a reason that each husband should love his own wife and children the most.

The focusing of love is a matter of temporary rather than ultimate importance and does not detract from the love for all which is always the intrinsic intention of unimunity. Focusing on the concrete for the finite is a matter of practical relevance. It is the way the world is made. It is the nature of finite existence. Therefore self-love and group love are more relevant than the love of all, but such self-love and group love can never become unimunity apart from a fulfilling relation for all from the individual to the total community of men. Thus unimunity goes beyond individualism and collectivism, beyond self-love and other-love, beyond selfishness and selflessness, making for the full appreciation of each; and with each one and each group finding his fullest self- and other-acceptance, appreciation, and satisfaction, with openness to all, acceptance of all, appreciation of all, and satisfaction in being universal man. Unimunity elicits both the most personal and the most universal man.

Let us consider some examples, first in the matter of race. Unimunity goes beyond being color-bound, or being shut in within the fetters of color prejudice, but oppositely it goes beyond being color-blind, which is the refusal to see and to accept or to appreciate the variety and richness of creation. Neither color-bound nor color-blind, unimunity becomes color rich, recognizing that each group must be accepted, appreciated, and given the fullest opportunity and power to become itself. In this sense and not invidiously and destructively, Black Power has rich meaning and there is real need for it. Unimunity similarly goes beyond both nationalism and one-worldism. It appreciates each national heritage, and for those within the nations the flag becomes more precious, not less so; but each nation can be fulfilled only insofar as it knows, observes, and implements its necessarily being one in creation and its purpose to be free with and for all other nations. Not to be rich in national appreciation is to forfeit the richness of creation, but to put the nation first or over against other nations is to go contrary even to one's own nature in creation and contrary to the grain of the universe. Unimunity is thus the fullest idealism but within the most effective and demanding realism.

In the same way individualism and collectivism with regard to economics should give way, *according to the nature* of things *actually* and *potentially*, to the kind of economic organization that seeks the full freedom and initiative for each person and group but always only as this seeking is consistent with and promotive of the communal good. Unimunity fulfills both private and communal enterprise. Unimunity comes neither deterministically in history nor by free creation dependent upon mostly hortatory motivation. Rather unimunity rests on the very nature of things, both by creation and by the only way man must go, but if he is to find fulfillment for the personal and the communal, he must go in understanding and freedom. Motivation thus becomes a matter both of true knowledge and of the good will. It would be exciting to write volumes on the reality, meaning, and motivation of unimunity. Particularly fascinating are the possibilities for an ethics of unimunity. Unimunity depends both on the nature of things and on man's freedom. Such freedom, of course, is always problematic.

If personal spirits cannot be created, or personal selves in human history cannot be manufactured, and if personal self-being cannot become authentic through mere biological growth, like the growth of a vegetable, how then can there be genuine becoming in the full sense of God's personal absence, not merely in the sense that he is not present because there has been no conscious invitation—perhaps no consciousness at all of the absence of relations—but precisely because there has been such consciousness and man has preferred his privacy and freedom for himself and his own purposes in such a manner that he has willed the absence of God?

When God creates man he gives him spirit, he creates man in his own image; he breathes his own spirit into him. Spirit is, one and the same; Spirit is entire; Spirit is never divided nor is it divisible; Spirit is no bit of matter, no small portion of substance. Man is no bit of God. Man is because God is. Man is in God and God in man. Apart from Spirit man is not. Man is Spirit and made to become personal spirit, living mature love. Man is made to be in love. Thus God calls into being out of Spirit a new mode or qualification with capacity to grow into freedom, to develop authentic self-being. Man as spirit is basically the capacity for freedom. Spirit is freedom, the power to transcend the local and the limited because of the inner nature of identity with the total. Spirit in personal spirit, spirit with personal purpose, becomes, genuinely *becomes,* through a process of learning love. That is what time is for; that is how eternity overflows into time; Love into love; Spirit into spirit; personal Purpose into personal purpose. How then does Love become? How does Love become love; Freedom become freedom; Spirit, spirit; the Personal, personal?

Spirit is; Love is personal, purposing. Purpose involves mind. Mind is awareness, awareness of difference, appraisal of what is and what is different. Mind is the power to discern, the power of knowledge, the capacity for self-knowledge, the ability to consider and to choose, the power to abstract, to symbolize, to imagine. Mind is the power to see what is and to imagine what can be. Mind is capacity for description and for prescription, for knowing what is and what can be. In giving Spirit, in being Spirit to and in the finite, the Spirit also gives mind. Thus the finite spirit, being Spirit in that perspective, becomes endowed with mind to know, to discern, to discriminate, to imagine, and to make choice. Therefore the finite becomes endowed with capacity to develop free ideas. The power to exercise free ideas, to symbolize and to choose, to abstract and to live in and by abstractions that are then referred back to color the concrete world is the prerequisite for freedom. Freedom is not of indifference, equal power for contrary choice; freedom is not of indetermination, the inability to predict the course of individual atoms, but freedom is self-determination, the power to become a self through finite choices. The self is and becomes its choices.

These choices are not only among concrete realities; they are among imagined realities, too, and among abstractions from concrete reality which have become deeply colored by man's appraisal of his experience, and that not only his actual experience, not only his immediate experience of the concrete world, but much more of the imagined world of free ideas, or of the world colored by man's history of ideas, and a world painted by man's appraisals. These appraisals, too, are not only direct and successive; they are not merely objectively accumulative, but they are also, and much more, colored by man's prejudices, by his limited views of what is self-promotive and self-protective. Man not only learns his world, but lives his world, and makes it a world colored by his experience in terms of the free ideas which are always deeply dyed by emotions, by affective paintings, and thus distorted. Within this power of freedom to build and to color one's world, God can be the void or the enemy, indeed has so to be until man learns that God is father and friend.

Man as an ego, then, underlaid by spirit and overlaid by self, forms his world through a process of freedom which is far more than the power of contrary choice. Man is free to determine himself through his choices and to color his choices through his own creative activity of abstraction of both knowledge and value. Man becomes his choices, and such a contained self creates external relations to God, the personal Spirit, the personal Purpose. The more man rationalizes his situation the more he builds walls which although they cannot keep out Spirit, although they are yet within the fullest circle of Love, can shut out the personal Presence of Love. The self can do this because it is made in God's image, with freedom to grow love, to accept or to reject love, with freedom to become or shut out love. God calls the finite person as a self to become a personal spirit of love, a *spirit-in-love.*

This call of God creates moral distinctions; man becomes not only self-aware but also aware of right and wrong. Man has the capacity not only for knowledge but for morality. The call to duty, and beyond that to love, comes on the finite side through conscience which can be thwarted, frustrated, and distorted. The conscience can be changed by man, personally and communally, to accord with man's desire for what he wants to be right and wrong. Man personally and communally, immediately and through a long building program can create a false self, a refugee from the very love man most deeply seeks and most deeply fears. Thus the self can not only change his knowledge but change his evaluations of experience so as to shut out God. But he can also invite God into his life. The self then becomes, in the roughest sense of distinctiveness, through self-awareness, not only intellectually but in a basic sense morally, and finally and most deeply, spiritually. He becomes through his decisions which themselves are based on a history of his own appraisals, not only objectively but with subjective bias. Bias turns distinction into division, and reason into rationalization. In this way the self becomes and establishes external relations to God as personal. He cannot shut out Spirit and Love without which he would not be, but he can shut out the personal wooing of Spirit, of Love; he can say no in such a way as either to rationalize away the presence of God in the personal sense or to turn God into an enemy.

Man can declare God dead by his guilty rationalizations. For Love to create the personal self who has the freedom to be over against God, to ignore or to defy him, is to effect the kind of becoming that is not only passively but actively and, in this sense, definitively distinct, yes separate, from the personal Spirit, and thus distinct *in* but *not* from Spirit. Love, then, is the fullest answer to this highest form of becoming, the becoming of free authentic self-beings, the fostering of personal self-beings in the Spirit. Distinctiveness, in one sense, is lowest at the beginning and at the end of pedagogical process and is highest where man dares to stand almost separate over against God, preferring his own rationalization of experience and his perverse use of freedom. Then the external relations between man and God reach their maximum. Such distinctiveness is separation, segregation, by means of external relations. Such separation involves breaks with God, others, and one's true self. Shall we say that such distinctiveness is the roughest, but not the richest?

The fact is, of course, that the more man's choices come into line with the will of God the less man becomes, in this rough sense, distinct, even though man is now far more real. We must look at this problem of the nature and meaning of personal spirits, their origin and end, ultimately and proximately. What are the fullest implications of the Universal Word, our central explanatory perspective, for this question? Spirit is; Spirit is in relations intrinsically, or can we say, even *as* relations? Spirit is eternal, ever self-identical, ever qualified. Spirit is one and many, identically single and communally many without the single being individual and without the communal being plural. Spirit is identical in the many and the many are one in Spirit, both equally and simultaneously true qualifications of Spirit. Or, rather, Spirit is thus the relating, the relata and the relations. And all such relations are internal with perfect coinherence and with perfect distinctiveness. Spirit is; Spirit is in relations and as relations intrinsically, but Spirit also creates and has relations, for Spirit is creative Love. Love that is self-sufficient is never less than full, but nevertheless it overflows; Spirit overbrims; Spirit is excessive generosity, not as forced water in a fountain having to overflow but as a self-sufficiency that remains still and selfsame and yet outgoing and creative.

Thus Spirit creates because Spirit is love; Spirit is self-sufficient Love that cannot be contained; Spirit shares; Spirit gives joy, and the highest joy is the attaining of love. Love can affect love only through growth and decision, through the processes and acts of freedom. Love grows through choices and the learning from choices; love grows as the finite freedom chooses more and more to receive Love. Love cannot be manufactured or given as a substance; love is not the product of a process. Love is a gift of life, a gift of love, a bestowal from Love. Thus Spirit eternally is, one and the same, and differentiated, *as* Spirit and *through* its creative manifestations. Spirit glories in the beauties of objectified nature and provides through nature the conditions for history, including the curse of nature for the sake of man's learning indirectly, or in freedom, from his choices, registered not only in the self but in the body, and through the body in and as nature. Spirit also creates life, life beyond the mere material world or the mere physical world. Life is capacity for response. Response grows over the long, long ages into responsibility, first conditioned responsibility, and merely or mostly conditioned response, and then into the responsibility based on free ideas, on understanding, on fear or consequences, on the acceptance of duty, and finally, on the promptings and constraints of love.

Spirit is and creates a pedagogical process, a cosmic environment from the lowliest beginnings of freedom through indirection, through a long process of inorganic evolution, through a long process of organic evolution, through a long process of what Teilhard de Chardin calls noogenesis, the evolution or birth and growth of mind, through the history of man and what lies beyond man. Streams of distinctions, slow and thorough, rough but exceedingly fine, qualify Spirit. Eternity as Love creates time as the condition for learning love. Time in nature is hardly time, as we have found, both the beginnings of time, the cradle of time, the conditions of time itself. But natural history is part of the history of life, not only externally or ecologically but internally and biologically. Nature and life lead to history and love. There is evolution of body and there is evolution of soul. In the last analysis they correspond, they are concurrent; they are part and parcel of one process. There is no progression without ingression; there is no evolution without convolution; there is no ascent without descent; there is no incoming of what is outgoing apart from an outgoing of what is Outgoing. Thus streams or streamers of qualification of Eternity by time, of Spirit by spirit appear, not as mere appearance in the sense of *maya,* not as illusion and lacking in true being, but as manifestations of Spirit through Spirit, of the Perfect through the imperfect, of the Infinite through the finite, of Love through the learners of Love.

Such infinite spirits, such personal spirits, are both Spirit in identity and spirit in "condescension." They are Spirit intrinsically in virtue of identity and also spirits learning love through a history of freedom, selves learning to become more than selves, but first having to become genuine selves. Spirit is true joy, the joy of being, Spirit spills over joy through the adventures of becoming, becoming free, learning to choose, learning to live, learning love. Spirit also finds joy through suffering, the learning through suffering, the learning love through suffering, the final learning that love can come only from the eternal Love that dares to become free within the bonds of servitude, free as light in darkness, free as love in hate, free as eternity in time (but never as time). The process is long and dark, harsh and forbidding, but the process heads in each manifestation for the light, for true life, for love and for Love. The adventure to find love in freedom by Love in satisfaction; the adventure of renouncing personal spirit to find personal Spirit, the adventure of believing in the light and recovering through and beyond the darkness the Light—that adventure is the meaning of creation.

Life becomes more and more informed by mind, life becomes more and more free through the power to abstract, life becomes more and more morally responsible through the understanding of choices, spirit becomes more and more personal through Spirit, leaving the joy, leaving the satisfaction, leaving the being for the becoming, for the suffering, for the struggle. Underneath all is Spirit ever selfsame; at the bottom is Spirit ever identical; in and through all is the Eternal creating time and times. Thus the inner reality of all creation, of all things, all life, all selves is Spirit. Spirit is and Spirit creates from the dust of the ground, from the physical resources of body and through the infusion and ingression of mind. Spirit creates through Love's inbreathing of spirit into distinctions of historic heritage of body and soul, finite selves. Spirit creates adventuresomely, often beyond what seems to us wise. Spirit overflows; Spirit descends and condescends to the depths, starting back to the heights.

Spirit is joy, intrinsic, indivisible, unspoilable. Spirit as Spirit cannot but have joy; Spirit is joy because Spirit is self-sufficient Love. But Spirit goes out, overflows, spills over, and in time. Eternity cannot enter as Eternity; Eternity enters as time; but time can enter into eternity, not as time but only as eternity or fulfilled time, and thus eternity condescends into time: love coming as time, as the chance and condition for learning love, and as the history of learning love. The Perfect can be nothing but perfect, but the imperfect can take on perfection, can accept aspects and powers of perfection, can be perfected. Time can be transformed and thus admitted into eternity. Thus life can grow, people can learn to love, and, being open to Love, can even conclusively live Love. Incarnation is not God walking on earth but the Son of God living the life of love. God becomes present not under the conditions of perfection but within the conditions of imperfection.

The more overagainstness toward God, in terms of conscious understanding and rejection, obtains on the part of man, the more walls between them, the more external relations, the more self-being of the finite person as a finite personality. The more man understands and rejects God, preferring his own self and his limited loyalties, the more genuine self-being grows into individuality, the more a person becomes a spiritual personality rather than a personal Spirit. But the more Spirit participates in struggle through condescension, the deeper is the intensification of the conflict of darkness with light, of love with fear, of gospel with law, of love with duty, of love with hate. Love shudders and shakes in sharing Love from Eternity to time the only way Love can be shared, by the creation of the conditions and risks of freedom, by effecting the struggles and sufferings of freedom to learn through what is not love that love may be real and prevail.

Love in such pedagogy is largely there indirectly, not as personal presence but as personal absence. Love is often there not as joy but as pain, not as satisfaction but as suffering. Love is frequently there not as attainment but as seeking. Love is usually there not as victory but as battle. Love is there not as resurrection but as cross. Love can finally win love only through suffering, preparing the will for acceptance and preparing the way of acceptance. The false self must be frustrated before the potential self can be fulfilled. Only goodness can lead to contrition rather than attrition, to love's repentance rather than fear's repentance. Thus personal spirits become through the establishing of external relations between spirit and Spirit, through genuine self-awareness and the rejection of freedom by freedom, through the history of choice as individuation and as identification not with universal Love, but with partial loyalties and limited causes.

But such becoming is of time, not of eternity. The more the finite person learns love and the more he accepts eternity, the more he rejects his individuality as such, the more he learns to understand himself as spirit within Spirit, as universal man within an Ultimate Concern and within a Universal Spirit. The more man learns love the more he becomes real, but also the less externally distinct he becomes. His distinction by becoming less rough becomes more rich. He becomes one with mankind in the unity of the Spirit and in the bond of peace. In the Universal Word, in "the one Love in us all," clearly recognized and fully accepted, man becomes both more real and more open; the external relations become lowered and less real as man becomes more real in Love. The more Love reigns the more external barriers are lowered. Thus the process from Love to Love through love is a long one with a long natural background, a long historical background and a long personal background, not only of evolution of body and soul, and not only of noogenesis or evolution of the mind as mind, but above all of the ingression of Love and the progression of love toward Love. The process leads, in fact, to the realization of unimunity where authentic oneness establishes rich distinctions.

How long in eternity that process will continue no one can know. It is beyond our ken. But continue it will until Love finds Love and is fulfilled in Love, through the learning of Love by love. Thus the external barriers make for the sharpest differentiations of self-will, of individuality, of self-being over against God. Here the becoming of differentiation is great. But the more the self as personality learns to become personal Spirit, learns its true nature and destiny, the more the barriers go down and internal relations become more operative. The internal relations are always there in the case of the all-pervasive Spirit as identity, but now, as in God, the internal relations can coinhere even in the personal spirit who is love of Love. Thus becoming becomes actual and distinctiveness real in the sense of external relations in order to lead to a higher form of becoming, the distinctiveness of personal spirit in Spirit, of love in Love, of man in God. External relations then differentiate without dividing.

At the conclusion of the process, at the consummation of spiritual history, man knows that God becomes all in all; this becoming does not mean the wiping out of the history of finite becoming as though man when he becomes one in God, with divisive external relations ended between him and others, and between him and God, now disappears in the undifferentiated Ultimate. Rather the history of richness, of struggle won, of cross and resurrection, enter eternity to be one with eternity, in the sense of the dropping off of all external barriers and the becoming one in Love. That Love is eternally qualified by self-awareness and by fields of qualified consciousness. The finite self now is fulfilled within that Love which is joy and satisfaction and becomes the being-in-Love. The self becomes spirit-in-Love. What that can mean man cannot grasp from this side except to know that it is the joy of sharing the Joy that truly is, the Love that is, the Spirit that is, the personal Purpose that is. The acuteness of that being in Spirit and being in Love not even the most swooning ecstasy can surmise.

In this way Love answers the why of being and the why of becoming. Material and efficient causes find fulfillment in formal and final causes. But all such whys of purpose give embracive meaning to the hows of process, and that not in terms of substance or process analysis, but in terms of Love's meaning through personal purposings and the multidimensional operations of Spirit. Thus Eternity fulfills time. Perhaps within that Eternity even the love that has become part of the all, and yet internally distinct, within the God who is all in all, the consummated love may once again want to dare to overflow and overspill and venture out again for some fresh finite process where love is tested and refreshed in finite adventure. Perhaps such love may want to dare the darkness by the light, the ill will by the goodwill of God. Or perhaps within Eternity exhaustless Spirit, which is no thing and adds and detracts nothing, and nowhere, as a total consciousness, coinhering its total field—to speak in terms of human extension and therefore only suggestively—will keep overflowing and overbrimming eternally and exhaustlessly, indeed enriching what is already fully self-sufficient as Love.

Thus Love becomes only to destroy the external becomings in order to make distinction within the ever selfsame Spirit. Division gives way to distinction; separation, to coinherence. Self-awareness, freedom, consciousness, love (and no substance or process, no thinghood or river), find fulfillment in Reality, for Spirit is, Spirit is in and as relations, but Spirit is Love at its highest meaning and direction; and Love is Spirit self-aware as Love and as personal Purpose. Infinite Love creates the finitudes of personal Purpose, not in and as relations of intrinsic coinherence, but as creative of, and as having relations, in time and for time. By such relations Love is, of course, not fulfilled, for Love is ever self-sufficient, but Love overflows to enrich what is ever without need in the sense of deficiency. Thus Love alone can answer the meaning of becoming, both the indirect becomings of finite history and overagainstness and the direct entering of love into Love, the becoming of love in Love, carrying with it the maturation of historic process.

We have now considered Love as being and Love as becoming; but Love is also the answer to non-being. In order for there to be any becoming there must be non-being. If all the being were that could be, then non-being would be an illusion. Then at best there could be change, but no becoming. Then non-being might be only the denial of particulars, that all is not everywhere, or the denial of the total presence of the total totally. Then indeed non-being might only be oppositions and contrac-

tions within the process, but even these are difficult to make plain if being
simply were being. Thus without genuine non-being, there could be no
genuine becoming, only a functional becoming as change and non-being
as the denial of particulars or as the opposition to the functioning of the
limited and the local, or possibly an opposition to the total's ever becoming the limited and the local. But when creation is real and becoming is
real, the becoming of time and of time into eternity, then non-being is
an essential characteristic of creative Spirit, it is the logical presupposition
for creativity, it is the guarantee of the genuineness of the new as new.
Thus the becoming of the order of nature presupposes, so to speak, less
non-being than does the becoming of selves and finally of personal spirits.
That self as an individual existence in time is new, even in terms of the
absence of God in the personal sense, and that spirit is new even in the
sense of the full presence of God, when the self becomes consummated
into God, with divisive external relations done to death and internal relations perfectly coinhering. The new is not the Spirit but the distinction
within Spirit, so to speak, the differentiation through a nonsubstantial
personal awareness. Then the new is real, becoming is genuine, but not as
substantive addition. The new is qualitatively authentic without constituting the accretion of any quantifiable entity.

Thus possibility becomes more than a word. Possibility is grounded in
the nature of deity always to exceed every actuality, or to have the capacity to exceed any limit, to overbrim and to overflow. Thus it is true that
"Being is what it is only by becoming what it is," when being is Spirit
and Love, and not substance or process. Already in *The Christian Understanding of God* this fact stood out. Creation is of the nature of Love,
creativity is characteristic of Spirit, but creativity and creation are not
necessary drives causing constant internal combustion. Rather, they are
the spilling over of what eternally is the Joy of Love, in order to return
to that Joy through finite adventure, and the winning of love by Love
through Love's suffering, not in Eternity but in time. Such becoming, not
so much of things and processes as of personal spirits and love, presupposes the possibility of Love to effect the new, to create history in Eternity
and to save history in Eternity, yes, to perfect history in Eternity. Such
possibility is thus more potentiality as the continuous relatedness of Love
to the ground of creation, as Love in such a manner that all discontinuity
of and in creation is ever related to, and relatable to, the continuity of
Love and the identity of Spirit, the ever-abiding faithfulness of God. Thus
non-being without being plays the logical and ontological role of the
open-ended nature of Love, the outgoing and creative functioning of
Spirit. Spirit is; Love is; and Love-and-Spirit both is and are through and
as the personal. These intrinsically is-and-are, and become in relations,
as relations, and through the creations of relations. Thus Spirit is identi-

cal and Spirit contains distinctions, is qualified intrinsically; but Spirit also creates relations, and not only external relations but abiding internal relations through the receiving of time into eternity, of personal Spirits into personal Spirit and into that Love which is Reality, in being, in becoming, and in non-being. These matters, however, await their thorough analysis and development in our final chapter on consummation.

Some misunderstandings may arise or objections be offered. We shall consider them and dispose of them as best we can. Spirit is, but is no thin substance; nor is Spirit some verbalism to avoid the problems of substance and of process. Spirit is no trick of word. Love is no spurious solution of what is unreal and, therefore, both unreal and irrelevant. The use of spirit can suggest the employment of such explanatory invisibles as genes, atoms, or the future. Such entities, of course, answer specific, not general, problems, and some of them are potentially visible. The Spirit, on the contrary, best answers the fundamental mysteries of identity and distinctiveness, of being, becoming, and non-being, and of meaning and purpose—when Spirit, of course, is seen as in itself personal, as in itself Love. The categories can be accepted as real when they provide the richest and most relevant scheme for understanding the totality of our experience. We have to have a framework, a universe of discourse, and the two main contenders, substance and process, find both their correctives and their fulfillment in the categories that have been developed. Life to grow and to flourish has to have overall meaning, judgment, power for newness, and directives for conduct. All these we find in the categories of spirit and the personal understood as Love.

Nor is the personal without personality, as William Hordern seems to think, the grin of the Cheshire cat without the cat, for Love is greater than personal presence; God can be present as Spirit even when absent personally, and the whole case of creation and the creation of freedom, the effecting finally of love by Love hangs on this contrapletal fact. The distinction between personal Spirit and spiritual Personality is of critical importance. Nor is the distinction between external and internal relations contrived and merely convenient. The whole case for doing justice to Love as contrapletal, of God being present and absent at the same time, of God's being identity and in control and yet the pedagogue who provides privacy and freedom for man to learn love, hangs, again, on this contrapletal understanding of external and internal relations. What we seek is the fullest and deepest illumination of experience as a whole and in all its aspects.

Some compossible we must have in order to offer ultimate explanations. Vacuous abstractions solve no problems. We dare not deal with an imaginary world. Love through its indirections and its direct relationships, through its joy and sufferings, in fact through its total explanatory power is our fullest and deepest provider of the compossible. Nor do such solutions in terms of Love analytically bypass the empirical and the rational. Our definitions and habits of thought with regard to the empirical and the rational, for that matter, have too long been associated by and colored with the history of Western metaphysics. Substance is now beginning to give way to process, but process itself needs to be seen in terms of purpose, and the purpose of Love. Substance and process have their proper and needed places in interpretation. The full proper limit of efficacy should therefore be granted to each category, but they cannot constitute the categories of Reality.

For Reality we need all the categories of Spirit, the Personal, and Love. I have offered this reworking of the basic categories to remove all unnecessary roadblocks for effective thinking and to provide an adequate framework for thought, both explanatorily and existentially, both as interpretation and for direction of life. These categories now need not only to be improved and developed but to be applied to all knowledge. A task for generations! At best I see only partially and suggestively. I offer them only and exactly as a proposal of the most general framework for our total thinking that can give unity to knowledge and meaning for life.

Part Two

THE
HISTORICAL
WORD

The Unique
and the Universal

ANALYTICALLY the Word can be universal as Spirit, but what can universality mean in terms of history? Can the Universal Word ever be universal in a genuine historical sense? Is not history characterized by uniqueness? Can the unique be universal? Or, vice versa, can the universal ever be unique? In the Christian faith there is, of course, the special problem, both central and integral to its nature, as to how Christ can both be the revelation of the universal God, truly incarnate in history, and yet also be unique. Are not the two terms, "universal" and "unique," analytically contradictory? Are they not mutually exclusive? We have already devoted some time to the problem of universality and universals. We had better now discuss the problem of uniqueness with reference to history. The problems connected with concrete claims for the Incarnate Word to be both universal and unique, or the question of the historical Jesus and the historical Christ, and the basic question as to how to relate the Universal Word not only to one religion but to all religions, I shall touch upon so as to indicate a *Gestalt*. For a fuller explanation the interested reader may consult the concluding chapters of *Reason in Religion*.

One aspect of our problem deals with the relation between uniqueness and finality. The unique is by definition not a comparative term. But finality is. It seems therefore that whatever is unique cannot be final and whatever is final cannot be unique. If Christ, for instance, is claimed to be final, as the World Council of Churches has taken as a specific aim, does this mean that Christ is thereby also declared by the nature of the case not to be unique? Or if he is unique, does this involve that he cannot be final? Are our difficulties real or only verbal? Can the words be made to yield genuine meanings, avoiding inherent contradiction? Or, perhaps, both words are totally inapplicable to history? Does the unique as the totally different have no place in historical thinking, where all is necessarily related and in some sense comparable? And does not finality involve some kind of stopping or transcending of history? Does not finality both denote and connote a coming to an end? Are not *finis* and history inconsistent terms? Where there is fully *finis* there is no longer any history. Uniqueness and finality seem both to be ahistorical terms, but finality less so, for cannot the end of history be its goal? But then, can finality be *in* and not rather *for* history? Does finality come with the ending of history? If so, finality does not belong for its discussion to this part but rather to the third, which will rightly be dealing with the Eschatological or the Potential Word.

What, then, can uniqueness mean, especially with reference to universality and the Universal Word? Especially what can uniqueness mean with regard to Incarnation, or the Historical Word? First of all, *uniqueness in all respects* is a meaningless term. Whatever is unique in all respects is totally unrelatable; it is completely incomparable. But whatever is completely unrelatable and incomparable is by that token also completely unknown. However knowledge is conceivable nothing can be known that is not in some sense relatable. It must be comparable to something else in experience. Similarity and contrastability have equally no meaning with regard to the totally unique. Indeed, uniqueness in all respects is inconceivable to man. He can conceive of sights that cannot be seen by the eye, or sounds that cannot be heard by the ear, especially by a human being, but he cannot conceive that which cannot be related in any way to anything in his total experience. But are we not now reducing the problem of the unique to the absurd? Surely the word would not have come into existence unless it has not only some recognizable meaning but also some genuine use. If the unique is the absolutely particular with no shareable universal at all, then obviously it must remain an odd and bizarre concept to the point of utter absurdity. Can we even conceive of a philosophy of such uniqueness, even a philosophy of the absurd?

Suppose we push substance thinking to its final logical absurdity. Suppose that there is a substance containing material in no way shared by any other material in any sense. Suppose that all its relations are external, that it is purely particular, sharing no material content with anything else in the sense that its content is never at any point or in any way common in nature with anything else, and that it has no form or shape or pattern that in any way has any common characteristic with any other form, shape, or pattern. Would not such a substance be unique? Suppose also that knowledge is not only of what is like but also of what is authentically different. In such a case could not such a substance be both unique and knowable in such a way that we could speak meaningfully of total uniqueness or of uniqueness in all respects? Even external relations, however, presuppose some likeness. Could the object be weighed? Then it partakes of the characteristics of space-time. But if it cannot be weighed, then it is characterized by the properties of the spaceless. In either case it is describable in terms of some characteristic. If it can be handled by sense experience in any sense, directly or indirectly, it is relatable and describable in its terms. But suppose that it cannot, and can be had only as a concept, not an imaginary concept, but a concept that is the conclusion of valid thinking. Such a concept could be arrived at only through some other concepts and therefore through relatable and comparable universals.

If, however, both sense and thought failed, and man could know this only in terms of some completely miraculous revelation of the unique in terms only of its own reality and not at all in terms of the knower, would not such knowledge be of the totally unique? By no means! Any recognizable knowledge, even though completely incommunicable, would presuppose some relation to the knower that would be more than entirely external to it. An entirely external relation, as purely arbitrary with no meaning of any kind for the knower in terms of anything else in his experience, would not be recognizable. Even the experience of externality would have meaning in terms of previous universals. Even a sheer or crass contrast from all previous knowledge would involve some confrontation. There can be no contradiction without content. An outbreak of the completely new, even totally *miraculously* new, would involve either that the knower existed or did not exist. If he existed, then in him the old ordinary world and the new had come together in some sense, even without integration, and therefore had in fact become related and in some sense comparable, even though only by contrast. If the new showed the knower that he, his life and his knowledge, were total delusion and that only the new was real, then the unique would become meaningless in the light of a nonexistent person and a nonexistent history but then that light would illuminate, and thereby be related and relatable. In the light of what it showed, the new relation, the knower might have to reject either the new or himself as existing, but there would be a relation and therefore no total uniqueness on the part of the new.

Thus Buddhism is more consistent than Hinduism. A total *neti neti,* not this, not this, can affirm the totally unique, but then such an affirmation becomes meaningless to human knowledge and experience. Then man must suffer from total *avidya,* or unknowledge. As a matter of fact, however, even the denial of the totally unique is an illegitimate contrast which implies and involves the breaking of the stark *neti neti.* How can anyone deny something that he cannot know in any manner whatsoever? The Hindu affirmation, on the other hand, that the deepest in man is nothing empirical but beyond all human qualifications involves and implies that the essential in man is both in some sense radically distinct and yet also relatable sufficiently to become a concept of the unique or "the one without a second." How else can the unique become a legitimate concept? But as such it is no longer totally unique or unique in all respects. There is accordingly no conceivable way in which anyone who takes human experience and knowledge at all seriously and who believes in human history in any genuine sense can ever meaningfully conceive of or use the concept of the totally unique. The unique in all respects is a fallacious verbalism. We should bear this in mind when theologians use such concepts as "the wholly other" or the completely unique. Then they engage rhetoric but not reality. Given human experience as real and dependable in any sense and human discourse as responsible, there can be no legitimate place for such expressions as the unique in all respects. No wholly other can be known, nor can it be logically inferred, provided our existence and communication have any reliable meaning.

Inasmuch, then, as "unique" must have a legitimate use and inasmuch as it cannot be used as "unique in all respects," unique must mean "unique in some respect or respects." But if this is what unique means, does it in fact mean anything, at least anything vital? Is it not true, as we saw in our discussion of universals in a previous passage, that everything in history is unique to some extent? Nothing is totally the same and nothing is even quite similar. We remind ourselves that no two fingerprints are exactly the same, not even two snowflakes, and all made products, even from the same mold, are microscopically different. What then, can it mean, in any significant sense, to claim that anything is unique? Is not the claim merely an affirmation that something is in history? If all things in history are unique in some respect or some respects, does the word unique add anything in fact to a description about a historical event? What does it mean, for instance, to claim that Jesus Christ is unique, if every person in history is also? He is unique in some respects, and others are unique in some other respects!

Obviously the term "unique" has not only meaning but critical meaning, for there are few matters that excite people at so intense a pitch as the matter of the uniqueness of Jesus Christ. If we are to discuss the whole matter of uniqueness and finality with regard not only to Jesus Christ but to eternity and history in general, we had better, then, go beyond both some merely general meaning that is in fact meaningless, like "unique in all respects" and also one which, to be sure, has meaning but no important meaning, like "unique in some respect or some respects," and tackle the legitimate meaning to see what it can and cannot convey for our understanding of Incarnation, of the contradictory formula of having the universal, even the universal of universals, unique in history.

Surely unique in this sense must mean nothing less than unique in some critical respect. Take some examples: there is only one surgeon who can perform a particular operation; in this sense he is unique; there is only one medicine that cures a certain kind of disease; in this respect this medicine is unique; there is only one telescope that reveals certain galaxies; in this respect that telescope is unique. Now uniqueness has taken on importance. But there can also, besides, be such a category as uniqueness of critical importance: there is only one surgeon, for instance, who can save that life; there is only one medicine that can cure that fatal disease. Uniqueness now takes on critical importance. Not that that surgeon is not like others in many and most respects; not that that medicine does not contain common ingredients, but that the surgeon and the medicine in question are different from all the rest with respect to the only issue that matters in the case of life and death. They can save when no one or nothing else can.

Such uniqueness, for that matter, can be either substantively or processively important. The personality of the doctor may in fact be such as a whole that he alone is competent to know and to do what is required; or the medicine may contain also some ingredient that can be found nowhere else. Thus for instance substantive thinking can form the background of uniqueness. Similarly one could consider some process of interaction that alone could secure certain desired results. But these questions of composition or interaction are of secondary importance to the question of saving action. In theology the matter should be put in such a way that the speculative consideration is far less important than the soteriological. As a matter of fact, people may not understand why the doctor can perform a saving act or what there is about the medicine that alone can save, while nevertheless they know the fact that the uniqueness is in fact critical. They may know neither the ingredients nor the working of the medicine, but they may know that it helps cure the patient.

It is all-important to keep this distinction between the philosophical and the pragmatic, or the explanatory and the directive, in mind. There may be a most important analytical or philosophical issue between a human being as spiritual personality or a personal spirit, but when it comes to performing that operation the distinction matters not a bit. Or there may be a critical question between a substantive philosophy where a thing is what it is and needs only itself in order to exist and a process philosophy where there is constant interflow and interchange among the areas and fields of the world's acting energy; but as to the working of the medicine there need be no fundamental knowledge of this distinction at all. What counts as far as uniqueness goes is whether or not that surgeon or that medicine can savingly perform that operation or cure that patient. The full relation between that person and other persons or between that medicine and other medicines analytically is another matter. Substance thinking may claim a total uniqueness which may be disputed by process philosophy; and a philosophy of spirit may not agree with either of the other two analyses; but which one of these is more right and more wrong is not of critical pragmatic or saving importance; as a matter of fact, it may be of little or no importance for the only respect in which uniqueness counts. Thus those who claim uniqueness for Christ almost fanatically may be right in their claim with respect to the issue at hand and still be wrong in the fuller analysis of what constitutes that uniqueness. There may be a saving, pragmatic uniqueness that yet may have different analytical and historical meaning than what is supposed by those who confuse saving uniqueness with analytical or historical uniqueness. The part can easily be taken for the whole, especially when what matters ultimately is the part! In what sense, however, can the Historical Word, or the Universal Word in history, be unique?

Later I shall at least discuss the question as to what the relation between the historic Christ and the historic Jesus can be, but that is mostly a problem of historical knowledge that I shall treat in a later volume. The issue now is in what critical sense, if any, the Universal Word can be unique in history. Can the universal be unique? Even more, can the universal of universals be unique? And if so, in what sense or senses? If later we find a meaningful place for Incarnation in history, if later we decide that the universal can be unique not only in some important but in a critical sense, what can that mean as to the uniqueness of the Universal Word? If the Word is God's own outgoing Spirit, as personal Love, in what sense can that Word be unique? And in what sense can the *Universal* Word be unique in history? The Word is unique analytically in the sense that there is only one God, one final power and presence of identity as he is in himself ever selfsame.

The universal Ground and Goal of all creation, the Fount or Abyss of all reality, is then unique. God is unique; the Universal Word is unique. Uniqueness in this sense refers to the reality and nature of God, of the Ultimate. The Word is then the outgoingness of God for community and creation: for community in the reality of the Love which is both One and Many, and for creation as God's sharing beyond himself by the causing to be a pedagogical process in which finite spirits can learn to understand, appropriate, and participate in the very nature and purpose of God. In this sense uniqueness belongs to "the Son" born before all ages, or before creation; logically the Son is ever the nature of God, and therefore is God as well as of God. But for our purposes here we must be dealing, not with the analytical Word, but with the Historic Word. In what sense can the Universal Word be unique in history?

Granting, for purposes of discussion, that God has come into history, and granting that God is unique as self-sufficient Spirit, the personal Love, who ever is and is the ground and goal of all creation and creations, and granting that God is utterly unique, qualitatively distinct from all finite beings, while God is also utterly universal as the most inclusive, all-embracing, and all-penetrating Spirit, can such universality enter history uniquely, and if so, what can such uniqueness mean? We have already seen that it cannot mean that God is utterly unrelated to all previous creation. Such uniqueness is analytically impossible, especially as God is creator, maintainer, and director of nature and history. Therefore God's presence in history in Incarnation cannot be wholly other or totally distinct from previous nature and history. Nor must we resort to some general uniqueness characteristic of all there is in history. What, then, is the relation of Incarnation as God's presence in history as he truly is, in some sense, and his presence in nature and history elsewhere in some other sense or senses? What can God's critical uniqueness in Incarnation mean? This question, after all, is completely vital for the question of the nature and meaning of the Universal Word, not only as analytical but also as historical.

If God were conceived of substantively, then he would be either present or not present in Incarnation, and if present there, God would have to be absent elsewhere. If substance thinking is right, Incarnation would have to be spelled with a capital and there would be no possibility of incarnation with a small letter. If God came in Jesus Christ, for instance, and never at all before, then God as God would simply have to be absent from all other occasions of nature and history up to this point. Furthermore, if God were conceived as a substantive personality with a unique ego in all respects, then if he had come not only in or with Jesus but actually *as* Jesus, then he could never come again unless, indeed, Jesus himself came again. Jesus then defines the eternal word. They are the same.

The presupposition of such theology would have to be either that the one eternal Personality came as Jesus and that Jesus is therefore the only God, although God beyond human history could take on different forms. Or else there could be a community of Gods, from two to more, and that one Personality, called the Son, came into history, even though there are other Persons in the sense of substantive Personalities beyond human history. An enclosed uniqueness, guarded by sheer external relations, would then involve a qualitatively unrelated once-for-allness of Incarnation. When people claim that Jesus was unique, they generally mean that he was God in human form and that he and he alone is God in human history. When they say that we cannot be Christs or that God cannot be in other human beings in the same sense as that in which he was in Jesus, this is what they intend to imply. In other words, such people are thinking of uniqueness within a substantive framework of thought.

On this presupposition, what of the human nature of Jesus? There are at least two main ways of looking at this problem. One is that the human nature was only an external vehicle of the Incarnation and never participated in God as God. The Word became flesh but the flesh never became Word. Therefore there was no intrinsic relation between God and man in Jesus, only an external instrumental relation. But that assertion must be obvious from the fact that substance is unique and can have no internal relations to any other substance; in this sense God's nature was unique; and the Personality of the Incarnation was unique, having no possible internal relation to any human personality. In this sense God himself entered history as God, was God from the beginning and was God throughout the Incarnation. At the end what was human simply fell off, like doffed clothes, and Jesus returned the same being to the same place from which he came. Such a position, naturally, is contrary to history, to the New Testament, and to the main line of Christian theology, but it very likely is the most common form in which the Incarnation has been held throughout the ages by people in general.

For this reason any suggestion even to discuss the question whether Jesus Christ is unique is a matter of life or death to the believer. The claim of uniqueness is bound up, almost always among the general believers, with the substantive form of philosophy. The Godhood was and is a unique thing, material, different from all other things or materials. Or Jesus was God as the eternal Personality who existed from eternity, came to earth using externally our human conditions, even human form, but was ever and remained ever fully God, and returned again from time into eternity, shedding his humanity, except for the work he had done and the experience he had had within it. This philosophy is unbelievably naïve, but it accords with gross human sense, especially with our optical experience, and has powerful appeal to the uncritically pious. It is amazing that the main line of Western philosophical thinking could have been immature enough for such a long time as to fall prey to this kind of simplistic thinking which does not solve and which in fact does not even face man's basic problems of interpretation.

Another form of this kind of thinking is that found, for instance, in the writings of as sophisticated a scholar as E. L. Mascall of the University of London who suggests that when the Absolute entered history and took on human form, it just forever became stuck with it. Once God had come as Jesus Christ into history, that was his human form. Thus the absolute presence determined once for all the human form in which it had once come. God was human once; there is only one God; this is the permanent humanity which has been assumed. Incarnation is once and for all and therefore we cannot discuss any other form in which God can or may come.

In this sense at least the humanity of Jesus is eternal. But if Incarnation is the eternal purpose and decree of God, then is not this humanity also potentially in God always? But if so, is it merely external and in no way intrinsic? On a substantive theory there can be no question, however, for God is God and never man. He can have only external relations to creation. Therefore there can be no intrinsic relation to humanity before, during, or after the Incarnation. On either this theory of Jesus' humanity, analytically for history, or of the one we have just discussed, there can be no legitimate hypostatic union. For God is God and never can be intrinsically united with that which is not God. Therefore God, being unique as God in the substantive or personalistic sense, can never become truly Incarnate. Incarnation is completely contrary to the substance thinking which is presupposed throughout. But it is precisely these people who have claimed hypostatic union for the Incarnation! The way out has been obvious and cheap: Incarnation is a mystery, a miracle, a contradiction of reason and of ordinary thinking.

Such a claim does indeed add zest to that longing of man to believe in something which he cannot understand. Therefore the very contradiction adds fervor and devotional acceptance, often to the point of fanaticism. But uniqueness in this way is logically impossible with regard to Incarnation, appealing only to those who worship the absurd because it is absurd. Such uniqueness, however, must deny universality even in the critical sense of God's presence in some genuine sense; such uniqueness is based on externality, on total exclusion (God and man can never be confounded!), and we seek a uniqueness, if this is a meaningful term, that is consistent with the nature of the universality of God in all needed critical senses and consequently of God's true presence in Incarnation. We seek nothing less than the Incarnation of the Universal Word, before, in, and after the Incarnation. Therefore we must proceed with patience and care in our analysis.

Uniqueness of Incarnation on the presupposition of substance thinking will not do. What, then, of process thinking? On the basis of process thinking uniqueness can mean only some critical presence in the sense of product of process. But whatever is a product of process is subject to repeatability. Therefore uniqueness does not refer to a historic uniqueness of emergence nor to a qualitative persistent uniqueness. Such uniqueness is a matter of finality rather than of uniqueness in the sense in which we have been discussing the question. Before discussing finality, however, we had better discuss the possibility of God's presence in the world before Incarnation on the presuppositions not of substantive thinking but of Spirit, the Spirit who is personal Love.

If we approach this same problem of uniqueness from the point of view of the main presuppositions of our analysis, we shall arrive at a widely variant picture that can do more justice to the facts of history and analysis. God is then no substance, self-contained, of one kind of material, so to speak, who can have only external relations to the world, but God is in himself, as eternal Spirit, creative Love, personal Purpose, the real potential of all there is and the fountainhead of all relationships, and he is so not as some external, final Source, but as Presence and Power in history in some sense, and senses. Thus God can come as the Unique, the only One, the one without a second, into history and remain the unique Word in history for all eternity. There is no One else, no Love else, no Spirit else, no personal, creative Purpose else than the ever-unique God. In this sense God is God, and is ever only God, ever and always unique, and unique as such in history. This Word having entered history in conclusive presence and power entered as the Unique in himself and will ever remain unique in this sense. There is no other God ever, God and with God, through whom all things are made and without whom nothing is made. This Word, this Logos, this God, this Son, is unique in eternity and is unique in history. He can only be his own initiative and power; he is "born" into history, not made. He is no product of process, but the Lord and Love of process. He is the Purpose of process. The deity of Christ, in this sense, is ever unique. There can be or come or enter history no other deity. Once come, no other God can come. Incarnation in this sense is unique and once for all.

But this fact of the eternal and historic uniqueness of the Word is at the same time capable of being universal, not only as Love and final Purpose, but as presence of spirit. Thus the same God who came in Christ is also present as spirit, as impersonal spirit, or as spirit in general, in nature. Spirit is present as creative, as groping, as seeking. Spirit in this capacity is not present as final or full Purpose, but as the power for the lowliest beginnings and the most preliminary feelings for order and destiny. God who condescends to create at all, condescends to begin and to be with the most tremulous stirrings for what is to become nature in our sense. He is inclusively and therefore truly present as God for the purposes of initiating the most vague, anomalous starts toward nature. He is present in and with every minuscule groping toward nature, proceeding with the process in nature, especially in its dawning life and mentality until it reaches what we now call nature, and can yet be with the pedagogical process through unimaginable developments that may be concomitant to his larger development of life and love, in this or countless planets or aspects of nature which we can never begin to imagine or fancy. But the final presence in all these stages is God himself in the form of spirit relevant to his creation then and there.

Similarly he can be with creation as it emerges into history. He can be present in conflict and cooperation, as operative and cooperative spirit, as seeking and as finding spirit, as permissive and as admonishing spirit, as guiding and as not guiding spirit, present in some respects and absent in others. Thus God who was uniquely present through a human being, in a sense which we shall soon discuss, was at the same time present, in a different sense, with all creation, according to relevance and need. Thus the Word who came in clarity and fullness in a critical sense in a certain life could also and was also present in all the developments of human history and of the various religions. He who came as Son in a unique sense of Presence at the same time was continually enlightening all who were coming into the world.

He was coming to conclusive fullness of the Spirit of personal Love but through a process that recapitulated all previous processes in the appropriation of our common humanity in a natural way and in the bringing these processes to a final or unique product in an exceptional way. But the uniqueness was more than a ripening of process or a choice of maturity by a deliberate goal-seeking. The uniqueness came mostly as the initiative and power of the Unique who had worked to prepare for such a "fulness of time" and came himself as the Spirit of personal Love into Jesus, not as a miraculous mystery contradicting creation and reason, but as the fulfillment of the whole meaning of nature and history within a genuine human being. We must look a bit more closely at the meaning of the Incarnation, which involves organically both true and final uniqueness and at the same time the universal potentiality of God within a genuine human experience. In what sense was the Incarnation universal? In what sense was it the Incarnation of the universal, but not in all senses universal, any more than in all senses unique, but rather both critically universal and critically unique? Surely God did not become Incarnate as fish or beast; or did he?

If the deity of Jesus Christ is unique substantively, then, the uniqueness, at least of the Godhood, is one and entire, having at most only some external relation to the human aspect of his life. The uniqueness was then so radical that only an inexplicable miracle, an impenetrable mystery, could describe the relationship of God in Jesus, or of God as Jesus, depending upon the conception of the deity; and so radical that only a total mystery or some paradoxical denial of relationship could constitute the relation of Incarnation to the rest of nature and history. If, on the other hand, we have in the Incarnation a product of process, however unique upon arrival and however repeatable thereafter, we have no Incarnation as a radical qualitative distinction between God and man. There is a new relation between God and man possible after the emergence, to be sure, but even the ingression is qualitatively continuous, as altogether natural inherently, with the rest of creation. Creation is then fulfilled according to its own potential nature, but not radically reconstituted *ab extra*. The ingression is not of the eternally transcendent in the unique sense.

As the product of process inherently there is no critical problem as to the relation of the new, even though it be new to the point of finality, for within the omni-relatability and omni-interdependence of process relationship is a definitively given reality. It is analytically assured. But there can be no uniqueness of eminent reality. Wherever there is uniquely eminent reality beyond process as process, we have more than process philosophy. There is no room in process as such for God who is God in radical self-reality as a qualitatively sovereign contradiction of nature and human history. In process thinking God is a pole of process and in some sense also product of process. Therefore neither substantive nor process thinking suffices for the Christian framework of truth; and the entire history of Christian theology must consequently be radically reshaped if it is to become adequate as the Universal Word. The Universal Word Analytical and the Universal Word Historical must come together if *theos* and *logos* are to form one intelligent and yet concretely given Word. Thomas Torrance in *Theology in Reconstruction* keeps worrying the theological bone that we must not slide over the difference between coherence statements and existence statements. He does so in order to safeguard the uniqueness of the given in revelation and to keep it from being dissolved into general meaning. His aim is so laudable and his work so diligent that one could wish that he had had better tools with which to work. He actually works with a substantive base and forfeits the truths of process, and neither is adequate as a genuine choice. When the Christian presuppositions are taken seriously, this question will be seen in a new and more satisfactory light. We must then proceed to approach this basic theological problem from within the power and reality of the Christian categories.

The Christian categories do not constitute realities in themselves. They are not abstract meaning. Neither are they subsistences, self-existent Platonic ideals or forms. In themselves they are aspects of the One who is Many, of the One Love which is Unimunity beyond the one and the many as we know them; the categories are real only within the Personal Spirit who is Love. In a way there are abstracted realities for the purposes of explanation. Only God himself constitutes the control to the wholeness of ultimate truth: namely that Love is and works on many levels especially with regard to the pedagogical process by means of which he shares and multiplies his Love. Thus when that Love is perfect in self-being as Spirit, he is both fully personal in himself and yet also impersonal where so needed. Love is neither personality nor process as such, but beyond both, while preserving all truth in both of them. Spirit is self-sufficient without being a closed substance incapable of internal relations. Spirit is self-sufficient without being a constant process where all parts, or rather fields of forces, need each other equally. Whitehead could never accept the full meaning of Incarnation because in his thinking God would need the world as much as the world God. There could then be no self-sufficient transcendent reality. God could not be conceived of as eminent reality but had to be understood as an analytical component of process. Whitehead opposed substantive thinking and considered such self-sufficiency as that of eminent being barbaric and immorally isolationist.

A theology or ontology of spirit, however, obviates the difficulties and deficiencies of both positions. There is eminent being but not as substance. Spirit is by nature both self-sufficient and relational. Spirit is capable of relational uniqueness. As we know, such a term sounds wrong because we have thought of uniqueness mostly as "in all respects" or as a general category of history whereas it must now be considered as "in the critical sense" of not only reality but saving reality and not only of saving reality but of consummating reality. There can accordingly, however, be an ingression into history which both saves and fulfills the total process which is both unique and final, unique with respect to its own nature, one without a second, and therefore always unique as such, and yet also final as the model and exemplar for all the rest of human history.

The Incarnation in Jesus Christ can thus be unique in that the Word as the Word is in himself always remains the Word and in that no human or historical process can ever reach or become the Word. The Word is God's self-sufficient nature who became incarnate. The Universal Word is God, in himself, analytically, historically, and eschatologically. As such the Word remains unique, unequalled, in a class all by himself. We have used the personal pronoun for God in this case because God in himself is personal, *is* Love. But the uniqueness pertains to the eternal Word, the Love that entered history, not to the historical as such. It is God in Christ who is unique and ever remains unique. Thus uniqueness is more than a relation; it pertains to ultimate ontology, to the theological foundation. The relation becomes unique as a historic ingression but becomes thereby also final as God's purpose for creation. In Christ God and man became conclusively joined according to God's eternal purpose and according to their respective natures. Therefore we have historic uniqueness wherever Incarnation ingresses *ab initio*. But God could and can come anew in human history and elsewhere where process is ready and yet without knowledge or mediation of the first or any other event or Incarnation, in this cosmos or in worlds unknown. It is in such possible cases the same God, the same Word, the same Incarnate reality, but in different historic media of Incarnation.

Thus the eternally unique and the historically unique are qualitatively different realities and must always be distinguished with critical care. The Ground of uniqueness is eternally the same with respect to the revelation of God, but the historic incoming is a particular event that may mediate God's presence from then on, but not necessarily as the only possible historic medium. "Most uniqueness" may become finality from then on, but there may be other unique historic inbreakings in this world or in other worlds. Eternal uniqueness or uniqueness on the part of God is absolute, whereas historic uniqueness possesses an absolute uniqueness only as one aspect of its reality in relation to all dependent appropriation of God's presence through the original event; but not with respect to the general potentiality of history as such. There is thus a congruence in the case of eternal and historic uniqueness with respect to the eternal, but an openness with respect to the historical. The eternally unique is both beyond finality and final. Before long we shall have to look at this question more fully, but first we must turn to the question in what way the eternally unique could be related in Christ to previous history and how. How could what is historically unique contain both what is eternally unique and also be intrinsically universal? What is the nature of a historic Incarnation that can be at the same time decisively unique in the critical respect needed and also intrinsically universal and open to all relationships? To this question we now turn our most careful attention.

The uniquely Incarnate with respect to the eternal, the self-sufficient Spirit who is Love, the eternal, personal Spirit, came as the ingressive emergent into human history, consummating process, ending history, turning Ground into Goal; but as uniquely Incarnate he was also, at the same time, uniquely universal, for only in God is the full identity of all distinctions. God becomes present when understood and accepted as universal Love. To be sure, God is more and differently present than the understanding and acceptance of him. The understanding and acceptance are human acts, relative, thin, and distorted. God, oppositely, is perfect fullness. But God comes as the objective, true counterpart to human understanding and the appropriation by choice. The invitation and the guest are not the same, but the guest does not come uninvited. God has thus made us for freedom and he respects with perfect integrity our need for self-being, for growth of understanding, and for growth of acceptance. But when he comes as his own presence and power, it is God who comes and not man's subjective awareness of him. Soon we shall consider both analytically and historically in what sense God came to Jesus. Now it is enough to assume that God so came and thus became effectively incarnate Love. The Incarnate Word became the Historical Word. The God who came was then the God through whom all things were made and without whom nothing was made that was made. The Creator became incarnate, to be sure, as Son, as Word, but it was none other than God who became incarnate. Now we must consider how, then, this God when incarnate as Son is related to all previous history.

He who ever is selfsame as the personal Spirit who is Love was always related to all creation as creating, sustaining, and directing spirit. The Incarnate Word contained as the fullness of God also spirit in general. Spirit in general is God's most general presence, akin to the presence of energy in all things. Thus the God who was in Jesus was not only God as he is in himself but also the God as he is in all creation. He was the God who is in the rock and in the fish, indeed! Spirit was no enclosed personality but a transpersonal Spirit who was also the porous, all-interpenetrating, coinhering, all-inclusive presence and power of identity. God is never less than spirit in general although he is, of course, more. The all-inclusive spirit is the creative outgo of the personal Purpose who is everywhere present, so to speak, but is never in itself purposeful or personal. Purpose, freedom, order, may be previsioned on all levels of biological life, as Hans Jonas ably advocated in *The Phenomenon of Life.* We have much to learn from men like Jonas, Whitehead, and Teilhard de Chardin in these respects. But here spirit nevertheless is not present in the developed form of conscious understanding or of personal awareness but is rather only incipiently operative as inherently attracted as ground to Goal. God is purposefully absent in order to allow that development of self-being through alienation and overagainstness which John Hick in *Evil and the God of Love* calls "epistemic distance." Thus there are incipient gropings through inherent attractions implanted in creation but no personal presence of God as Purpose. In this way in the Incarnate Word God is present as personal Purpose, as conscious Love, and yet also inherently present as transpersonal spirit or as "spirit in general."

Similarly God is present as the Spirit of God, as we have long called God where he is operatively and not also cooperatively present in the sense of an understood companion or cosubject. There God is present as providence in a more exact guiding sense. God acts in history not only in his Son but also in his Cyruses and in the processes of nature, in his unwilling agents, and in his unwilling tools. God works through conscious urgings in the conscience and also through the general working of conscience as man's drive of duty. God works through the intricacies of desire, pulling man; and through the complexities of law or duty, pushing man. God is one, and when he becomes present in man as Incarnation, he is not only present personally as the Spirit of God. Thus God can be present and absent in history in different ways. The God who becomes incarnate conclusively as Agape has before been present in nature and history as the creating and sustaining reality in whom all things and all selves have their being. But as such he was and is present not as *who* but as *which,* not as *he* but as *that.* He is present impersonally.

The transpersonal Word becomes personal as the Incarnate Universal Word, the Historic Word, but he does not cease to be the creative ground and goal of nature and of human history. He also becomes present in a mixed reality which is sometimes as impersonal as conscience, driving and drawing through duty and desire, but which is also sometimes personal, as for instance when God is understood as the God of history and of encounter, but nevertheless not as yet as the God who is universal Love.

Indeed, God is present in the same person sometimes in all three senses at the same time. As long as that person lives, God has, so to speak, to be present as impersonal spirit all-inclusively. Perhaps spirit can become so purely personal beyond creation that spirit in general becomes present only as potential for creation in full ecstasy, and therefore absent in the fullest reality of God himself as he is in himself, and of man's relation to God in man's highest fulfillment. Perhaps spirits even in this life can be beyond the body in God, as Paul wonders; but, in any case, in relation to previous nature and history the Incarnate Word is open to all there was and is through spirit in general, which is intrinsically derived from, dependent upon, and inherent in the nature and reality of God, the personal Spirit who is Love. God always was so related during history and remains so related as Son incarnate. The full nature of God became incarnate and therefore the Incarnation, which is of the true God and is thus eternally unique with respect to all creation, is also by that very fact completely universal and related to all creation. Whether God is beyond or within creation, not separately but qualitatively, God is always fully related although not fully personal. Spirit is the category of all-inclusive identity. There can be no Incarnate Word who is not the God of personal Love and yet also the all-inclusive Spirit who is the Ground and Goal of all creation. God is fully related according to the need of the relation. Where there is need for privacy of person God's personal absence is the most fulfilling relation and is therefore positive and not negative in the sense of want of relation. A deficient relation actually becomes efficient. In this sense the distinctly unique can yet be universal. When absence is better than presence, absence is perfection of relation according to need and no lack of relation according to a want of it. Such absence is not ultimately negative but positive. It is part of personal Purpose. This fact we must stress emphatically. No wonder the true light that was coming into the world was also lighting all else. To understand the nature of Logos as Love, the personal Spirit, is to understand how the eternally unique was also by his very nature inherently universal. God remained selfsame and yet also all-related in the Incarnation, for he who became incarnate was of God and was God, God the Son, God the Universal Word.

Naturally we can see God related in Jesus Christ himself far nearer and clearer than in previous nature and history. He was related to Jesus Christ peculiarly through nature in his body and through history in his humanity. The body of Jesus was, after all, nature which as such was neutral territory between Jesus, creation, and God. The general spirit of God created and sustained the physical material out of which Jesus' body came to be fashioned and continued to be fashioned while he lived. His body, too, changed completely every seven years! The Incarnate Word was thus present as creating, directing, and sustaining spirit all through the organic chemistry of Jesus' physical life. Creation affected Jesus not only as nature but also as history. All previous history, relevantly channeled and focused, became his heritage through the history of his people which he appropriated. In every present Jesus was living, breathing, and acting within such a medium of God's indirect presence through not only nature but also history.

Both spirit in general and the Spirit of God were operative in the divine milieu which constituted Jesus' natural and historical setting. Nature worked there as did history, but neither nature nor history can work apart from the creating, sustaining, and directing presence of God as spirit in general, and as Spirit of God. But God also worked personally calling his Son, speaking to his Son, guiding, inspiring his Son. Jesus responded not only through nature and history in general, even beyond the most special influence of all, that of his own family, but particularly through his own personal choices, through his own self-responses. Thus God became incarnate primarily through his own choosing, his own calling, of his Son. Or the eternal Son called for the response in the human son, until through the appropriation, over time, in freedom and in growth, the Son of eternity and the son of humanity became the one personality of history who was in one true personality Son and son, neither one nor the other, but both; and not both as such, but the one unique historic personality. He was God and man in the fullness of time, the fulfillment of God's purpose in man's nature by the effective right relation into which God and man entered dynamically in him or *as* him. Thus the eternally unique became unique in human history, to the best of our knowledge, incarnating in free understanding the personal Spirit who is Love, the eternal God himself. The fully universal who remains unique even in all history thus became historically unique in order to constitute the finality which is the meaning of all history and which actually ends history, not through destruction but through fulfillment. Christ is the end of history as its true and final meaning; and, therefore, when he becomes real, human history has been fulfilled in meaning.

The pedagogical period is over when the meaning of history has been fulfilled. Thus the eternally unique for history becomes also final for history. Let us look then at the Historic Word, the Universal Word in history as the fulfillment of history, to ascertain in what sense it is final in history and for history, and in what sense what is final must thereby also end history. God is uniquely universal. When he enters history truly, ground turns toward goal and the eschatological Word becomes determinative. The Universal Word passes from Historical to Eschatological. Before we leave the Historical Word with respect to uniqueness, then, let us have a look at the fuller meaning of finality. After that we can at least suggest the historical side concretely in the relation to the historic Jesus and the historic Christ. That done, we shall finally then proceed from the Analytical Word and the Historical Word to the final part of this work, the Potential Word. First, however, we must examine more closely the nature of finality.

The eternally unique, we have shown, can be universal and what is uniquely universal can also be final for history. But what can finality in history mean? Obviously what is historical cannot be absolute. Every historic event is born in history and dies in history. On this point Hinduism is right in its main contention concerning the nature of history. Or the way we would put the matter is that when the eternal becomes historical, it thereby fulfills history and thus ends it. Human history, at least, points; it has a pedagogical purpose. God the eternal Spirit is present in history and works in history, but he remains ever the same with regard to his eternal self-sufficiency. He is not made to live by history but rather ever makes history live. He is eternity as lived Love while history means learning love. The eternal Spirit is ever dynamic, ever active, and as creative, ever "historical," but only if by that is meant *living*, not inert, not static. The eternal Spirit ever *is*, and is ever the creator of the conditions of history. God is Love and lives Love beyond all finite creations, sharing of his love. Thus he is in, with, and for history, but he himself is not of history, or in that sense historical. He helps man learn love in history while he lives love as eternity. Only the finite is historical in this sense. We can say, of course, that God's experience is "historical," that one aspect of his being is creative of history, but we may not say that God the Creator and Lord of history is by nature historical. He has no need to *learn* Love. Thus the historical Word is historical only in and for history. The Universal Word enters history to fulfill it, to finalize history, to complete the purpose of history. The eternally unique Word is thus not historical; the Word becomes flesh as it joins the finite, even as the Word is in himself, "full of truth and glory," but the fullness is ever of eternity, the fullness that fulfills history and creates the fullness of time.

If we keep assuming, then, that God entered history conclusively in the sense that God was truly present in himself, and if we keep assuming that man can become fulfilled only by the understanding and appropriation of God's presence and power as universal Love, and that human history has for its goal the finding and the living of this creative, adventurous Love, then the incoming of God in human history by the Incarnation signaled the finalizing of history, or the ingression of its final purpose. The Ground became Goal in Jesus Christ—if here the nature and purpose of God as Agape became centrally and conclusively understood, accepted, and disclosed. But what was final about the purpose, the pattern, the model for life and history, was God and not the historic event. God's nature and reality were final, not the particular historic relation. The finite as finite can never become final for history. Thus the relation that was established in the concrete event of the Incarnation cannot be final, for the relation comprises both the eternal and the historic, the infinite and the finite, God and man, the Word and flesh. In other words, what was final was not the Historical Word, but the Universal Word that became historical in Jesus Christ. No one else can ever have the same ego Jesus had; no one else can ever have the same experience Jesus had; no one else can ever have the same spirit Jesus had; no one else can have the same family Jesus had; no one else can ever have the same world, from the perspective of a particular self, that Jesus had. Thus Jesus is unique in at least three senses. The eternally unique is unique in him categorically, by Incarnation, but is unique with respect to his own reality and not comparatively. This uniqueness is *an unshareable historic uniqueness*. Secondly, although Jesus Christ had a unique relation to God that no one else can have, nevertheless he also had a shared uniqueness in that the same Word in a different concrete relation can come to all those who are given to become sons of God and to share in his fullness grace for grace. In them too will be established a unique relation to God. There is no sameness, and not even any "quite similarity," in the creation of God. Universals never come, apart from saving particulars even in man's relation to God. The like is not completely like; there is ever distinction. This "open" uniqueness is of critical importance as to *historically shareable* reality. In this sense Jesus was not only unique but final, the inaugurator of a new possible relation to God. Finally, Jesus was unique in a third sense as a human being within all his ordinary humanity. Jesus had a uniqueness all his own as a human being regardless of his relation to God. This kind of uniqueness is, of course, common to all men. Thus there is in Jesus Christ a threefold uniqueness that illuminates the meaning of historic finality. What is of critical importance for mankind is not the first or the third kind of uniqueness, but the second, where Jesus becomes a model for all men in his relation to God.

Until man understands and accepts the proper presence and power of God, Jesus Christ remains critically unique. Until then he stands by himself. What is different about him is all-important. The difference constitutes the very nature of God and the central purpose for man. If Incarnation indeed became a fact in Jesus Christ, the eternally unique first entered history conclusively in him, to the best of our knowledge. At least finality of history became effective in him as a proclamation for life and an understanding of God, the nature of ultimate reality. The meaning and nature of things became finally disclosed in Jesus Christ. By that fact the way to right relation with God also came through him. Knowledge here becomes saving knowledge, critically important, showing man what is wrong with him; and also how he can become right with God, with himself, with others, with history, and with nature. With respect to those who afterward understand and accept God because of his life, Jesus Christ is unique as the bringer of finality, the meaning of their lives, and the goal of their lives. He is, to use New Testament language, "the firstborn among many brethren."

Jesus Christ, as such, exhibits historic uniqueness. This uniqueness is, of course, a fact of history to be investigated. If God is Agape, did Agape first enter history in Jesus Christ with effective understanding and acceptance? This question has been my concrete concern for a lifetime of writing. Whether or not Agape first broke through in Jesus Christ with decisive understanding and power is, of course, not an analytical matter but one for historic investigation. If it did, then with respect to all his followers, he mediates for them the meaning, reality, and right relation to God. In this respect he is unique. For them he is a necessary "mediator" of God, but the necessity is one of a historic situation or option and not an eternal necessity. It is conditional and not categorical. "Christians" come to God through Christ. But can we equate Christ as a historic event with the eternal, Universal Word? Is Christ not the Historic Word? And does the Historic Word need to be once for all? Can the Historic Word, in fact, by its very nature be once for all? Is not the Historic Word final rather than unique in the full saving or critical sense of that word?

We have to look, then, more closely at the question as to what that mediation means. What is the nature of historic mediation of the eternally unique? In what sense is Jesus present to his followers? Are they really *followers* in the primary sense? Can they be related to God only through Jesus or also apart from him? If other Incarnations come into history or into the history of other planets, to what extent is that Incarnation or are those Incarnations of Jesus Christ? Can Incarnation ever be plural or does it ever remain sovereignly singular? If the latter is the case, what can such a fact mean? If the latter is not the case, what can be the nature of God that allows for plural Incarnations? We are now concerned with the meaning of personal Spirit in God and personal spirit in man and what Incarnation can actually mean as a relationship in human history. If Christ is the permanent pattern for the right relation to God, what is the nature of God, of man, of human history? In what sense can Incarnation be repeatable? Only the understanding of repeatability can establish the meaning of finality. How, then, can the eternally unique also be final, a repeatable reality in some meaningful sense for human history?

Uniqueness and Finality

I N WHAT SENSE, to become more specific, can Jesus Christ be said to
be not only unique in the critical sense of being the bringer of Incarnation but also final for human history? Thomas Torrance insists in
Theology in Reconstruction that "in Jesus Christ and only in Jesus Christ
do we have the one Logos of God," with no other way, ever, to the Father. Such a uniqueness presupposes a substantive, a Greek, view of God,
a complete discontinuity between Jesus Christ and all men. We cannot in
such language genuinely speak of other men, for the unique Godhood of
Jesus Christ constitutes an incomparable human nature, a miraculous
mystery of union, never achieved, except in Christ, before or since. Thus,
when all is said and done, he was not really man, a human personality.
Therefore Jesus Christ cannot be final within such a framework of
thought in the sense of having introduced into human history a relation
to God that is in any meaningful and effective way repeatable.

Torrance holds consequently that only the original disciples can be
apostles or "cardinals" of the faith. He also holds, however, that "the
Holy Spirit is God himself insofar as He is able, in an inconceivably real
way, without being less God, to be present to the creature." God creates
this unique relation, which, on the contrary, should be an obvious observation regarding God's relation to man in all dimensions. Metaphysically,
however, there is only one God, and Torrance would be well advised if,
since he stresses God's real relation both in Christ and to man, he could
accept the New Testament teaching of the actual presence both of Christ
and of the Holy Spirit as actually constituting the inner central life of
all believers. But if he did so, then the one Logos of God would be both
in the Christ and in the Christian, in both Jesus and those who come to
God through him. In that case it would be the Logos, the Word, that is
unique and not the historic personality of Jesus, except as a historic personality among other personalities and except as the original Event, the
determinative Ingression, the foundational Incarnation. In that case the
historic personality of Jesus is supernormal but not unique qua history.

What is unique is the Word, God, the decisive Cosubject of the Incarnation, which in and with the human constituted the historic personality

of Jesus. In relation to people before him Jesus was, rather, supernormal but in relation to those who accept him he becomes the norm, or normative. The basic decision as to Christology comes in at this point. No wonder many in The United Presbyterian Church U.S.A. fought the word "normative" for Jesus as suggested in the revision of its creed. They wanted to consider him unique in the sense of substantive philosophy, as the only God on earth. Their trouble was at least philosophical!

Winston King in *A Thousand Lives Away* has well said that the Buddha is "only a Man" although as such he is supernormal, not without capacity of emulation or repetition, but in a class so utterly by himself that the millions of people and the countless ages have little hope of attaining to who he was or of seeing what he saw. He is thus decisively different and yet not qualitatively distinct in the sense of man's full and true potential. For Buddhists, then, the Buddha can be final but not once-for-all unique, (being one of many manifestations through countless ages), for he did obtain the final *moksa* or enlightenment. Men now come to enlightenment through him. Therefore he is unique historically for Buddhism, but not more than that unless what was unique in him was also universal. The whole question of once-for-all uniqueness in and for history centers in whether or not the manifestation is final for all forever. If Jesus as Agape is final forever as normative life and regulative pattern, no other uniqueness more critical and fulfilling can ever come to this or any history. If the question is open, then the uniqueness is historically normative only to the best of our knowledge in present history, and even for such claim the vindication is practically beyond human competence. The most we can get for a warranted faith in a decisive uniqueness is an open road, some veritable process of dynamic self-verification both intellectually and practically. Similarly Moses and Mohammed are unique but only as prophets and founders of their respective faiths, not qualitatively unique as gods nor as normally necessary mediators for all men.

The problem is this: If the Logos was present in Jesus only, then we have to deny that he can be present in any other man, not even as Christ or as the Holy Spirit. Then we have no Universal Word for men. By such teachings we not only deny the central New Testament teaching on the subject but we also make an arbitrary and divisive myth of Jesus. The New Testament insists that if we have not the Spirit of Christ we are none of his and that Christ in us is the hope of glory; that actually for us to live is Christ. To hold anything else is to deny the nature of the Universal Word. Under such denial we are left with a uniqueness external to man's nature and destiny. We have a Christ who cannot be final, only unrepeatable, an external savior. There is, of course, another choice: Jesus could be different because he was not truly man; but in such a case we have forfeited Incarnation. Rather, the truth is that the Universal Word became incarnate for all men, to bring in the full saving relation of God to men, which God alone can bring, which God alone can *be*. Jesus cannot differ from other men either in the sense that the Logos came to him and to no other man or in the sense that he did not have a genuine but only a unique human nature. Uniquely victorious over sin, and that by a new and fuller relation to God and the incarnating of God, he was like us "in all respects." Incarnation is the incoming into human history of the uniquely Universal Word, the only true and right relation to God and in God.

But can it now nevertheless be true that Jesus is necessary as the only mediator? If God came here and came conclusively, can he ever come *as* anyone else? Is not God one? Is not Jesus then necessary in order for us or for anyone to come to God? Can we abstract from history what God has put there once for all? What God has joined should men put asunder? What do we mean now? Do we mean that the eternal Son is necessary; do we mean that he who once came in Jesus is ever more necessary? We cannot mean less. But if the center of Jesus' historic personality was this incoming of God, this product of the process of humanity, can we abstract the Historic Word from the Universal Word? The Historic Word is, of course, the Universal Word, but it is still the Word that is unique and not the historic form. We cannot freeze the form of history and maintain that the relative form, the flesh, the bearer of the Incarnation is eternally necessary. That is to finalize the finite; that is to eternalize history; that is to make man God. The trouble with Kierkegaard's distinction between "the Socratic occasion" and "the Christian moment" comes just here. He makes "the Socratic occasion" a generalized, abstracted truth, a mere meaning, whereas Christ as "Christian moment" becomes the messenger who is the message. He thus presents us with a false choice between abstracted general meaning and personal truth, concretely embodied. The truth of Christ is always personal, but personal truth can also generate and constitute meaning. The life is the light, the person is the truth, as well as the way and the life. Indeed, this truth is the way; it is the model; it is the pattern for all men.

Nevertheless, how can we take the color out of history that Jesus gave to it? Does not his concrete personality and nothing less become the way, the truth, the life, that man enters into? How can we speak of man's having direct relation to God when that relation is in fact mediated by the concretely historic person? Two observations are necessary at this point: for one thing God could, can, and in all likelihood does, come originally to other people as Love, as for instance, to those of the myriad planets that know nothing of our tiny little earth. For another thing, the critical mediation is of God's nature and purpose, of his presence and power and not of the historic Jesus. Then may not Jesus himself always be present to each believer? What life is like beyond this earthly existence we cannot know. Perhaps a body beyond the limitations of space can be spread unimaginably so that a mother who is dead on earth can live from beyond earth at the same time with several children in widely separated earthly places. Perhaps we shall be so disembodied that spirit with spirit can meet, not only God with man, but human beings beyond earth with human beings on earth *at the same time* even in different continents. We cannot rule out such possibilities. But what it can mean for a created personality, even when fulfilled by God's presence, thus to be with many at the same time we cannot now know. Perhaps spirit can so be identified with Spirit that Jesus can be thus mediatingly present in a direct way. Perhaps in a new life one finite person can become plurally present beyond all space. Perhaps our godly friends can thus be with us, the "cloud of witnesses," not only in general, but actually at the same time with innumerable persons in widely scattered regions of earth. We dare not rule out such presence, but actually he who is present in the universal sense is the Word, is the eternal Son, the divine Logos who came not as Jesus, for Jesus was also truly human, but in, with, and through Jesus, making Jesus Christ for us the normative historic Word, whereas the full Historic Word is wherever the Word is genuinely present in human history.

What, then, is supposed to be mediated when it is said that we cannot come to God except through Jesus Christ? Is the human Jesus, the historical ego, the bearer of the Word, effectively constituted by the Word in the new creature of the new man; is that historic Jesus present to each believer? Does each person experience the historic Jesus? If the answer is "of course not," who then? The Word as he came in Jesus? What does that mean? Not Jesus but the Word? No, this answer would have to be within the assumed presupposition of substantive thinking that the historic Event of the Logos is necessary. Then, not Jesus as a historic personality, but Jesus as the Christ? What can that mean? Can it mean that the Word becomes seen through a particular Event so that the Word can never be had except through history? Does it mean that in Jesus alone the Word became incarnate and that therefore the Word must always come through him, but that nevertheless it is not he as a historic personality that matters but the eternal Son? We wonder what this can mean. Not the man Jesus, not the human being, not the flesh, but the Word. And not the Word as Word but the Word seen as flesh in history. Not the Universal Word as such but the Historic Word.

Does it mean that the Eternal Word alone saves, but also that the eternal must be seen necessarily through the historic Event where alone that Word broke into human history? In any case such an explanation would under all circumstances preclude the Universal Word's coming originally either to other planets or in human history elsewhere. What we are discussing, however, is what the nature of historic mediation can mean once the Word has become historical and works for and in others, truly mediating the presence and work of God. Can it be that the mediation can be one of coloration of the Word for history? Men cannot understand who God is and what his will is. In Jesus, God has come and therefore revelation has taken place. Here God has come and performed his act of salvation and therefore through Christ the act can be appropriated. Here God has come for fullness of life and therefore through this mediation life can be consummated. What then is transmitted into and through history? If not Jesus' concrete and actual human ego, literally present, what is literally present in the mediation? A new understanding? A new power? A new presence?

Surely we have to accept and to affirm the new understanding, but what is its nature? Is the understanding merely one of memorial? Is it mostly memory? Is it a matter for the most part of recall? If there is no pastness as such, such understanding would be a misunderstanding. If the wasness of the past is gone and only the isness of the past remains, the presence of new understanding from the past, when genuinely accepted in the present, is no escape into the illusions of the pastness of the past, something that merely has happened, but is rather the affirmation and the appropriation of the living meaning of that past in the present. In this sense at least Christ becomes contemporary. Revelation does not point backward as something that is now happening. We do, rather, repeat the past forward through the present as something that is now happening. We do repeat the past forward in true repetition, as Kierkegaard saw with flaming poignancy. Rightly to entertain the past is no mere memory but memory turned into hope and hope turned into realization. Thus even knowledge is dynamic. Revelation is alive; Revelation is active history.

But history comes not only as understanding but also as power. History is a stream and man chooses the part of the river in which he must swim. That river is never totally still. It has its eddies. It has its stagnant side swamps, but even here the water can never be totally cut off from the mainstream of life and all life must be related to it. Waters from the past do get stopped for a time and times, and there are the dead ends of history, but even here there is at least a minimal connection with the river of life itself. Thus genuine understanding is not only a swimming out into some still lake but involves, in differing measures, also the acceptance of the power of the past as it hurls itself into the present. Abstraction means understanding; false abstraction means false removal from the mainstream. Relevance means a being related to the stream. Most finding of relevance in people's minds, however, is finding the places where the river is resisted by rocks. There is friction. There is conflict. There are waterfalls and swirling eddies. These can be readily seen. Relevance often means attention. It means the places where the running can be observed. Relevance frequently stands for public noticeability.

But that is not what true relevance means. Genuine relevance, as strength of force, involves being carried at the main depth of the stream where the movement may not even be seen but where most water comes through. Popularity is treacherous because it can be confused with true relevance. Publicity is dangerous because it may mean a bubbling and boiling over some rock close to the shore, well seen and much admired, but without much forward movement. Then there are the deeper rocks and the stronger resistance, and at these points there is more relevance to the flow of the river of time. And most of all there is the relevance where the stream has found its way unhindered and is now flowing unobstructed into the future. A piece of flotsam splashed by the near shallow resistance will be most seen. The flotsam against the deeper rock may come up to the surface now and then. But the flotsam at the center of the river will be carried deep in its bosom until it comes up quite out of sight of the spectators on the shore. The deep movements of history are seen least, but they carry along the most water, the most life.

Thus Christ may not be most relevant where he is most confessed and most discussed. There he may be largely an ineffective stereotype, a misdirected and misleading abstraction, a side eddy with shallow water getting nowhere, but only a cork playing against a rock near the river's edge. Christ may be most relevant where his "protoimage," the type of experience he was and offers, runs mostly in the subconscious depths, in the way of life that is taken for granted. Thus the understanding in itself is not the main criterion, but the understanding coupled with power. It is not the form of godliness but the power of it that counts! The power depends upon the way the understanding is involved in the total life of the confessor or in the entire life of the believing community. The depth of the faith may have become almost a matter of course, the unostentatious presupposition of the requirement of life as such. Not those who say, "Lord, Lord," but those who do his will are the ones who join understanding with power; and not those who do God's will as he came in Christ with conscious, deliberate effort, but those in whom God's will has become a second nature, a new being, a new man. What is past alone is then not only a new understanding, it is not only a new way of accepting and appropriating life, but also a new power generated not mostly by will or by deliberate trying but rather by the stream of reality, which in Bultmann's terms clicks into authentic life. The mediation of Christ in this sense is a historic Word, concretizing the Universal Word, coming not mostly as thought in itself, but as the living Word where Meaning is Motivation, where Concept is Purpose, where Thought is Power, where Life is Light.

Understanding, however, and power are not enough. They do not by themselves constitute God's presence. There can be no genuine presence of God that is not a living presence. God is alive even on the level of spirit in general. How much more obvious that there can be no presence of God in Christ which is not the presence of the living God! This presence is of the same God who came in Jesus. This presence is the same Spirit who came in Jesus. This presence is of the same Son who came in Jesus. This presence is of the same Word who came in Jesus. When we then say that Christ is present as the mediator we should not think of a human historic personality. Jesus was Jesus, and Jesus remains Jesus as an ego. If his ego became more than human, as it developed as a historic Ingression, Emergence, and Incarnation, then what is more in that ego is the presence of the Uniquely Universal, the Living God, the eternal Logos, the Son of the Father, in a new fulfilling relation to God; but the specific historic consciousness of Jesus, that specific historic personality of Jesus, that particular historic ego of Jesus, never becomes the main medium of transmission. Rather, God is seen through that Event of Jesus as the Christ; God comes as power through that event; God comes as presence through that Event. The particular Jesus may be granted to return to earth after the resurrection, as the Bible hints that Moses and Elijah returned to talk with Jesus. We do not deny that Jesus, the historic personality, may have spoken as an individual directly to Saul, who thereby became Paul. We do not deny that "heaven" may be open for such particular communication on the part of Jesus and of all the saints. Is that what we may mean by angels, at least for one thing, spirits disembodied of our kind of flesh? But the main transmission, the main mediation, is the revelation of God, the power of God, and the presence of God through the historic Event, through the historic personality of Jesus. The Universal Word comes to all who come to know him mediately through the Historic Word, the original pioneering breakthrough of the Word into history.

What is mediated, then, is a pattern, a model, a general reality beyond the special. Such a general reality in terms of memory, however, is not general in the abstract except as a directing of the past into the present. The general reality is nothing less than presence, the living reality of God's self-communication. Therefore God's living presence comes interpreted through the medium of the past. The mediator is, then, no go-between who tells of or who points toward the reality. He brings the reality. He brings the reality not personally, or as being himself present in the mediation, but rather by the way his life and the meaning that is put on his life color or picture the living reality that is transmitted in the mediation. The mediator mediates a living relationship to God. That is why the interpretation that is put on Jesus Christ is of such importance. But finally the relationship is living and the original historic initiator of the experience is not determinative but the experience itself. Thus when the experience is authentic, there can be correction and growth in the meaning of the experience from within the experience itself. There can be and should be ever-open appropriation of the fuller relationship. What the mediating agent brings, then, is not the actual human historic person come back to life on earth in the experience nor a heavenly being coming between God and man, but rather the model, the pattern, the form that directs the believer into the living experience of God himself. This, as we have said, can and should correct the original picture and cause personal growth of understanding, power, and presence.

What is thus mediated is the essential meaning *and* reality of Jesus Christ, for the Holy Spirit himself constitutes the living relationship. He can guide into all truth. There is ever-new truth to break forth. But if that is the case, how can we speak of the finality of Jesus Christ? Finality comes accordingly not as a human being, not as a historic person in whom the Word became flesh, but as the only right way to become related to God. Consider carefully: a way is not the goal for anyone. If the goal were reached, there would be no way. No one can reach the goal directly or immediately by going through Jesus Christ as the door. The door is rather the gateway that makes available the right road in which all are invited to walk. Does this then mean that since Jesus Christ reached the goal of understanding, power, and presence, no one else can go beyond him? Of course not! He reached the right way; he opened up the normative relationship; he definitively interpreted the experience. Therefore his experience, his life, his relationship to God as Spirit, Love, and personal Purpose, are normative, but not exhaustive. He himself is free to go on growing to all eternity. He himself is free to keep walking in the right road. But others may pass him on earth or in eternity. We are speaking of the fullness of time as the entrance of eternity, as the passing from the learning to the living of love, but we are not saying that the fullness was a quantitative attainment, an unimprovable relationship. What was mediated was precisely the right road, the only true entrance, the definitive pattern to follow. Whatever be the picture or understanding of finality it is directional and dynamic, not positional and static. The Universal Word is ever essential. The Historic Word becomes the normative necessity for those who can reach God only through him. The Historic Word is consequently factually and not categorically necessary. It is necessary for a particular history and for particular believers, and not for eternity nor for all historic instances and for all believers.

We have, then, a finality of pattern, a finality of model, a finality of life, a finality of general teachings like Spirit, Love, and personal Purpose, not as general abstractions of meaning and not as separate directions for walking, but as a Whole-response, a Total-event, a concrete Life, the Historic

Word. The Historic Word became concretely living in a particular life, but what matters is the determinative meaning of that life: not meaning as such, but meaning in life and for life. We respond rightly not to categories but to the "Savior." We respond not to generalized abstractions, but to a concrete Universal, to use a Hegelian phrase in our own context of thought. This fact we must stress, and then stress once again, that God never relates himself to anyone through anyone in such a manner as to take away the full originality of the individual. Individual self-being must be most dear to God inasmuch as each person is invariably unique. There is thus a Unique Universal constituting the finality for history but the finality is generally directive, offering the only right kind of relationship. That relationship, however, has to be fulfilled by each person in his own inimitable way.

Thus imitation is both right and wrong. Of course we must imitate Christ, but of course we cannot imitate Christ. We must follow him and we cannot follow him. We must find and follow the only right road but the road itself is no highway but is the blaze mark on trees in the woods where each person both follows the same directions and yet makes his own way. Finality, then, is of a kind of discovery that is so personal that when it has been mediated to someone else that person must find for himself even what he has been told is true. He must walk for himself in the direction that has been shown him. Finality is, then, both repeatable and nonrepeatable. It is repeatable as a way of walking, a truth, and a life. It is repeatable as the only right door, the only right way, but it is never repeatable as sameness or as "quite similarity" of experience. All and each must find the living God finally for himself, but no one can finally find the only true God except as Spirit, Love, and personal Purpose. The kind of experience will be the same for all, for there is only one God, but the nature and the concrete content of the experience will also differ for each person.

Thus, finality is both singular and plural. There is only one God. Therefore when God once enters human history, however relative and limited the means through which he comes, no other God can ever enter human history or any other history anywhere. There is only one Universal Word; therefore there can be only one Incarnation as far as the presence of that Word is concerned. That Word is eternally unique and historically final. If this is what we mean by Christ's being unique, there can be no question about that fact, provided that God has actually come here, provided that Incarnation is a fact. But if by Christ's uniqueness we are intending God's presence in history, that is purposed for all men. Only God can fulfill man; only the right relation to God can consummate man's nature and destiny. In this sense, from God's side, Incarnation is sovereignly singular, once for all.

Nevertheless Incarnation can also be plural in the full and final sense of God's purpose—to fulfill all men by his own presence—and of man's main potential as essentially made for God. The uniqueness is God's part of the relationship, the Universal Word. The finality is the kind of relationship that he offers. If in Jesus Christ the God of Agape who is personal Spirit became conclusively or effectively present in human history, then Jesus Christ is final forever as the only right kind of relationship. He cannot be final, however, in the sense that no one else can have the same kind of relationship to God. No one else can take his place in history, for history is a factor with regard to its pastness. Wherever, therefore, he is concretely mediator he is in a class by himself. That relationship is irreversible in concrete history. The very nature of finality in history, however, is for the sake of all men to walk in the same way, to enter into the same relationship, not in terms of the concrete historical meaning, not in terms of having the same flesh, but in the sense of having the power to become sons of God with Jesus Christ, being rightly related to the Universal Word. Here history's meaning reaches fulfillment.

Right here the importance, the critical importance, of the Christian framework of thought becomes vividly apparent. If we work with the presuppositions of a substance philosophy, Jesus Christ can differ substantially from all men. Then the eternal Son could come only once into human history as Jesus. The eternal Son was then the constitutive ego of Jesus. There can be no genuine Godman, as a dynamic relationship to God, as a human personality finally fulfilled lovingly by God's presence. The users of substance philosophy have to make a claim to that effect contrary to all the presuppositions of the theory. They have to affirm the absurdity of the Godman. Thus Christ became man by a miraculous mystery, unlike all other men, an unrepeatable miracle of relationship. When we understand the nature of the Christian categories, however, the meaning of coinherence, of cosubjects, of perichoresis, of God's intended relationship to man whereby he himself fulfills man by his presence, we can understand how what is from God's side a singly sovereign uniqueness becomes from man's side a universal finality, a repeatable relationship into which all men may enter. We have been seeking so far the meaning of eternal uniqueness in relation to historic finality, of the Universal Word in relation to the Historic Word. Let us at least suggest how we can think of the historic Jesus in relation to the historic Christ and how we can picture the relation of the living God to all creation, especially with regard to the religions of the world.

For some the distinction between the historic Jesus and the historic Christ is merely a matter of words; for others it is an old theological chestnut. I am not, however, dealing with the distinction between the historic Jesus and the eternal Christ or the historic Jesus and the Christ

of faith. I am rather discussing in the case of both the historic Jesus and
the historic Christ a *historic* personality, asking how far, in what manner,
and with what effect he can be known. By the historic Jesus I mean the
concrete, human personality of ordinary human history. The historic
Christ connotes, rather, the *kind* of person Jesus was according to our best
reports of him. By the historic Jesus I denote the full course of an individual in all the complexities of detail from day to day. By the historic
Christ I understand the main impression that life made on people in
terms of what he was and taught. The historic Christ is the concrete
universal, which the historic Jesus enacted. The exact human personality
we cannot know with any certainty. We have a hard time knowing even
those with whom we have lived well and long, let alone a vague historic
figure of a different age and as reported mostly at second hand long afterward. But an impressive, distinct pattern comes through the New Testament, a model for living and thought that has captured the imagination
of centuries.

Professor J. Arthur Baird has devoted years to developing a complicated
method to discover a historic figure, a pattern, a picture. In the original
draft of this book I prepared a long chapter implementing my claim that
whereas the historic Jesus in detail is beyond our ken, we can know reliably the *kind* of person he was. I believe a critical historian can feel
assured, too, that the life created the community, and not the community
the life.

This life was one of Agape, the universal for-ness, the open, accepting,
freeing life. (Years of work and several volumes stand behind this assertion!) Such a life lived power into history. It became the focus of new
understanding of God and of our relation to other men. We can readily
trace a *Gestalt* which calls in turn for definite implications. A competent
historic picture is more historically reliable, moreover, than any detailed,
unsorted, unscrambled assemblage of facts. Every historic life that counts
enough to be worthy of investigation either stood for something significant or did something that is distinctive or worth knowing. Life moves by
meaning. The meaning of Jesus' life was God as Agape, or more fully,
God as Love, Father, and Spirit.

Jesus lived the categories in which the New Testament defined God and
which I am suggesting give us the basic keys to the organization and interpretation of all truth. The overwhelming testimony of his teachings witnesses to this fact. The main import of his life strongly corroborates his
teachings. Jesus lived and taught, or taught and lived Agape. We dare
not place them in order one before the other because life itself is formed
by meaning and yet meaning seldom rises to a focused drive without the
investment of life in it. When that meaning in its wholeness and power
is pioneering, life is the more indebted to the truth it appropriates; and

like that life, pioneering teaching does not come strong and clear apart from consistency of life. Besides the teachings themselves, moreover, there are the continuations of them and the developments of them on the part of the earliest interpreters; and besides the original life is the vindication of that life by the way the early disciples accepted it and were willing to pay the price for such acceptance. In the case of the historic Christ we have an unusual wealth of both first-line and second-line vindication. Even though we cannot develop this discussion at any length in this volume, we can nevertheless suggest what the distinction between the historic Jesus and the historic Christ is and why the distinction is important.

The upshot of our findings is that what we can know is the living of a kind of life in concrete history which has full relevance for man. The eternal reality of that life challenges a new age of universal man. The inner and deepest meaning of Chalcedon asserts that man becomes truly man only when he is rightly related to God or enmanned by God. When God becomes cosubject with man cooperatively, man becomes genuinely man. The more man is "inlived" by the Spirit the more man becomes truly man. Chalcedon stands as the perfect formula not only for normative theology but for normative anthropology: God in man, without division or confusion, making one integrated, fulfilled personality. The Chalcedonian man is the man that through the Spirit's indwelling, through coinherence, I repeat, is rightly related, fulfillingly related to God, without division and without confusion. Chalcedonian man is the more unified or integrated the more he exhibits an authentic relation between his source from identity and his source from distinction. Thus the more God is known through such a life, the more God becomes relevant to man; and the more man is known through such a life, the more fully man finds the searching judgment that can clarify his condition and that can prescribe his way to salvation. But this chapter or this work must not be devoted to this thought, however important. In later works I may be privileged to develop the subject in proper length and scope.

Another topic which I can only suggest here is the relation of the Universal Word in this historic setting to the living religions of the world. Obviously the Word is ahead of all religions, a center for them which is always beyond them. The Christian faith has the same center, by historic good fortune, but not the same circumference! All religions belong within and through the Universal Word. Or to change the figure, the future of universal religion for universal man calls all religions to realize the truth of the Universal Word. But such a truth will be unimunity even in religion. Each religion must first find its own authentic self, its proper and distinctive heritage. Each denomination may have a historic heritage which should be preserved and fulfilled rather than ignored and destroyed. The Universal Word always comes "not to destroy but to fulfil," as Eric

Sharpe develops importantly in his book by that title; and historic faiths and traditions are precious realities at their inner best. The Universal Word of God's complete for-ness is not the for-ness in Christian form alone. It is for all men and for all religions that they reach the fullest possible release, creative attainment, and living satisfaction in their own way.

We must not aspire to a monolithic universal faith; neither will eclecticism do. We can neither have nor deny one religion or many religions. The Universal Word is normative but is normative in the field of religions as unimunity. The gifts of the Spirit come in the forms of many religions, according to need, background, and response. Religion is never a matter of theoretical revelation or of merely rational fulfillment. Nor are the many faiths and traditions responsible to and reducible to only one historic set of events or dogmas. The eternal faithfulness of the Spirit, the inclusive Love, the Universal Word, is and always will be one. The Source of Significance is one. Yet that one is an eternal unconditional for-ness in human history that all religions find their own proper nature and fulfillment.

The day Christ becomes "Christian" in the sense of the Western development of dogma, that day Christ becomes a sectarian label, the divisive Word of an ingroup religion. At the heart of the Christian faith is the Universal Word, the universal for-ness and faithfulness for all religions, the call of the future that all religions, the Christian included, find and develop their own specific heritage as concrete universals, cooperatively and fulfillingly, the real meaning of Spirit and Love. The full development of all religions within the creative, unitive reality of unimunity can never come apart from rich, satisfying diversity.

Part Three

THE
POTENTIAL
WORD

The Problem
of the Potential

THE PROBLEM of the potential underlies both creation and consummation. If creation and consummation are real, whatever leads from one to the other also becomes profoundly important. The topics of this part are overwhelming. I shall develop analytically and in succession three chapters on creation, continuation, and consummation respectively. First, however, I must bombard the reader with a barrage of unavoidable questions, and then sketch the barest of summaries to give a preliminary indication of the direction in which the ensuing, detailed discussion of topics will move.

The problem of creation is whether anything is "brand new." Is creation from nothing in fact? Or is creation merely transformation or shaping? In the Greek terminological distinctions, is it *neos* or *kainos*? Is creation some inherent capacity within the whole or within the parts, or within the whole and the parts together, to "desire" not only change but meaningful change? Or again, is there reality prior to, at least logically, the existent realm that produces change inexplicable in terms of what we now know or can know? Can there be what is new for us, categorically, and yet not new in itself? Is creation, to revert to Greek distinctions, *ouk on* or *me on*? Can there be reality that exhaustlessly creates, and is never limited by what is? Can *reality at its heart* be creative, producing the new, rather than merely open to new arrangements, or to realms or kinds of reality unknowable from our perspective? If such can be the case, what are the presuppositions for it, and how can we know that what is new to us is not merely transferred from realities beyond our ken? Or can we know?

Is creation sheer miracle in terms of the power to do what we would apodictically call impossible from our competence to judge? Or is the impossible in fact the possible to realities other than those we know, with resources other than we can ascertain? Or can we in fact know that the nature of things is creative? Is the power to create a "given," characterizing what is ultimate? If we give up the inadequacies of both substance and process thinking, while remaining fully hospitable to all their truth and strengths, can we understand the nature better in terms of God, not only as eternal and unconditional Love, universal For-ness, but also as inherently Creative Spirit? If the final appeal must be to the convincingness of the total seeing, in length as well as in depth and breadth, can Spirit in the service eternally of personal purpose and creative Love, make intellectually inviting the general nature and meaning of the world we know? Does the power to create, as a given, help to explain more consistently the world we know? Such is our first problem.

If creation is real, however, can what is created also last? Can there even be a meaningful development that persists permanently? Can there be growth, in, for, and by God finally, or is creation merely of a temporary nature? Can anything in nature or history *become eternal?* Or is Hinduism right in its confident assertion that everything that is born in history also dies in history? Can the permanent never come to be? Must what comes to be also come not to be? Must all that is made perish? Or can there be some other choice? Can what is eternal become distinct with newness, so that what becomes in some sense is and is not? Is creative change both real and unreal in some sense? Can there be a new in nature and history that must disappear by its very nature while there is also a different category of newness that is both eternal and, even so, becomes radically and genuinely new? If anything is eternal, if there be eminent reality, can *that really* change? Can eminent reality grow, become enriched, genuinely create?

Is consummation, furthermore, whatever it is, a matter of the "parts" only? Or are there no parts in the consummation of the new? Can there be eternal identity that remains selfsame, the given, that is yet given to change, not only in function or attention, but in reality? Can there be change in the whole that is not only functional or a matter of rearrangement, of shaping, but also a matter of authentic enrichment? To change our language, can God create what is new and make such creation eternal? Or, to speak theologically, can God share of himself in such a way that some created and creative part becomes distinct from him, enriched both as a part and also a matter of enrichment to God? Can there be lengthy purposes of God, creative visions, that have to be worked out in eternity—the learning of love for the living of love, the final fulfillment —and then come to rest?

Would such epochs in eternity, moreover, involve both God and what is created in urgent purpose, with seriousness of destiny, in such a manner that what each distinct entity did would matter profoundly not only to present satisfaction and attainment, but also to the permanent result? And would it matter to some, one only, or to all others, and in what way? And in what way could such success or failure be said to be eternal? Can there be any real change in the created order that fails or does not need to affect God? Would such results involve God intimately and ultimately? If total results are achieved, in what sense can they be said to endure in what lies ahead? Do they endure in themselves, in God, as an accomplished fact only, as life or reality itself, or in God for future realities? How could they, and in what sense, be of importance beyond themselves and how would God be affected by the results?

Does eternity, to proceed, involve some eternal "succession" or, only the attainment qualitatively of living in love? Is the final merely the ultimate or also more? Is consummation a state of being permanently perfected, finished, finished for what, or in what, or in what sense? What is the ontological status of possibility in creation, in creativity, in the light of, or in relation to, consummation? How does potentiality differ from possibility? Is possibility a "weasel" word, a trap? Can possibility mean anything at all apart from the potential? If so, what can it legitimately mean and what are the presuppositions for the distinction both ontologically and epistemologically? If God creates *ex nihilo,* how does this fact affect the understanding of consummation? If God creates from resource merely unknown to us, how does that fact alter our understanding of eschatology? Must we settle the question of creation as *ouk on* or as *me on* in the case of protology before we can discern it adequately with regard to eschatology? Or is there a sense in which we must go beyond such alternatives radically to find a fuller context for explanation?

Creation and consummation are basically two sides of the same question. Can a new light on creation open up new possibilities for consummation? Or can a whole new range of consummation make more understandable the problems of creation? And what bearing does creation, or consummation, or creation and consummation together in some new combination, have on the question of what comes in between? How is *continuation* to be related to transformation in the light of either, or both, ends of creation and consummation?

What are, then, the problems of continuation? The problems of continuation depend, naturally, on the nature of creation and consummation. Does creation involve a closed chain of causation, fortuitously operating or by some preestablished harmony? Or is creation fought with freedom as well as with lengthily enduring purposes? Is there a conservation of matter, so to speak, under constant rearrangement? Or is there a conservation of energy, pliable to both constancy and change, and change even by the redirections of purposive initiative? Or is newness in the sense of the "brand" new, added to creation? Is there not only creativity as the fresh, adventuresome reuse of matter or energy, but even as the incoming of the genuinely new, authentic novelty? How does such novelty relate to what continues, in whatever form or manner that continuation may take place?

If there is such newness, does that add to the world already in existence? And can such accretion be a matter of quality only or of both quality and quantity? As a matter of fact, can quality even be considered in relation to accretion? In what sense is waterness more than hydrogen and oxygen combined? It certainly is "other than" but is it authentically "more than"? Is love real as some combination of the psychosomatic situation and functioning, or is love an irreducible reality, irreducible to the basis for it which is needed in this world? Can quality exist, or if not exist, be, and what is the meaning of "the being of quality"? Can it be that love remains when the material basis perishes? Must love be confined to personalities or can love be more than and before personalities? In what sense, in any case, is there continuation, continuation of the basis in time, continuation also beyond time, even from within time?

Are we naturally too substance bound, too completely brainwashed to think in any other terms than of being in the sense of objectification of the existent, of what can finally, in some sense be quantified, or related to what is quantified? What must we do to be saved from our equating, however subtly, our world of reality with our world of sense experience? How can we open up to real possibility in fresher and fuller terms or how can we entertain the notion of the impossible in adequate explanatory terms without breaking reason? Or is Shestov right in his *Athens and Jerusalem,* that to be fully open to reason one must accept faith at the sacrifice of reason? Is man's original sin after all, to take of the tree of knowledge when ultimately he should and must live by faith? What are the presuppositions for possibility in terms of honest and competent thinking, or must we abandon thinking to accept the facts of faith, the imperious discontinuities that are finally irreducible to some causal network of complete continuity?

What are the possibilities that make potentiality a primary category of experience? Can the evil which is adjectival cease to be? How can we correctly handle the opposite of positive possibility? What are the possibilities for *cessation of being* as well as for the creation and the continuation of being? In what sense does such possibility depend upon the nature of creation and upon what is created, and in what sense does it depend upon the nature of the consummation of creation? Continuation is surely more than mere persistence, at least if creation is more than a closed causality, but without persistence and dependable persistence the new would also be impossible, at least to be known by us as new, and impossible as the creation that is "more than," that is fulfilling. Persistence or continuation underlies discontinuation in terms of creation, while, on the contrary, continuation denies cessation. To account for all aspects of experience, thus, there must be discontinuity as creation and discontinuity as cessation. And both can be related to continuation in some form of reality, for the new may fit into and either disturb the old, or the old may cease to be, in some sense, even while persisting as a result in the ongoing continuation. In some sense transformation involves cessation of the old, some possibility for non-being. In what sense and how is such cessation related to potentiality? And furthermore, how is such cessation related to potentiality for consummation?

Relativity and dysteleology, moreover, can add and detract as well as complete and distract. The meaning of the "in some sense" is thus important in either and both instances. The potential may be a potential to be born or to die, to come to be or to cease to be. Possibility in either direction will depend on the potential as that in turn relates to what is more than, or at least in some sense other than, potential. Our contention is that all such questions must submit not merely or mostly to some descriptive "how" of human or earthly experience, however much measurable within certain limits and for certain purposes, but must rather be ascertained in relation to the Universal Word, or the fullest and most adequate total meaning man can find. The "how" of possibility or potentiality awaits the more embracive and decisive "why." Thus the problem of the potential underlies both creation and consummation while in between it concerns also the questions of the continuation of creation.

If creation is for consummation, then continuation may exhibit an important element of transformation. Transformation is then purposive, qualitative in terms of some "why." What is the nature of such transformation with regard to the original creation, to the continuum of continuation, and to the final meaning and nature of consummation? We shall develop our answers to these questions, not entirely seriatim, for we raise the questions to pose the problems and to prepare the mind for the focused answers. Before we enter into a more detailed discussion of these questions in the three remaining chapters, however, we should profit from a preliminary sketch in this chapter of the central vision that underlies our fragmented posing of the questions. The total focus can thereafter be brought to bear, at least as an acknowledged assumption, on the separate topics we are to consider. As we have already discussed the Analytical Word and the Historical Word, we now attempt, then, to sketch in the nature of the Potential Word.

The Universal Word is God's all-inclusive, in every way complete Forness. The Most High is the Most Real. God is Agape through Spirit, ever exercising personal Purpose. The hows of existence finally depend upon the whys of God. The Sovereign Lord is Saving Love—all these expressions point to our decisive assumption throughout that Truth can be trusted, that God is faithful, that no matter what good we can think, Reality is better. Our assumption, which is our ultimate faith judgment, that is, our All-governing presupposition, that is, the Master Model, must

180 The Potential Word

in no way deny or distort any factual observations. The ultimate perspective must unexceptionally acknowledge and give the fullest available explanatory adequacy to the world we find in terms of our most critical and creative reason. We have to live by faith, but no faith is warranted that neglects or avoids the most reasonable accounting for facts, including all the facts of being, becoming, and non-being, of essential, transforming change, of genuine, accumulative, fulfilling novelty.

Nor do we ever dare even to breathe that we see as God sees, but only that we have become open to see as best we can from his point of view, or from the posited viewing point of what is ultimate, what gives cohesion and unified meaning to the universe of our discourse. Thus, we never become *theos* or see as does *theos*, but we acknowledge that *theos* has come, and comes, as *logos*, bestowing on us the duty and the joy, the privilege and the challenge, to participate in the central viewing in some sense, "to think the thoughts of God after him." The following sketch, then, is the vision that constitutes our hidden assumption: God is creative Spirit, Spirit motivated by love and exhibiting personal purpose. As such God is, and is self-sufficient, that is, he need not be explained in terms of anything else or in terms of any aspect or function of his being. No presupposition can be explained without ceasing to be a presupposition, and some presupposition we must all have. We simply cannot think as beyond all knowledge but rather only from within knowledge. From such a focused perspective we hold that what eternally is, is not thinghood nor process, nor even personality, but dynamic creative Spirit. Even though reality is creative, there is rest in eternity, for God is love, and as love is perfect. The perfect is, works, and rests. Activity is only one aspect of reality.

That God is eternally creative, then, does not mean that God is eternally restless in the sense of dissatisfied, but rather that he is eternally unsatisfied with any and every creation. The goal for such a ground of creation is his own perfection. But the finite by self-choice never reaches the infinite, in the sense of perfection as self-sufficient Love. Thus, eternity as God's living and enjoying Love has always as its other side the adventure of creation. God as Spirit is ever multidimensional, as an ever outgoing Love, as Purpose ever planning, continually not continuously. Thus God is, and at the heart of reality is Love, Peace, Perfection; but from that heart there is also ever the creative outgoing of spirit as Love. Hinduism speaks of God as the creative artist, the player in the drama of the world, and with the drama of the world, the dreamer of dreams for the world, waking up to his own perfection only to dream new dreams for it. This eternally creative drama I take to be the heart of the *lila* theory. The theory can be universalized, and thus be fulfilled, too, while also fulfilling the Christian understanding of creation. We need a universal interpretation.

Some religions have God as only the good side of the drama, struggling with the evil. These positions in whatever religion (for the positions overlap and intermingle within and among the religions) contain some eternal dualism, or some given for God besides himself, some external factor limiting God, or as in Edgar Brightman, some internal aspect limiting him. At his self-acknowledged best writing on God, as in *Process and Reality*, Alfred North Whitehead had all there is ultimately in God in terms of both his primordial and his consequent natures. Such a position is a semipantheism, or a pantheism, with God in some sense in all and all things in some sense in God. Such "mutual immanence" characterizes the process in parts as well, but not in the same totality of vision as it does God, who alone sees and experiences the eternal possibilities in relation to himself, experiencing them both as eternal possibilities generally and as actual potentialities for the world.

The longer I live and think, the more real and grasping Whitehead's vision becomes. His view of God, he affirmed emphatically to me in conversation, was personal in the sense of self-conscious, as well as totally initiating the concrete world, and in the sense of the "companion who understands" on the level of human history. But for Whitehead's God, experience is ultimately, predominantly tragic insofar as the finite must continually frustrate his vision and cause his envisagement to remain unfulfilled. Thus Whitehead called himself, in this sense, more a Buddhist than a Christian. The names are secondary! They can become misleading tags. What matters to me is whether or not life basically is tragic. Is Whitehead right in his appraisal of life? Is God's lack of attainment so profound that frustration is uppermost in the experience of God? Are exclusion of possibilities and the forfeiting of potentialities on the part of the finite experiences so predominant that they must be more aware of the problem of evil than the power of the good?

Here is one place where I differ strongly with Whitehead. With Tillich, I would rather hold that experience at the depth is joy, that love, to be sure, suffers frustrations that are real and that matter even to God and particularly to God; but that nevertheless, the abiding vision at the center comes from a constantly self-fulfilled and ever other-fulfilling reality that even in his self-giving for the evil, experiences an indescribable satisfaction. Whitehead himself acknowledged such creative satisfaction as the highest kind and as having a genuine measure of attainment with God and the finite occasions of experience. This love and joy at the center can be shared. The nearer one comes to God's kind of experience, the more deep and real love grows and the more it experiences redemptive as well as creative satisfaction. Such has been both my own vision and my own experience. Therefore, I shall endeavor to spell out this fulfillment as ultimate, first in a brief introductory sketch and then in a longer follow-up discussion.

The question is, then, of the final ratio, so to speak, of frustration and fulfillment. In eternity, I believe, attainment subsumes the lack of it; the good, the pedagogical process, without any denial of the reality of frustration or finite lack of attainment. Whitehead, admittedly, never got beyond the universals which fundamentally express our earthly history now, our present cosmic situation. He had no doctrine of life or reality for the finite beyond our present attainment, as a standard, either in this world or in any world to come. His view was thus not decisively God-centered, but predominantly geocentric. He confessed this fact to me frankly and hoped that some theologian would lift the discussion to a different, a distinctly theological dimension, for he himself felt this task to be beyond him as basically a philosopher of science, and only nascently a metaphysical thinker. He wanted to go beyond "cosmological" to "metaphysical" universals, and that in theological terms. It is this very task to which I now address myself.

My own vision is, then, that God is creative Spirit, motivated by love, and characterized by personal Purpose. Eternity is the living of Love. Love in itself, Spirit in itself, Purpose in himself, all one—is joy and peace, is perfect experience. But love longingly goes out in creation, seeking to multiply its joy, bursting to share its own experience, overflowing its own plenitude. For such eternal Love, ultimately creative, inherently free, there can be no fixed pattern, nor limited finite vision, nor exhaustible goal of creation. Eternity is Love's Abyss for living, creative satisfaction. And Love's Abyss is inexhaustible joy, reality, the why of all. The goal remains ever the fullness which can never be reached, and which must yet always be approximated. The infinite revels in the creation in and with the finite; the Perfect revels in its relative creations. The approximation of appropriation, moreover, is no mathematical or geometric end, but an ever-flexible, eternally inexhaustible vision, ever creative, ever creating, ever attaining, ever falling short, but always and ever sharing in love of its own fullness not only of being, but of possibility and potentiality, of its own pleroma as multidimensional Spirit.

In eternity—that is, in God's life of love—there is an ever-ongoing life of being, of peace, of resting and of joy, but also an ever-outgoing process of creation, of planning, of sharing, of constructing fascinating dramas, creating not only the plot but the creative characters, and watching them perform in agony and ecstasy. Not only watching them perform! But of changing the scenery, of rewriting the lines, even of redoing the drama itself, and possibly of changing the main acts at will and wisdom.

This earth, from which we must view the whole, our particular time, is at most only a scene. A few million years ago God was at work mainly on the stage and scenery, but he had also begun to plan and to start some actors. For that matter, the stage is indeed part of the play. Nature and history combine not as externals, but as ingredients to the great purpose. From this little scene we try to understand the Playwright! And other planets and stage settings beyond anything we can imagine God provides. How much fun and how much frustration the great Adventurer, the great Lover, has in his life we cannot know. But Spirit is, Love is, Purpose works in personal vision, God sharing our hopes, God being our fellow sufferer as well as the "companion who understands."

Each of God's visions keeps developing in eternity until every part reaches its utmost possibility, until the whole and the part are as close to life as they can be, sharing his peace and joy, and partaking more and more of his creative identification of love with the rest of his creations. The life of Jesus, as conclusive in love, in joy, in peace, in redemptive suffering, best presents the picture of the Creator Spirit and the Redeemer Love. His life and teaching give us the best clue to the nature of the drama.

God, being Love, participates in the processes of creation both by activity and by passivity, both by presence and by absence, and, in that he is multidimensional, by activity and by passivity, by presence and by absence, at the same time. God is thus *for* creation, *for* the finite, in whatever manner or sense is needed, at his own will and wisdom and in response to the call of the creatures. God is the unconditional, universal, all-temporal For-ness. But the rate and quality of attainment in any cosmic drama depends upon the creatures. God watches with fascination, with hope and pain, for each and all to do his and their best.

The choices and carry-through of each and all affect not only each and all, as results in history, but also God in and beyond human history, and in the end affect the final result of any creative epoch. Such an epoch may not even be rightly called "cosmic," but may have to be conceived of as some unimaginably larger unit, for lives may span countless cosmic epochs, until God has produced the best possible results for that combination, or combinations, of creative adventure; until he has exhausted the potentialities which have turned abstract possibility in vision into concrete potentialities of creative process. All the processes, too, may be open to unthinkable creations and cessations from God beyond any imagining at the start of the process or, for that matter, during inconceivable durations of the process. What possibilities God can use depends upon the response of creation throughout its whole history of capacity to respond.

Thus, we see evolutions that God has tried to bring into fulfillment that instead led to frustration and death. At the lowest edge of creation God may use possibility as the vibrant capacity to work, akin to some quite open or flexible energy that can be used, transformed and made to function in many forms. The dynamic drive, desiring, may be mostly neutral, generally seeking, nearly blind groping, feeling for, and hitting on new expressions in the inexhaustible possibilities of creative Spirit. It is the nature of deity and Creative Spirit, ultimately, always to exceed in possibility any and every actuality. Potentiality, thus, is creative of dynamic newness at every level and in every dimension. Only by becoming, in some sense, and freely at will and wisdom, can Spirit become what it in fact is; or Spirit is by nature creative, starting with the most neutral, undiscriminating, unfocused beginning, as vague evolution, a begging to be, a pleading to become definite, some unstructured flair for fulfillment.

God may thus start many creations with a mere creative drive to fulfillment within some kind of creative order. He may experiment, through untold interest, with many kinds of vibrant possibilities, general expectancies, seeking some unknown goal, far, far below any conscious level. The life in him thus bequeathed, thus externalized, thus objectified, may seethe and swirl and strive, whether to succeed or to fail. But God's nature is always opulent and excessive. God's creativity abounds and overflows, as he, no doubt starts many of these creative epochs to have only a few find some way of operating, of coming together, of reaching toward some creative goal. Possibility is, thus, more than Plato's receptacle; it is both preharmony and predisruption; it is sheer vibrant waiting: dynamic seeking, unbounded longing, outreaching, onreacting, upreaching (to use symbols), seeking, striving, finding and refusing, finding and accumulating, finding and retrying, finding and to some extent succeeding. Such energy is not God directly; it is a posited capacity to work with an inborn nisus. It is the spirit of God as the principle and power of identity, but with an integral creative drive for distinction. It is God's spirit coinherent and congruent but allowing and abetting differentiation, craving manifold manifestations.

Continuation may be basically defined as the history of this given, which itself varies with an undetermined response, a basic seeking below the level of conscious seeing, up to it, through it, and beyond it. It becomes for us the history of nature and the course of history. In it there may be loss through cessation of being, through a cancellation of drive and return to the state of precreated possibility, with separation from potentiality. Death becomes real as ceasing to be, even while what was goes on, in some sense, becomes also a frustrating or a fulfilling part of nature and of history, and thus also of the life of God. The negative as defect or distortion or as plain absence may vitally affect continuation. The continuum of continuation is vitally altered through anti-being in whatever form of failure-to-be it may come. Such lack of being or distortion of being, thus works in and through the continuum. Thus, the negative cessation also has as its complement the positive persistence of the force of that cessation, and the multidimensional Spirit is the all-embracive referent to all such forces of operation.

Into the continuation, furthermore, may come from God new possibilities which turn into active potentialities for choice, and which may enter the history of nature or the course of history to enrich them, or, in the fuller sense, into nature-history to help fulfill it, or into the total region of a concrete creation to effect all possible consummation. All the while God, process, and participants in the process, according to their stage of development, may affect the nature of continuation by their response to the process with its potentialities as they are relevant to the parts or the whole. Thus, God and process are affected even as the continuum of continuation changes. Thus, there may be new additions to process in terms of possibilities for God that would not otherwise be except for the new nature of potentiality which God finds due to the choices of finite occasions of experience. All parts, thus, affect each other, God, the process, and the parts of the process. These parts, of course, are neither disjunctive parts as in substance thinking, nor mostly fields of experience as in process thinking, but open, overlapping areas where cosubjects make both for identity and distinction, both for total immanence and for privacy of parts, increasingly so the more the process develops toward God's goal for it, the flexible end in terms of the highest of each and all in their concrete togetherness as bundles of potentialities with regard to their concrete kinds of attainment. In this way continuation becomes always a blend of the given, of added possibilities dependent upon the chosen potentialities, of cessation of being and the cancellation of being, as irrelevant to potentiality, of the creative transformation and growth in nature and history, and of the incessant fight within the continuum for attainment or against it, of seeking chance for constructive choices, or the evading of them until the reaching of the final consummation which will be determined concretely as a whole and in every cosubject by what success the Universal Word has with possibilities, as that Word has ever worked concurrently, turning possibilities into limiting concrete potentialities for future process. And, in the end, God the eternal Spirit, the creative Spirit, the Love that at the fullness of Spirit is personal, beholds that it is very good. Thus, not only at creation but at consummation God pronounces his "very good" for that cosmic epoch.

Consummation is surely no fixed goal; it varies in satisfaction. The numberless creative epochs, whatever they be called, all fascinate God, the period for learning love, with whatever variant conditions for learning, toward the best possible result. Each creation is a riskful adventure and a luring challenge. God never gives up until each creature has reached the highest possible fruition within eternity. God enjoys each end, in its wholeness and in every part, but is never satisfied that the result could not be better. Thus, there is always joy of attainment in the harvest, but also invariably the zest for the new sowing. There is the seventh day of rest, but also the starting again, the thrill of a new week of work.

Epochs are not closed, but open; they are open to each other, so that the startlingly exceptional creative members of an epoch may possibly "skip a grade," entering some other of the myriad epochs, or may become transposed, "translated," into the living of God directly, into "eternity his due." Thus, not only are there myriad lives, changes of lives and conditions of lives, but also far deeper relations and junctions than any transmigration and reincarnation may hint at, for such doctrines speak of individual souls that are disjunctly eternal, ever living within the "wheel of existence" or being fulfilled within the *Brahman* of *nirguna*, that is beyond qualifications. Even within such Hindu teachings that destroy the individuated soul, the soul as such is not necessarily eternal, but only capable of a certain coincidence with the ultimate.

The life of cosubject, or coinherence, can handle the problem of congruence better. No life is an island, a separate self, except for periods of discrete consciousness and bits of personal histories. Man's distinct spirit as such is not eternal, but created. All Spirit is one, but engenders myriad manifestations, creations, to live as finite existences, to enrich life and to multiply it, but the creature's coconsciousness can be done to death by cessation or fulfilled by identification. The rivulets may enter the ocean of Love to be fulfilled, losing the conditionedness of their concrete histories of limiting banks and raspy bottoms, only to catch again the urge for concrete living, for creative outgoing, for the odyssey of adventure within finitude. Thus, God is both eternal as full Love and also ever creating new riches of histories that are learning love, for God is the joy of love and the love of creative spirit, seeking new trials, experiments, and histories of love.

Is then nothing finally done in history? Each history is real and matters profoundly to God and to the participants, while each participant also matters profoundly beyond himself to God and the others. Thus, to be concrete, we can know each other on "the other side," and, in fact, on countless other sides. And finally we can know each other at our best in the light of whatever conditions we have chosen for ourselves. Such variation of "best" may, by not being good enough, filter away some from the more intensive creative adventures and fulfillment within the satisfactions in love. They simply will not make it in a satisfactory sense. Others, however, become so perfected during the process that they coalesce in God in unimaginable manners, and all in every epoch may at its fruition stand fulfilled, ripe and ready according to their manner of attainment for some total acceptance in God and new appropriation of creative tasks within his outgoing as well as his incoming love. Such may be the fruitions and the creations of eternal life.

The final result, accordingly, is a matter of true attainment or lack of attainment. It matters to God and to all. Succession and accumulation may have meaning only in time, not in eternity, but there they matter profoundly. The sense of eternity as completion in the sense of no more striving is always the longing of the finite, the weary, the failing, not of the perfect love nor of the vigorously creative. In God and in the saints attainment in love is ever real and satisfying, while yet ever seeking new and further creativity. Within the exhaustless Love there can be no eternal recurrence, which presupposes ontologically some limited substance theory, but there is eternally the chance of fresh attainment, the seeking for fuller attainment in the Spirit, the resting with joy in God, perhaps even inexplicable identification with him, and then again within the eternal depths a reaching out and forward to new creative satisfaction for the recurrent trying for the highest attainment goal of the finite within eternity, itself an inexhaustible goal for fresh enrichment and fulfillment. There can be no satiety in God nor any lack of creative challenge, but both full rest and peace and creative satisfaction are promised within his love.

The few who beyond others find and know this love during cosmic histories can so love and make available the eternal resources that all of history becomes changed through them, not forced, but as creative options, as radically new potentialities. Hence the power of the Buddhas, the Christs, the Mohammeds, the Gandhis and the Baha'u'llahs of God, who often summarize and sometimes more symbolize the unattained resources for created and creative living. Thus, creative love can find the pain and joy of *identification* with God and with the other members in the process, where love can find joy even in suffering, and attainment even in self-diversion.

Thus remains forever God as creative Spirit, the planning, personal love, who lives and loves ever, within concrete epochs and concrete lives, and who is ever ready as the fellow sufferer and as the companion who understands, but who also can offer to such created spirits as are ready to receive him his eternal joy and peace at the depth of their own experience, where love becomes concern for all, and becomes creative and redemptive within such concern. Eternity is, therefore, always more than time, but eternity can participate in time and ever more fulfill it. Eternity is man's fullest and final help and hope. God is ever God, but man can become more than man by his participation in the life of God. He can win, even now, fullness or freedom in some measure by his living the life in God that is eternal, within the genuine resources of love. Such then is the brief sketch of the final meaning of existence. We turn now to consider in fuller detail this preliminary understanding of the Potential Word of creation, continuation, and consummation. The preview awaits the full picture.

Creation

W E ASSUME the fact of creation. We do so, not as some arbitrary postulation, but as the best understanding of modern knowledge. In other words, we begin by accepting the history of cosmic process which science gives us. Not everything has always been here. If that is true, so is creation. The assumption of creation, then, does not depend on any Biblical myth. It hangs on no special creation, as primitive man once assumed. He took for granted that the world had been made. From our background the Babylonian creation myths and their later revision or reappearance in the Biblical accounts are the most relevant. The reason primitive man used such myths, however, was surely more than his seeking escape from the proximate by finding some resting-place in ultimates. It was more than the mind's tendency, on whatever level, to absolutize somewhere and somehow his fragmentary and fugitive knowledge.

Primitive or premodern man, too, experienced newness, and within the depths of his groping for explanation of such newness felt that somehow the world he experienced was not all there was. In or beyond this world he felt that there was "the more" that alone could account for what he experienced. How developed these thought forms became within his consciousness we cannot know, but they must have been the same in nature as the deeper running of man's consistent explanatory curiosity. In any case, we appreciate the nature of the facts that Eliade has uncovered in his many volumes, and we acknowledge the doctrine of creation as a common and steady heritage of Western man. We wish to affirm how deep and important is the primordial feel of man for the meaning of his life and of his world. The creation stories must not be dismissed. Often sophistication, as represented by our best medical research, for instance, finds truth that men discovered from general experience long before the microscope and modern medical techniques. Recall the case of antibiotics!

Nevertheless, our own assumption or acceptance of the fact of creation is one, rather, with our assumption of the veracity and general reliability of man's knowledge. To be sure, man's whole structure of interpretation may be conventional rather than objectively referable. Man may have invented his knowledge more than discovered it. Knowledge could be a comforting make-believe. Knowledge could be a long and impressive conspiracy, some accumulative man-made universe that is more in man's mind than in the world beyond it. Many, if not most theories, of the origin and length of life on earth may in fact be bolstered by precious little objective evidence! Nevertheless, we have no way of disputing it as a whole. If knowledge in general is deception, there is no point in discussing. Man's whole language, his total communications, for millennia on end, are involved and we choose to call the fact of creation an assumption, an act of faith, but as warranted as man's best knowledge in general. We choose to believe in the best, most careful knowledge as at least on the way to truth, a beginning to walk in a reliable way, however many times we must correct our direction. A fascinating discussion of the topic is R. H. Overman's *Evolution and the Christian Doctrine of Creation*. What we are saying, in fact, is that we are accepting at the outset that not everything that is has always been. Something has become. There has been some history of development in such a way that we can know times when some things were not, or that our whole universe of discourse, as we now use it, if we could have been there to observe it, would have recorded a different world for knowledge. Perhaps that world at some point would have contained no developed life, perhaps no human history, perhaps not even any organic life at all.

Does not creation, however, refer to the idea that once there was nothing at all? Can we call creation simply anything coming to be in such a manner that something that now is has not always been? Should we not rather properly speak of creation as *ex nihilo*, as coming from nothing? Does not the doctrine of creation presuppose there once being no creature at all? Only God or whatever may be eternal could then observe or know creation in its full, proper sense. To be sure, such an assumption, in any case, could hardly be known by us. We could not by definition have been there to observe it! Thus, there could have been no direct knowledge of such a creation. We cannot know any creation totally *ex nihilo,* or entirely out of *ouk on.* Why then do we say "could *hardly* be known by us"? We make such an affirmation because there could, of course, be indirect suggestions of such a total creation. For instance, if what we now know showed us a steady proportionate increase of being, we could deduce that at some point mathematically the whole process had its very first portion of being, and beyond that none.

Such a proportion by itself, nevertheless, would not demand absolute beginnings in terms of a creator or a transcendent Spirit in ultimate terms. There could be some realm of reality, invisible and unknown to us, but still of a finite order, a creative rather than a created given, from which through processes and powers entirely incomprehensible to us the world in the first place came to be and since then has been coming to be. We do not, of course, want to get mixed up in any irrelevant controversy between the "big bang" and the continuous creation theoreticians. Our assumption lies at a deeper level than either of these theories. Even if at the present the big bang theory seems to go about conquering and to conquer, such supposed facts are completely secondary to the kind of initial assumption we are accepting.

The choice does not lie between assuming a finite or an infinite universe. Indeed, for the finite to prove an infinite universe is a rather comical procedure! Infinite is always symbolic and conjectural. Yes, for the finite the infinite must always remain presuppositional, inferred knowledge, a heuristic device, a faith stance, more or less, and more and less strongly suggested by knowledge or warranted by total thinking, but never demonstrable or reducible to the kind of knowledge we have of the finite world. Man can quibble about mathematical definitions of the infinite or the infinites, but such projections are the extension of man's nearer knowledge and more limited thinking; they are frankly suppositional rather than supportable by knowledge. We believe in creation, then, because we believe in knowledge. We do not start our investigation with any assumption of creation as necessary on Scriptural grounds. Nor are we invoking any revelational authority apart from the revelations of knowledge. Nor again, do we appeal to man's primitive depths of natural assumption. Rather we acknowledge all leads toward the assumption of creation as mutually or complementarily supportive of our own assumption, but not necessary to it.

Nor are we in fact resorting to any absolute beginnings of cosmic process, as though such beginnings could be proved within what we know. John Dewey surely is right in his *Logic* that absolute beginnings, and absolute closes, are mythical. To prove that what we know as present actuality has come to be from nothing is to destroy the reliability of reason as adequately accounting for its knowledge. Reason itself rests on the assertion *ex nihilo nihil fit,* which the proving of creation from nothing would contradict at its heart, and therefore, such proving by reason would in fact amount to the dying or the destruction of reason. It would be tantamount to the primary sacrifice of intelligence. Those who try to evade the dilemma of reason, as posed by creation, to accept honestly and competently both the reliability of reason and its explanatory capacity for the history of becoming, either evade the problem itself or sacrifice their integrity along with their reason. These are harsh words, but they are true and necessary observations. If the facts are what the history of science indicates, as far as reason goes, we are left either with faith or with agnosticism, either with some adequate assumption, warranted by or at least suggested by knowledge, or with some mystery that leaves open the whole question of origins, a mystery springing not from ignorance, but from knowledge. The fact of creation, the assumption of knowledge, explodes all claims to the power of reason to account for all things. Reason, to be reliable, must stick to grounded fact and consistent thinking. The reality of creation defies such a combination.

We are making only modest assumptions. We assume the reality of creation as the task for creative and critical knowledge. We presuppose, then, no special creation of man or nature, which may perhaps now be beyond our ken because of a sinful fall from original innocence, nor any primitive myth as man's common groping to account for his own origins, but rather that there has been some evolution, some history of development, some true becoming in the history of the cosmos and in the history of man. We make a total assertion as to the state of knowledge and explanation as a whole, not merely some analytical claim to specific novelties or discontinuities, inexplicable from the ingredients of some limited "ingression." We build theology, then, not on gaps in knowledge, as Bonhoeffer pleaded with us not to do, but rather, as he advocated, upon the main strength of man's total edifice of knowledge. The assumption of creation is the acceptance of knowledge.

Usually, when the matter is considered at all—the worlds of creation that cannot be denied without the denial of the development which is taken as public fact—the explanation is given in terms either of emergence or of ingression. Emergence involves evolution; ingression, creation. Or, at least, such is the general, superficial distinction. Emergence adds up to a history of evolution, surely not necessarily of a Darwinian kind but of some kind, whereas ingression presupposes, it is generally assumed, new reality coming from outside into the world. The most common thought connected with such coming is God's creating the world, either out of nothing or else out of some reality beyond our ken. Thus, many today like Teilhard de Chardin are substituting "the within" as a source rather than "the without." Matter itself becomes mystery. Many prefer to think, if they think at all, that what is now actual somehow just has come from, or in connection with, what is.

The world, it is supposed, evolved from an inorganic to an organic world, to a world with high forms of life in it, and to the world of the history of mind. With Herbert Spencer, many have thought of the simple evolving into the complex, the world of nature into the world of history, the biological process into a so-called personal and even some alleged "spiritual realm." Of late, not only has Teilhard de Chardin made popular in some quarters the talk of from "within," but Paul Tillich also has termed the source "the dimension of depth." Somehow such language, as Bishop John Robinson insists, comes more easily to modern man, trained in depth psychology as he is, than does supernatural or "transcendent" language in terms of "above." Alfred North Whitehead tried to avoid both the arbitrary transcendence of the Christian faith, at least of one of its views, and the arbitrary immanence of evolutionistic thinking. Both he considered to be unwarranted faiths in view of the total evidence. Both the Christian faith and Whitehead, however, frame their answers mostly in terms either of the work of the eternal God beyond the world (the Christian faith) or (Whitehead) of the primordial nature of God who works ceaselessly with the world to create a better world through a more satisfactory ingression of eternal objects, the full harmony and relevance of which God alone can envisage.

Surely, however, for thinking people such terms as "within" or "above" are practically meaningless. They are equally inadequate. They are not paradigmal. They are not primitive. They are not basic. Such terms are adverbially used, and never ontologically in any regulative sense, and therefore say nothing at all as to the nature or reality of the new. They in no way explain the new. They are directional or dimensional but not ontologically material or explanatory. Evolution and ingression are both picture words, let us elaborate, indicating direction; or if the word "direction" implies too much a stratified, "level" picture, we may take them to indicate dimension. But both direction and dimension are spatial locations, without ontological pregnancy. They describe, possibly, the manner of birth, but never what is born.

But man, willing to hide from himself his guilty ignorance, his self-deceiving double-talk, has simply expressed the matter in terms of evolution, sporting some high-flown phrases about the survival of the fittest with no honest or at least adequate explanatory account for the arrival of the fittest. Covering his track with a flow of words he has, nevertheless, meant to account for the track by them, and the world as a whole has accepted such fuzzy, misleading thinking, and blithely gone on prating about evolution as though such a term somehow could fill in the problem of the becoming of history. Even if creation as the coming of the new cannot be accounted for even in principle, without the denying precisely of the reality of creation, nevertheless, a purposive process of organically accumulative newness, continually ready for the actual and fulfilling it, cannot be attributed to a combination of chance and nothing without full forfeit of reason as a responsible and reliable activity. The facts beg for some principle and power of creation and continuity, and perhaps consummation that at least suggestively indicates the kind of reality that can make such a creative process possible. Evolution as such gives no answer.

The kinds of evolution, furthermore, are irrelevant to the matter, if the fundamental question remains unanswered. One does not answer who or what came through the door, at least not adequately, by replying that what came was not walking but riding, or that it came from an airplane or a subway. Positing a creator or some other realm of reality from which ingressions came, on the other hand, answers the main question no better. The fact is that if we have knowledge at all, or a history of creation, there has been a history of development. The real question is then: What has come, and can we give any explanation, or must we simply accept it as that which has come and which cannot be explained without denying it? Are we within or beyond the reach of reason? And can we keep the idea of accounting for—the *ex nihilo nihil fit* final criterion of reason—or must we sacrifice the adequacy of reason, not in the interest of faith necessarily, but in the interest of sheer honesty? Have we come up against a wall? Shall we simply ignore the wall, deny it, or try to scale it? In this study, we choose neither to ignore nor to deny, but to make every effort to scale this formidable wall.

Eternal recurrence, moreover, is no more of a solution than evolution or creation. Eternal recurrence solves no ontological problem any more than does emergence or ingression. It is not only that it is speculative. All abstractions are in some manner and in some measure speculative. Our own thinking is admittedly speculative, but we hope needfully and responsibly speculative, always seeking to account the most fully for all facts within the most adequate, coherent reasoning, thus affording us the most warranted faith possible. Such is our intended use of abstractions! Abstractions separate in terms of general ideas, and general ideas can never be nailed down a priori to any particular situation; yet apart from such general ideas we could not think in terms of any free and advanced ideas or in terms of a complex situation. Therefore, it is not abstraction or imaginative interpretation (another word for speculation) that is at fault. But recurrence is an inadequate abstraction. Recurrence offers no explanation of the new. Recurrence as such simply says "over again." It affirms that the same situation keeps coming back forever. Eternal recurrence insists that the same things keep going through the same door eternally. The interpretation involves that nothing is new, that every-thing has happened that way through all eternity. Therefore recurrence denies the fact of newness. What you seem to think is a new person going through that door is in reality the same person who had gone through that door infinitely and will keep coming and going forever. But he is not the same, of course, as the person just before, or the one who came a century ago, or a thousand years ago. But, they too, will similarly keep coming back. It is just that eternity in the end, exhausted of all other possibilities, starts the same rounds all over again.

What does that mean, however, except a denial of newness as such? There is nothing new under the sun, but whether or not it is vanity or triumphant living again, and what lives, are in no way accounted for by saying that all eternally recurs. But what is far worse, newness is denied not only in eternity but also in history, for everything that comes has already come. Therefore, nothing new ever comes into being. Nothing becomes. Thus, the doctrine of recurrence never accounts for genuine newness, but only for apparent, but unreal newness. It is strange, indeed, that Altizer with his strong stress on history should also fall back on eternal recurrence.

What does eternal recurrence mean? Does it mean that all that we know only seems to be something new coming through the door of time? But why? The seeming is due to the fact that eternity contains in itself all there ever was, is, will be, and can be. Is it not then true that such recurrence has to take place because some underlying substrate, some eternal substance, shows one of its infinite aspects at a time until all aspects are exhausted only to begin the eternal rounds all over again? But such a process presupposes substance quantification as the ultimate nature of things, making all becoming an illusion as becoming. It denies the reality of creative history. Is not what seems change merely the appearance of the coming of some other aspect, not a new aspect, without our being able, so to speak, to see the process of change from one to another aspect of the infinite continuum? Then what is actual, in any case, is not more than an infinitely small part of the reservoir of reality. The world of knowledge is then only the most infinitely minute part of what reality, in fact, is. *And* what seems genuine becoming is not at all so in fact. Even when there was only inorganic appearance, as far as cosmic process goes, reality was full of Jesuses and Judases, of Beethovens and Shakespeares. These characters, moreover, had to return over and over again. At least such a theory does not limit reality to the world that we know or to the history of what we know. Reality is, in such a case, far vaster since we see only some small segment and know only some cosmic seconds of history.

But are the Jesuses and the Judases who keep coming back only "there" potentially when they are not actual in human history? Do they exist beyond our earthly sphere eternally or can eternal recurrence involve countless cessation and coming to be? But consider the implications of such a presupposition. They negate the very reason for the theory of eternal recurrence. What then can be the nature of the substrate capable of such unimaginable newness, such enormous pregnancy, and yet represented in any one moment only in such a poverty of appearance? Why should such an unimaginably small slice of reality ever appear while in eternity almost everything is dormant as the hidden background of such a minuscule of reality? What bursting frustration or else what poverty of being! What waste of life and beauty!

What kind of eternity, after all, is that which can be exhausted in time? What kind of infinity that can be emptied of creative possibilities? Is this not some logic of large numbers, of some finite substance however vast, and not some inexhaustible infinity? What bottomless abyss is this where we can finally scrape bottom? Are we not up against some kind of ultimately limited number, posing as eternal? Eternal recurrence, as a theory, is devoid of both the reality of becoming and of infinity. As far as dealing with creation goes, the theory is bankrupt, a mere pushing it back into a presumed infinite process without infinity. Are there not merely a fixed number of characters that come through the door in such a manner that when the end comes to the number of characters, they begin the march all over again? Thus there is neither infinity nor eternity? Deity in this instance does not exceed in possibility any and every actuality? Reality is not at heart creative? The masses must be slaves, the superman must come and recome. The inorganic period must return! Nietzsche was a poet, and a prophet, but he does not qualify for a hardheaded philosopher. His thinking was creatively seminal but not rigidly systematic and coherently controlled.

Where in the meantime, we ask more fully, do the characters go after they have appeared? Do they go somewhere? Do they come from somewhere? Where are they when they are not in history? What is the total route of such a lengthy marathon in some circled racetrack? In what form, in what manner, for what purpose do they exist? Why excoriate slave morality? And why speak of freedom? Why exhort to braver worlds? Why covet authenticity? What has been has ever been and will ever be. In what sense and in what manner? If what is actual does not persist as it is, then what persists, and why must the same forms come back unless they always are the same? Many, many serious questions, analytically and of ultimate and proximate nature, regret to be asked, in creative cross-examination of such a poorly protected pretender to God's throne. And Thomas Altizer, modern thinker, blends Hegelian emergence with Nietzschean recurrence! What faith, perhaps glorying with Albert Camus, in the absurd, but how little such faith will stand the test of hard thinking!

Are possibilities ontological structures, characterizing eternal Being, or are they mere appearances? Or are appearances all there ever is? Is not even actuality real? Does eternity recur out of non-being, with what is ceasing to be as well as coming to be? But why then the same again? What positive structures can non-being possess, necessitating eternal recurrence? Even the *skandhas* of Buddhism have more reality than that! Or does everything drive or drift to perfection in the end? Does creation point to consummation in the full circle of eternal recurrence? Is Altizer justified after all in combining Hegel's emergence with Nietzsche's eternal recurrence? When perfection wearies, does the cycle of getting to be perfect start over again, while possibilities are so fully contained or exhausted that the same forms and routes must be taken? Eternal recurrence is another simplistic solution, not deeply conceived, with limited presuppositions, which denies in fact the full meaning and reality of the new. The new seems to us to be, but thought must finally bow to some limited order where the means and forms, the material and the possibilities, the substance and the potentialities, must be reused, and reused in the identical way seriatim in eternity, however much the seriatim recurrence may give the appearance of newness to a minute section of the circle.

Does eternal recurrence, to continue, work like some unimaginably huge nitrogen circle with exchange of carriers, with the plants, and the animals, being born and dying, but with the operation of the chemical circle unbroken? Is not each plant, each animal, each bit of time in some sense new, unique, unrepeatable, and yet does not the whole process keep on, and keep keeping on? Where did the newness of each plant come from? Was that particular newness there before, anywhere, in any sense? Or was it just possible, something that could become, given the sun, the soil, and the seed? Is history itself any different, basically? Is a cosmological epoch some large circle of interchange and transformation of elements where the carriers are only illusions, temporary productions, to us seemingly real but never real in fact? Is all knowledge of our historic process some vast *maya,* some preposterous dream, some seeming without being, some appearance without isness as such?

Are there not given conditions, given elements, with man being born and dying just like plants and animals? Are men to be treated differently in kind? If not, why should history be? That is just the point. The primary evidence we have of cosmic process is not of some closed circle of operation, not of some causal chain of continuity, changing merely individual form, but of one special cosmic history, going in one direction of development, conspiring toward some operational unity of universe, with interdependent parts, from the salinity of the ocean to the tides of the moon, which in their total interaction sustain life; a process beginning with non-life, proceeding toward the organic, and then arriving at the organic, perhaps now to go on to the heights—and depths—of human history, beyond Socrates and Jesus, through the present explosion of creative knowledge, which is not only accumulating but accelerating, and that not only gradually, but with an unexplained suddenness of spurt, threatening a new age or drastic destruction, or a new age of unexplained creation and creativity. The facts of creation bespeak a different conclusion than eternal recurrence.

The totality of our history of evolution, ingression, development, creation, use whatever name we may, is the main content of our knowledge. Therefore, *the assumption of creation,* we repeat for emphasis, *is the acceptance of knowledge.* To flatten out the evidence by some assumption of eternal recurrence is to deny primary data prima facie. Thus, creation, in this sense, is a matter neither of emergence nor of ingression, in the first instance, but is, rather, the acceptance of our total knowledge, the history of becoming, the nature of the cosmic process itself. If so, the question concerns the best possible accounting for the cosmic process as a whole. We grant that the uniqueness of each tree and animal is important. We must not deny clear facts of constant newness. Can there be no such thing given, however, as a concrete entity of Spirit, Love, personal Purpose, capable of producing unlimited, exhaustless newness? In eternity why must trees and animals recur? Why such a limiting substance view of eternity? Is treeness itself eternal, or animalness, or manness in our earthly sense? Cannot newness be real as the product of the exhaustless Spirit, the creative Spirit that exceeds not only every actuality, but every kind of actuality? We are not limited to substance thinking! We must be free to think creatively in terms of our total data.

Possibility must be defined by creation, not creation by possibility. To accept knowledge is to accept creation, and not some vague, mystical creativity. Creation is the vast sweep of cosmic history as a whole that has come within cosmic seconds, mathematically speaking, and has accumulated with spurting, plunging, and of late, dazzling acceleration. How did such creation become possible? No amount of lengthening the low beginnings in any way alters the basic facts of the history of creation; rather, such attempts intensify, highlight, them. What is then the ground, what is the goal, what is the nature of such creation? A few cosmic seconds ago, to the best of our knowledge there was no universe at all, in our sense. A few ticks and we have an inorganic creation. Then the organic, then life, then human life, and, as a cosmic microtick, the dawning life of reason and of love. Whence? Where now? Where to? That and only that is man's main question for his creative and critical reason. *What is the relation between the whence, the here, and the thence?*

The golfer must not lose sight of the ball and the interpreter must not lost sight of cosmic process as a whole, of the miracle of creation, the mystery of becoming. What minor importance the from "above," from "below," from "outside," from "within," now have. We pursue primarily not the direction, not the adverbial question, but the heart of the matter. What is the nature of the whole process, plus its whys, its hows, and its analytical whats? That inner meaning, the constitutive quality, the determinative nature of the whole cosmic process we have suggested is Spirit focused and directed by Love. Can we from within our cribbed existence, our nascent beginnings, venture to stammer some understanding of this process in terms of the whole?

The answer has surely to be Spirit and the "direction" *spiritward,* the fulfilling the creation begun by Spirit, motivated by Love. The meaning of the process is *spiritwardness:* from Spirit, in and by Spirit, for Spirit that

life may have all possible fruition in love, an ever-growing love, in freedom, seeking unity as a goal, but with a goal characterized by the richest
and most extensive possible creative distinctions: unimunity. The fullest
inner unity, the unity of the Spirit, manifests creation in the fullest possible variety, under the initiative and sponsorship of the eternal Spirit, the
perfect Love, seeking ever the living in Love which engenders also the
processes of learning Love. Whatever is most consistent with the central
vision becomes the steadiest perspective and the fullest viewpoint for
defining possibility, possibility for this cosmic process to erupt in eternity,
plus countless others, world without end.

How is it possible to effect and to fulfill each process and each person,
for the best of both, creatively including the results of freedom? And what
happens to process and persons when that fruition is reached? Or can
there be no final fruition for Love in eternity? Does God, remaining as
Creative Spirit "stretch" the infinite with every creation? Is the perfect
the ever omnicompetent that, to speak in human foolishness, can add the
one more and the many to infinity? Can the finite objectification have
only temporal reality, as the carrier of the conditions of learning love, and
then cease to be, the heavens and the earth at last fleeing away, leaving
spirit free, free of space and time, free of mathematics and numbers, the
eternal Creativity, including the eternally creative? If so, possibility must
be radically reconsidered.

Possibility in any case, in order for creation to be real, for the new to
be authentic, must finally mean the impossible for us. The ultimate nature of possibility as the power of Creative Spirit must in the last analysis
contribute that which for us human beings, not for all finite creatures, is
impossible. Possibility must be defined in terms of creative Spirit when it
is taken seriously from its meaning for the nature of creation. We can
predict possibilities from within process. They are opportunities for
change, for making, for growing, for becoming, that we can observe from
what we know and perhaps to some extent control. Thus they are aspects
of what already is. They are powers for change understandable, at least
descriptively, from within our observable data. They can be handled
by reason. Insofar as they are causally predictable, they are controlled or
determined aspects of the world we know. Insofar as they are possibilities
for choice, they are, one way or another, finite opportunities, capacities
for conditional operations.

In either case, controllable or conditional, they are potentials, potentials for causal sequence or for previously established conditions for
choice. Pure possibility modifies the ultimate creative order, of which
man, to be sure, can become participant. Thus cosmic process came to be
although what now is could not have been predicted a billion years ago
from what was then present as the basis of prediction. Ah, but "flower in

the crannied wall," root and all, could we know it, we'd know what both God and man are! True, in one sense, but we should have to know not only what was there but the total source of whence it came, to what it is related, and where it is going; in other words, the whole ground and goal of the cosmic process, of which the flower shares an area of distinction. Then possibility would not become the impossible to reason but rather the potential for true seeing. But then we would see as God; and not as man now must! In such a case what now seems impossible to us would indeed be possible. Then possibility would find its explanation ultimately in what is now for us humanly or naturally impossible. Possibility is never fully defined except in terms of the necessary presuppositions for creation. Thus possibility always outruns what can be predicted from within the present actual order.

Thus the potential, the predictable under the conditions of knowledge, is for reason, while possibility is for faith, the recognizing that the possibilities of creation, properly speaking, are impossible in the light of what is now known by us. Possibility always plays havoc with our understanding of what is potential. Thus Shestov is right in claiming that man's sin is the eating of the tree of knowledge in the sense that he now thinks he is God, that what he knows has final control of truth, instead of his being open to faith. Being open to such faith involves, in fact, man's recognition of the truth of the radical discontinuity which characterizes creation as well as the mammoth sections of continuity that also are true. Possibility, at innermost, is the vibrant, open, ready capacity for the radically new, the implications of non-being for creation. It stands guard over the irreducible reality of the new. It is the vital, dynamic, "electric" energy, the capacity not only to work but to appear, to become, that roots not in what is as we know it and reliably can know it, but in the further uncharted reaches of Spirit, condescending, becoming neutral, becoming prime material not as substance but as the flexible capacity for the yet untried, the yet uncreated, possibly even the brand new, the fulfilling dimension of novelty.

In short, Spirit is multidimensional and as such is also, on the appropriate level or in the proper dimension, the capacity for creation, for becoming even the candidate for creation, the vibrant outreach of God, the dynamic non-being, unsettling, striving, transforming, fulfilling "substance," the capacity for God to create that which is not, and to make us with him, as spirits, creative as well as created. Such possibility alone is full possibility. It modifies the creator, not creation. And even so, possibility is not unrelated, it is not sheer possibility, it is no self-subsistent being or "thin" substance, because possibility is related to the eternal Spirit, to creative Spirit, and thus finally not without meaning, without relation, without control, without belonging. The knowledgeable reader may want to contrast this analysis with Barth's distinction between *das Nichtige* and *das Nichts*. Creation and possibility are both related in our analysis to the ultimate categories of Spirit, Love, and Purpose.

Thus the possible is no mere potential in God, as we know what is potential, for possibility is the power for the impossible for us, with God, the responsible power for the brand new, for creation, for becoming. The possible is the genuinely new, but not the ultimately unrelated. Even for us genuine possibility is the relatable new, the responsibly new. Possibilities turn actual, are *realized* in creation. Human beings in creative faith also share doing the unpredictable, as creative spirits, that which is both potential and thus discovered as well as created, but in some sense authentically new in history and thus created. Will and imagination can write poetry, compose music, or write theology, that is inspired, creative, not entirely brand new, yet brand new in some qualitative sense. Possibilities ever seem to hover over us if we are free to entertain them. The creative spirit, the creative creature, can share unimaginably in the process of creation if he dares open up his thought, imagination, will, and deed, in full faith, to what can be, to vibrant unmeasured possibility.

We are discussing creation. Let us keep that in mind. We are not discussing possibility as such, however tempting such a philosophical disquisition might be! We are discussing possibility with regard to creation. Therefore we are not denying possibility in the sense of what is potential from within process, either causally or conditionally. There is possibility as the causally predictable, at least roughly speaking. There is possibility as conditional for choice, at least on the whole. These kinds of possibility are amenable to reason either for controlled observation or for descriptive discovery. But these possibilities, humanly speaking and for our purposes of discussion, can be foretold, can be ascertained in advance. As predictable they are standard opportunities. What matters for our discussion, however, are the possibilities for creation which as such are unpredictable, the unexpected, the "brand" new, not the unrelated and unrelatable once they have come, but the ones not reasonably potential. What counts are possibilities irreducible to present process.

Creative possibilities, however, are for faith, for spirit, for becoming. All talk of their being inherent within or ingressing from without, furthermore, is beside the main point. They are now new. They are not what was there before, as far as normal, competent observation goes. It is no use to deny the newness by calling it "possible," as though possibility were a resident power. The power is the power of the new, or the power for the new. Possibility in the creative sense is unexplainable in terms of persistent process. To be sure, what was there was part of a reality in which such creation is possible. Reality cannot thus be limited to what can be observed. In other words, creation is real. It must not be reduced either to what is or to what is not, and thus in effect denied.

Hydrogen and oxygen combine to make water. Such a combination is now a potential of a causal process. It is a predictable reality of relation within present process. It helps not a bit to call water either an emergent or an ingression. Water is now possible, and it always was possible whenever such a relation obtained. But water when it first came into being was neither oxygen nor hydrogen nor just a relation or a combination unreal in itself, merely reducible to other elements. Water is precisely water. After the fact we can describe and predict what water is and how it can come to be, but water is water and is real as water, not as hydrogen or as oxygen nor as any mere relation between them. The relation with its creative result is as real as the elements which combine to make the product. The relation is a possible new, a reality in itself not merely as a relation. Thus also oxygen and hydrogen can ever be broken down, now, or in some unknown future, to other combining elements; nevertheless oxygen and hydrogen are what they are. Electrons, atoms, molecules, cells, are what they are and are real as they are. All elements and functions, moreover, are what they are. Whatever forms of energy we have, the forms are what they are and are not reducible to energy. They are what they are, energy, function, being, relation; and work in their own capacity. We cannot, then, reduce what is to anything else as though it were not. Possibility is not a matter of words but of power. Buddhism's stress on *tathata,* true suchness, is very much needed in its proper place.

What is, is, and is what it is, when it is, in the form it is. Such is the reality of the created in terms of what we know. All is real in some real sense. The fact of interdependence and interaction must not be denied, but neither must interdependence and interaction become smuggled in as explanatory principles or powers. This power to be and to remain in being while it is in being is also the truth of substance or of being on the level of objectification. Objectification has its own kind of credible reality. On the level of objectification things are what they are. They cannot even be reduced to spirit. They have the reality of genuine distinction. When they are, they are distinct, and real as distinct. But they can cease to be as they are by being transformed or by ceasing to be. There is possibility for becoming and for ceasing to be, for birth and for death. Spirit is the ground not only of being but of becoming and of non-being; and all must be seen in their own true light and for their proper purposes. Possibility is adjectival to whatever can be under the conditions for coming to be. Thus we do have the causally potential and the potential for choice, which define certain kinds of possibility with which reason can deal. Reason can handle what is predictable or what is ascertainably conditional.

But creation of the new as such, at every stage of primary coming to be or of related coming to be, is possible only in terms of the basic nature of things. The basic nature of things does not in any way deny cosmic being and its conditions for being, becoming, and non-being, but it relates the whole cosmic process to its own ultimate meaning, to creation as a whole, to cosmic process in the light of its own ground and goal. To accept creation in this sense is to accept knowledge as a whole, the use of reason which acknowledges and therefore neither fights nor flees from the proper meaning of faith. Faith is affirmation of meaning, the fulfillment of reason, in the light of the fuller facts which add to what was not previously present or previously explainable. Thus possibility as the unpredictable from within what now can be is the impossible for reason, the proper object for creative faith, the daring acceptance of the unexpected, what seems to be impossible to us because we have not yet sight of the full potential. And what is potential for faith is not even merely related to creative Spirit, for the potential for Spirit is what is related to his own power to create. It is not before it is. Spirit can create, cause the new to be. What is possible is the miracle of the creation of the brand new beyond the establishing of a whole new circle of what is potential. Thus the possible in terms of creation is exactly the miracle of creation, the power to effect the new, to *create.* Such possibility is not unrelated within the new circle of fulfillment and therefore is not unrelated to the potential. It is responsible. But it is not reducible to the potential. God creates new heavens as well as new earths! The nature of Spirit *is creative,* or has the power to create. Non-being is both real and important as the presupposition for creation, God's power to create.

We are not speaking then of the principle of incomplete predictability in terms of knowledge, human or divine. Possibility is no mere matter of our insufficient knowledge to predict nor is it even a matter of God's lack of knowledge of what the future can bring. God creates the new, and knows it only performatively in his creative envisagement and causing to be. The new, literally, in the full creative sense, was not there before *to be known.* Possibility is thus not a matter of ignorance but of knowledge, the knowledge which comes after the fact of creation. Faith turns into knowledge as creation turns possibility into fact!

What we are doing, of course, is to fill in distinctions between Whitehead's cosmological and metaphysical universals. *Cosmological* possibilities are within the created order, mostly as potentials of that order, whether then as causal predictables or as conditions for choice, or as finite creations of spirit, the inspired work of imagination, of creative outreach or intake. But *metaphysical* possibilities, in the final sense, are the radical capabilities of God for new opportunities not only as potentials, expanding or enriching creation, but as radical capacities for the brand new which revolutionize the old, to which the old becomes related rather than the new to the old. Pascal speaks of the audacity of trying to see as God sees, which is ever beyond us, but of our need to see in the light of God, or as from the direction of the central meaning and purpose for existence. We seek in line with Pascal's directives to define creation in the light of the central, total fact of the history of creation, of the cosmic process itself, and the presuppositions for it and the implications of it.

We start therefore with God as Spirit, as Love, as Purpose, and try to understand the movement of the process as a whole in that light. The transcendent is not superdescriptive as revelation or reason-killing creation. It is rather reason open retrospectively and prospectively to the facts for faith. The theories of evolution constitute inadequate bases for faith. Few considered carefully their total presuppositions and their total implications. As a philosophy such evolution begged the main questions. As faith they were arbitrary, inadequate myths. Faith needs to be warranted by both the creative and the critical reason. Then creation becomes real, not as sameness, nor as sameness in some new form, but as genuinely *creation,* as the new which is real, which is more and other than what was describable before it came. Reason can then acknowledge the mystery of creation, the conspiracy of the new toward a unity of a universe, the fact of process as cosmic, the truth of the history of creation in its wholeness. Within such a position creation never becomes explainable in terms other than itself *as far as* previous process goes. It becomes the reality of what was possible and has become actual. Creation is acknowledged as real. Reason can accept fact, the fact of what is, what has become, and can remain open to faith, as to what can become.

In this sense the assumption of creation is the acceptance of knowledge, and the acceptance of knowledge is the acknowledgment of faith. Meaning and mystery combine to challenge both faith and reason, and both are called into the service of knowledge and life. Creation is then dependent upon neither external Scriptural authority nor primitive myth. Nor do we reduce creation to the causally continuous and thus in effect deny it, hiding it behind ontologically prejudged conditions for the consistency of reason. We look, rather, at the main evidence. We accept what we find and try as best we can to interpret the facts both of continuity and of discontinuity. Creation then, in the long last, is possible because of the nature of Spirit as creative, of Love as outgoing, and of Purpose as directive of a process which seeks both inner unity and the enrichment of distinctions. The history of creation then defines revelation, the history of revelation *so far.*

Continuation

CREATION not only becomes; it continues. Creation not only continues; it seeks consummation. Our present task is to consider the nature of continuation with reference to more than analysis; with regard, in fact, to the meaning of the various aspects of such continuation. The whole cosmic process we view in the light of Spirit: Spirit, motivated by Love and directed by Purpose. We come to this discussion with creation as a given, a background assumption. Creation is the outgoing of Spirit, causing the new to be. The new is new, and in one sense brand new, but never merely brand new, never only discontinuity, but rather, in the final analysis related to Spirit, and Love's purposes of creating. Insofar as the new is mostly an extension or complexification of the already existent, the new is potential. It is predominantly continuous. Possibility, in such a case, is defined basically in terms of relationship. From within creation itself, finite personal purpose alone can occasion what is thus not potentially about to become, even as on the cosmic scale personal Purpose has the exclusive power to initiate possibility in terms of discontinuity, the coming of the new which basically changes the nature and meaning of what was previously in existence; the way life and love revolutionize the whole meaning of nature by effecting nature-history, where history and not nature governs the main meaning of the relationship.

History revolutionizes the meaning, not by the imposition, but by the eliciting of regulative relationship, where continuity not only continues but exacts its own strange and wonderful power, even affecting what is discontinuous at the center of its nature, meaning, and function. Thus potentiality can be a matter of possibility for causal predictability or for chances for choice, that is, for conditional predictability. But potentiality on such a level is mostly created rather than creative, whereas in God, potentiality has an unimaginable range of creative expression, unpredictable except for its basic characteristic of being fundamentally related to previous creation. Creation as utmost possibility, moreover, in its fullest sense, is the Universal Word which is mostly discontinuous with previous creation and therefore by force must revolutionize it. For God, so to speak, potentiality relates to cosmological universals wherever possibility has to do with metaphysical universals. Possibility transcends relationship to any and to all specific cosmic epochs.

In a way we have already laid down certain conditions for continuation in our main discussion of creation. The reason for such a situation is that creation cannot be totally disentangled from creativity. Creation, as we have observed, is never brand new. Even a new cosmic epoch is started by the Spirit who has within him an infinite experience of backgrounds for creation, and who thus acts not only with reference to pure metaphysical but also with some reference to cosmological universals. Spirit acts, however, as the one eternally seeking fuller approximations of the finite to the perfection of the infinite, of time to eternity, of love to Love, of spirit to Spirit, of personal purpose to personal Purpose. Thus there are no pure possibilities in the sense of totally unrelated possibilities, or as in no sense potential. Even so, such is the exhaustless creativity of creating Spirit that always there are more chances for the radically new. Continuation means that when a concrete epoch is started there is a limitation of relevance for that order which must be respected. Continuation means that each cosmic continuum creates a defined direction, a proposed route which in eternity selects possibilities for time. Metaphysical universals give way to cosmological conditions. Each cosmological epoch defines a route of relevance which determines the nature of possibilities.

In one sense, therefore, and importantly, continuation means re-creation. It means a route of recurrence for objectification. We would call this God's maintenance of what has been created. But we do not want to fall prey to some basically static substance thinking, for spirit is ever dynamic, ever active, ever vibrant. The atomic order of constant activity underlying all that we call settled substance or solid matter illustrates what we mean. Nothing in creation just is and remains in a state of static isness. Even in any section of time, so to speak, it is what it is only with reference to what else there is. It is as it is when it is in interaction with other forms of isness, first of all with the Source of its activity and then also with creation, and in particular with what is relevant to its own form and function of being. This dynamic situation is, of course, the truth of process thinking in its rejection of substance thinking. Reality, in one sense or in one of its aspects, is obviously in process and in processes. What we call things and persons, objects or living creatures, are not only definite forms of being, as they are when they are, but also dynamic processes interactive and interdependent making them also, at the same time, more and other than they are, even when they are as they are. In other words, distinction is real but not the only aspect of reality. There is also the unity, the "inner" identity of what is distinct with the total reality and meaning of Spirit, *in ipso et in aliis.*

Therefore re-creation is more than any external act of causing anything to be again, as though it were only a special object or occurrence. Re-creation is the continual dynamic creation of what is distinct, what is objectified, with reference to what else it is, and with regard to the manner in which it is more than mere repetition, to what keeps it in being and keeps keeping it in being. Therefore, re-creation is more than creating again, in the sense of substance thinking, nor is it mere arbitrary acts of re-creation from beyond or from within itself. Re-creation is neither merely evolution nor ingression. It could be thought of in terms of some substance, but whatever truth substance thinking has over against process thinking is now supplied by the category of spirit, to the effect that reality cannot be dissolved into relations. Re-creation, again, simply cannot be solved by process. It cannot be reduced into continual interchange, if there is no "related" or relation to interchange. A form of flux as flux is nothing in itself. There must be some doctrine of aseity, some ultimate of self-being; and therefore re-creation can be understood only in terms of the meaning of, as well as the creation of, distinction in terms of the foundational activity of Spirit as the power both for identity and distinction.

Re-creation of the existent in one sense can be thought of as concurrence. The intention of concurrence is plain. On the one hand, God is with all creation. *Pronoia* or providence accompanies all creation without violating its integrity. But concurrence based on a substance doctrine is either useless or externally interfering. Either God accompanies whatever happened, helplessly letting it be itself; or else he interferes externally and thus violates the created order. He intrudes. On a substantive basis for analysis these are the only two choices. He can, of course, so have made the world in the first place that there is an order that has to be carried out to a good end, some Leibnizian preestablished harmony. But in that case, God's accompanying the created order is ineffective and superfluous. Better, then, some deistic order, with substance needing only itself to exist and to function, with no need for God's presence in any sense. Occasionalism, the constant re-creation of the substantive order, also seems needless except to have God present somehow and give him something to do. If the order of creation is God-centered, it tends to be deterministic, as in Islam, with no real place for creation as such. There is then constant creating, but no creation.

In pure process thinking, on the other hand, there is no eminent being, no aseity, no permanent reality as such. Within such thinking, concurrence can only mean the guiding of parts by some sense of participation in the whole and the whole in the parts, but what is in the whole and in the parts beyond the relations which are always being made is never clearly explained. The ultimate question of isness, as Paul Tillich kept insisting, will not be downed. It comes back and keeps coming back to plague us unless we come to terms with it. Substance thinking has a case that cannot be dismissed out of court and cannot be defeated in court unless its truth is granted. The truth is the reality of what ultimately is, the ever-recurring question of why anything is rather than is not, and in what form and manner it does exist. We have rejected the substance formulation, but we have kept its truth of aseity, of being in the sense of spirit, which is both everywhere and yet can be simultaneously absent in some dimension, allowing for different types of distinction from matter to persons.

In the light of the meaning and power of spirit as multidimensional, expressible only in terms of contrapletal logic, a concurrence becomes a matter of flexible cosubject. Concurrence now becomes neither lacking in final reality and power of self-being, as in process thinking, nor superfluous and ineffective, or interfering or intruding, as in substance thinking, but a distinct entity congruent with creation according to need, at Love's will and wisdom. Thus concurrence can be mostly passive and permissive in the physical order and in the biological order generally, while becoming more active on the level of the Spirit of God in conscience and in inner group directives, whether of the racial unconscious or of the accumulations of civilization through institutions or records such as books and tapes; and finally most flexibly present in the "area" of the Holy Spirit, or qualitative distinctiveness, within the workings of the Holy Spirit, where there is actually encounter between the uncreated and the created, eliciting from within or arranging circumstance without, in such a way that the finite is fully respected and yet also, as far as possible, aided with direction and with enabling power. Thus concurrence now becomes a matter of congruence, of the presence and power of Spirit both as inner identity of the finite and also as a flexible accompaniment whether permissive or active according to the requirements of circumstance and condition. Concurrence, in fact, gives way to coinherence. Concurrence smacks of substance; coinherence requires the category of Spirit.

For Spirit re-creation is no occasionalistic *de novo,* denying in effect the reality of the created order except as the concomitant qualification of the creative activity of the absolute, the sovereign Creator, nor is it a matter of some deistic objective order of creation from which the Creator is absent, except for his interfering. Concurrence becomes a congruence of identity not only of Spirit, but of the distinction as such, and of the distinctions collectively, in such a way that both unity and disjunctive effectiveness are maintained. Thus coinherence or perichoresis, in other words, circumincession or interpenetration as both identity and distinction, becomes the proper clue to the relation of God to the world, or of Spirit to the created order. In this sense there is re-creation of the already existent without the denial either of the persistence of created order or of its constant activation within the eternal spirit, its ground and its goal. Thus creation not only continues; it becomes and keeps becoming even as it continues. Creation and continuation are not only distinct functions of Spirit, but so to speak overlapping operations. One suggestive way of looking at this dual functioning, or relation, is that re-creation is concurrence, based not on substantive or process thinking, but on Spirit as co-inhering, as the dynamic congruence of identity. Spirit sustains the distinctions within identity and supports the reality of created distinctiveness as such.

What is, however, the nature of sameness on the part of the existent? *What* continues? We reject the concept of substance; we declare the idea of process as such to be inadequate. When anything has come to be, nevertheless, in what sense does it continue? We accept, as we have shown, neither occasionalism, or God's continual re-creation of what is moment by moment, nor deism's self-existing creation, which involves substance thinking, nor, again, nature's being some form of the consciousness of God, organized and functioning for a particular purpose in the divine economy; nor furthermore, nature as some form of flux, basically lacking self-identity. What then is the sameness of nature? Is it energy objectified for the purposes of constituting a pedagogical medium in such a way that the energy, material or immaterial, remains a continuum in God with spirit as the principle and power of identity, but with the energy in whatever form, functioning or structuring, having its own created nature, real as an enduring distinction? The created order would not remain the same apart from God as the cosubject, the congruent and ultimately directing and sustaining reality. It would not be at all! Apart from spirit there is no creation, no power or principle of identity or of coming to be.

But the created order remains as the cosubject of distinction, congruent with and distinct from spirit. Nature is not spirit, but is "in" spirit and "through" spirit, not of course originally in a spatial but in a qualitative sense. There is thus a double sameness, the reality of the eternally generating reality of God, always re-creating nature, not as things, but as the vibrant continuum colored by its particular history of creation: The reality of the side of the distinction is derived dependence on spirit, but having being also for its temporary purposes, and, as of the kind it is, existing in various forms and degrees of distinction. There is the distinction of the low grade of experience, to use Whitehead's terms, and of the high grade. The degree and kind of independence of a rock differs vastly from the kind of independence of a mature human being. The human being exists as cosubject with God, in this sense congruent or coexistent, a being coinhered by spirit, but develops a mind that discriminates and makes man increasingly a distinct entity, with a history of choices which makes him more and more distinct. We then have a degree of distinctiveness, a power to be, without separation from its inner reality, its "ground of being."

The sameness of the nature of what we might call "things" differs from the sameness of what we call animals, and that in turn from human life at its genuine scope. The difference is chiefly one of persistence. The rock tends to persist or endure in a more stable manner than the life that is influenced by will. Mind is the capacity to entertain the emotion of distinction, in function and in interpretation. The higher the development the more the mind furthers distinction. It distinguishes and makes for distinction. Growth introduces accretion which involves change, but can also introduce qualitative differences or discontinuous distinctions, at least relatively speaking. Such growth not only adds to, but transforms the present creation. The new is surely not brand new, but rather continuous and discontinuous, for the most part; but it is not only more than (except for mere accretion which is hardly true growth), but also in some sense other than, or alteration.

What then remains the same? The underlying spirit and the distinctive function? Yes, and more. To be sure, when a new ax comes off the handle and a new axhead is put on, the ax is still the same in the sense of function, but it is yet partly new in terms of material. This kind of sameness, if it is treated neither as merely re-created nor as merely self-existent, is the truth of substance, as far as material goes, and the truth of process, as far as function goes; but beyond both substance and process we have the truth of the coinherent spirit and the kind of persistence which distinction has, according to its nature and function in spirit. Such sameness and newness not only as accretion but as qualitative transformation of some degrees and kinds (if the words be not contradictory sounding because of old associations with words) make it possible to understand how creation is not apart from God and yet also has its own distinct drives, functions, successes and failures, even on the level below developed life in any form. Thus there is "purpose," "mind," goal-seeking present, not as totally distinct from God and yet as a creative, generative reality which he has let loose. Such creation works neither as the objectification from outside God's own work nor as a preestablished harmony from within, but as a genuine power for creation, beginning at the lowest levels and groping, fumbling its way. And God watches each process with fascination!

Let us look more closely at this matter from the point of eternity. Love, creative Spirit, the artist God, starts new processes within his own ever-creative life. He gives each new epoch wherever it starts, certain characteristics, certain general potentials, certain inner drives, and certain feels for goals. These urgent potentials, these restless drives, these feels for goals fumble and fail, fumble and find, fumble and freeze, fumble and race.

God watches in fascination. What are the endless possibilities? How structurally tight can they be and still be creative? How creatively flexible, and still focused? Some evolutions may creep and crawl; others may run and leapfrog; others, crash and die. What remains stable and steady is the inner reality that just is: spirit. What remains relatively persistent are the successful adaptations, the creative adjustments, the imaginative relevant newnesses which add to and transform what is, including both what is transformed and the transforming power of creative being.

There is no exhaustion of the infinite; the eternal Spirit, the Love that is, seeks ever further fulfillment, ever newer and better creations. God seeks to arrive at some new height of creation where the process contributes the best possible chance for further process, where the product that has become and dynamically is the new continuum makes relevant the best possible opportunity for what can be made with it. At the lower beginnings the seeking is more dull and slow, but conditioning, critically preparatory. God watches for what kind of potentiality, what kind of relevance, becomes practicable by reason of the route that particular creative epoch has taken. When the process makes basic mistakes it may stop, or may have to start over again, handicapped that far, for the fullest exemplification of final creativity. Every stage on the way counts. Every life matters. That is the reason that every creation is a challenge, a risk, a burden, a joy to God. The creative spirit concurs, sustaining, permitting, possibly at times offering some extra inflow.

The extra inflow may come from time to time at low stages. The creative fumbling, however, may be left mostly on its own. God is ever preparing for the heights of cooperation by means of the early and real distinctions in the pushes and pulls of process. But surely as the process progresses there comes to be an increasing openness between identity and distinction, between base and function of being. When mind differentiates on the highest level we know, or in the most intensive spiritward quality, in the deepest dimension of depth, whatever the name or symbol, there is still further openness. At the highest level of human spirit that we know, there arises personal cooperation, a seeking by the finite spirit for the fuller reality and power of the Supreme Spirit while the Supreme Spirit offers his collaboration in creative newness. There thus comes to be a double search which results in collaboration of the part of cosubjects that remain real while there is also, on the part of the finite, a new enabled subject without division or confusion, the exemplification in both identity and distinction of the Universal Word. At the highest there is unimunity, in Spirit, fulfilling unity, and fulfilling differentiation.

Without the Word nothing is made that is made, but what is made is not God, but in and of God, real in itself on every level of being, in every dimension of depth, in all kinds of qualitative Spiritwardness. The Word can be made flesh on the highest level of Incarnation, which is the life of love, with God and in God, as in the beginning, possible now, and in worlds to come without end. And God sees that it is good, in fact, very good. But some creations go astray and must die, go down in the flood of destruction, start again, as each age starts toward the fullest goal creatively potential according to its past history which constitutes every new vortex of creativity, every new dynamic continuum for further growth.

Endless questions come to mind that are not for us to try to solve, even for our wrestling. What can constitute possible configurations of growth? How can we know the relation of continuity and discontinuity except for our scale of scope? And how utterly, ridiculously narrow that is in eternity, in God's time for creation! How can we ever know rates of creation, the speed of the currents? What we call a slow beginning may be unimaginably fast in relation to countless other creations. What we call a fast speedup in one cosmological process, even a blitz emergence may be a slow camera, indeed, in comparison to the regular rate of some creations. What we call mind may be like the purposive seeking of an amoeba in comparison to our best brainpower in eternity, and even that analogy may be presumptuous. What can be the configurations of newness where deity exceeds in possibility any and every actuality, and that not only of finite disjunctive occasions, but also of the myriad total cosmological epochs? Our minds may possibly imagine the billions of billions of galaxies and speak of the trillions of trillions of light-years, but what is that to God! How can we ever know the openness and the limits of nature except from our own narrow base of potentials, and even then with what woeful limitations with regard to the cosmological epoch as a whole?

Who will do a thorough, yet imaginative, job on spirit as order and spirit as the revolutionary power within the order of nature? Here more is at stake by far than we can even imagine, even in the knowledge that we can have of the relation, in conflict, tension, and possible symbiosis, of teleology and dysteleology. Determinism and freedom have little meaning and less reference in this area of investigation. Can such terms as "freedom" and "destiny" have more than a minuscule appropriateness? And if we can know something of these matters in our nature, can we even hazard some guess as to the countless creations of unimaginable different orders of being? Who will speak for what to us must be the eternal silences? There is a different routine of operation in rocks and in rabbits. Will chemistry presume to reach the bottom of that mystery by some controlled comparisons? Who will bring to the bar of all possible interdisciplinary studies the whole context of nature which must have bearing on each of its regions; and who will know enough to bring the best results from any region to the far-stretching and ever augmented reaches of man's total field of knowledge?

How does nature participate in spirit, and spirit in nature, in the running for safety of a rabbit and in the will to live of a strong-spirited terminally ill patient? What are the healings that cannot be denied? What are the operations of spirit in heart trouble and in cancer, and what the stable and steady working in these cases of nature as an objectified realm within spirit? In what sense is nature "alive," vibrant, dynamic, seeking, perhaps even begging? In what sense is it dormant? When and how does it operate as asleep? When does it work as unconscious guidance, or as a habit that needs no deliberate attention? What is the running down of nature in relation to spirit?

What is the Second Law of thermodynamics, deep down? What does it signify for creation? What for continuation? What for consummation? And what are the potentials for the opposite building up? What is the effect finally of the creative new, the complexity, the high-grade experience in that tendency to sameness, and what is not only a tendency to conservation, but a running away from creative reality, that downward drag toward sameness, the neutral, toward the undifferentiated? These questions may receive some proximate answer of description, of the how, of a few whats, but what do they all mean in the total light of creation and continuation, not only now, but with regard to the total meaning, the pointing meaning, the Supreme Spirit, God?

From the previous analysis it becomes evident what the bearings of spirit are on natural theology. Some believe that we can know nothing of God from natural theology; on the other extreme, there are those who would fashion a whole theology based upon knowledge. In between there are those who believe that we can conclude from nature both that God is and what he is not, but not what he is. That must be a matter of revelation. Others still hold that we can know something of God from nature, perhaps as with Paul, "his eternal power and deity," but not his eternal purpose and inner being. There are still others who would have two interrelated dimensions of knowing God, a preparatory knowledge through God's work in pedagogical process and a fulfilling knowledge in the life and teachings of Jesus as Love, Spirit, and personal Purpose.

Both the claims for no natural theology and the claims for a natural theology, if taken for full value, are in fact impossible in the light of our analysis. From what we know we see the coming together of creation into a universe for discourse and discussion. We have an interrelated cosmic process, with a history of its becoming, exhibiting not only increasing complexity but also increasing interdependence where the newest and most delicate levels of life and love are most fragilely sustained on the basis of the previous process and yet not explainable in terms of it. The meaning of purpose, even as a topic for discussion, comes only on this come-lately level and can be seen most clearly only on the level of organic and superorganic life. What we cannot see but can surmise (what we *suggest,* is even in such cases far more important than what we *say*) are the ages of superlife, of the ultrahuman, that seem to be waiting to be born, the newer birth of God in human history, far beyond any stage in evolution we can call human history. Evolution, ingression, creation, whatever the term, is vibrant with the challenge to change.

Possibility continues. Creativity continues. Creation continues. The future speaks of purpose as well as the past, and the present has no full interpretation except with relation to the processes of the past and its pointing to some future. That is true of all growth and is equally true of cosmic growth, of the newness which awaits cosmic process. A fascinating study of Teilhard's concept of pleroma can be made at this point. Creativity, order, conspiracy of purpose, life and love, speak of the eternal Spirit, the creative reality underlying all things and working to set free whatever can be more fully and flexibly free. Not to include this data in one's interpretation of the meaning of what is, has been and can be, is not only to be arbitrary but to decimate explanation from the beginning. Whatever the final view of the whole, of the most important, of the most real, of the process as it moves, of the process as it points, of the process as it seeks consummation, the cosmic process itself obviously constitutes paradigmal evidence, regulative in some sense of the theology that alone can claim warrant in the light of what we know.

But to try to picture God in himself, the eternal Spirit, in terms of what we now see or in the light of what we now know is preposterous as a procedure. What an inadequate view of God we should get! And what other views we should get from the cosmic process a billion years ago or a billion years from now, if it keeps going. What other views might we get from myriad other cosmic processes that could constitute the basis for picturing God. No picturing models, no disclosure models, no analogic models have anything but a most indirect relation to God. If the cosmic process is taken as a whole, if we use nature as the pedagogical process for a model, what kind of eternal Spirit would correspond to that? Surely not one to account for the creativity, the order, the general order as well as the best we know.

Suppose a carpenter made doors, and chairs, and ladders, and rolling pins. Which product would best help us to picture the fullness of the carpenter? If we saw these being used and knew that they were made, we could conclude a purpose for them, a reason for their being produced. But would that purpose adequately represent and describe the maker? Could we construct an adequate image of the carpenter himself? The closest we could get would be to some cybernetics machine that could simulate any carrying out the orders of men, but even that would have to be programmed by a purpose other than, more than, and previous to the machine. Who upon going into an automation center could picture the whole life, even the home life, of a man? But our process is surely only one of myriads and obviously only in its most uncertain beginnings. Perhaps it is soon to become directively open to the culminating purposes of God far beyond our ken. Can we from what we now see, systematically interpreted, envisage the full nature and reality of the eternal Creator? Just as no natural theology is a denial of what we know, even so natural theology is also a denial. We can neither have it nor not have it. What then?

The question is vastly, as a matter of fact *immeasurably,* complicated and multiplied by the fact that God as spirit is neither absent from creation nor fully present in it. God endows creation in its distinct reality with the creative power to seek distant goals, to seek creatively for these goals, sometimes to reach them and sometimes to fail of the search. But more than that, he does not offer set goals but rather gives the world he makes an active part in the process of creation. He makes the world itself creative in such a way that some credit and some responsibility rest on creation itself from the lowest levels of groping to the highest levels of choosing. The higher the reach, the more open nature becomes to spirit. Thus, in one sense, God is more present there and, at our highest attainment can be ever more personally present. Yet at the same time God can also become more absent there as he is refused entrance or as he intentionally withdraws—on all levels, to be sure, but especially on the highest levels where, for instance, the saint knows the reality of the dark night of the soul or Jesus, full of the Holy Spirit, goes out into the desert to be tempted of the devil.

In such a situation there can be no constant picture of God's direct creation. The conditions and results are both too variable. Much of creation is made purposefully to be indirect in its operation as a medium of communication between man and nature, man and man, and man and God. Thus here, too, there can be no exact ascertaining of God's presence even as an ideally possible knowledge. There is no direct, constant, predictable ratio to be established. When such indefinite and unpredictable situations exist and persist, how can we picture God in terms of his creation or as any necessary implication of nature? How can we induce or deduce the nature and reality of God from nature? How can we infer not only that he is but who he is and what he wants? How then can we have any reliable natural theology? We cannot, to be sure, and certainly not from such an approach; but, on the other hand, how can we neglect using the complicated knowledge we do have? We must not, on penalty of forfeiting the truth, avoid the question of what may be the import of the purpose we do see in creation, even as a descriptive rendering of final cause, and even more, with regard to the meaning of the history of creation as a whole.

But can we not use nature as precisely this kind of pedagogical process, and then use history as its highest level, and finally go on to use the kind of life and teaching Jesus was and gave, as the tip-top outlook of history? By using all three together imaginatively, can we not arrive at a natural theology that would be as adequate as anything we can have and therefore as reliable as man's knowledge can provide? Must we dismiss, or at least underrate, *analogia imaginis?* Are we not entitled to the best possible warranted faith? Would not such a procedure combine what is actually in most careful use of both the creative and the critical reason and therefore be our best clue to the nature of God? Since to be human we must believe, is not such a conviction the best account that we can render of the total cosmic process in its central meaning? It would seem so, and yet we cannot give an answer of simply yes or no! Such a view of nature, even nature in the light of its central meaning of history, and history at its center at that, would give us at best a view of God in terms of cosmological rather than of metaphysical universals.

The God we would see would be the God of this kind of creation without benefit of other creations in eternity. This planet, as some of us have written years before the recent interplanetary exploits, may be only one example of life in one infinitesimally small fraction of our universe. No life on Venus? What, then, of the billions of billions of galaxies and all possible life at whatever stage and of whatever kind? But what is all this *analogia imaginis* except a most minuscule scene in God's eternal drama? Are not our most daring dreamings presumptuously belittling God? Thus even if we saw the best possible interpretation of God in line with his highest presence as love or personal spirit, we should see him only in terms of our knowledge, in terms of our nature as human beings, in terms of this cosmic epoch, and only, at that, from the point of view of life on earth.

But it is important that we see that. It is important that we understand the best we can. It is after all we who see and who see for our purposes. It is important, therefore, that we try to see, but not try to be God, for we must ever long for and seek the central purpose of this cosmological process and of our lives within it. For us such seeing must constitute needful, responsible knowledge within a warranted faith. Thus we cannot deny natural theology in some sense without being guilty of that false sophistication which denies and deprives us finally of needed knowledge. We have then what we may properly call, with many others, not a natural theology but a theology of nature, of our nature, which shows us something important about God and which we must neither minimize nor deny. We find the meaning of nature not only in nature as a process but in nature as seen in the highest purposes of persons.

We understand nature best through the love we find in the master model of the Universal Word. Such a theology of nature is not natural theology in terms of any direct knowledge of God. It is not only two-dimensional but three-dimensional, a flexibly complicated knowledge for seeing and believing. Nature must be raised to nature-history, and nature-history must be seen in the light of the fostering of love, the effecting, or the eliciting, of the fellowship which God both is and ever seeks to create. Thus through the life and teaching of Jesus and history's best everywhere; and through the meaning of history as being pushed by need to together-ness and pulled by liking toward cooperation and understanding, and at its highest drawn by love, we begin to glimpse the creative faithfulness of God, who lures us on, who puts the searching for creative satisfaction at the center of life, a drive which can be fulfilled only by man's finding his outlet in creative love, love in communal and creative release within the community of creative concern.

Restlessness comes in part from possibility as the vibrant striving, the seeking of the created order, from within its own endowment of distinc-tiveness and from its stimulant congruity with spirit as its dynamic basis, its inner double reality and power for objectification in potentiality; and in part from the power of non-being as the promise and threat of cessa-tion. Restlessness thus roots both in being and in non-being because of its ground in the multidimensional reality of spirit. There is thus the pull of creativity and there is the pull of cessation. There is the drive to con-tinuation and there is the lassitude of retreat, the concomitant of failure. There is the positive restlessness of becoming and the negative restlessness of coming not to be. There is the will to life and the wish to death. All of creation is permeated with this dipolar tension, this divergent seeking. Evolutions on the lowest levels go on and find newer channels; or they stop going on, gliding down to perish. To persist or to perish, that is the constant question of creation as continuation. Consummation and cessa-tion are constant contenders within the cosmic process on every level. That is the way creation becomes vital in its suspension between being and non-being, between becoming and perishing, between continuation and cessation.

This total double-goaled process rests within the identity and power of spirit, within which and from within which objectification or disintegra-tion are ever vital options. Creation is always real as distinction but never on its own basis. The power for distinction, for growth, creativity, free-dom, is due to the reality of spirit.

Thus purpose is always contingent and not final with creation, both in the ultimate and in the proximate senses. In the ultimate sense there is no preestablished harmony, no unilateral goal of creation, no fixed, far-off event toward which all creation moves. Creation is flexible. The goal is cybernetically adjustable within the dual search. The end of creation is conditional on response, and on Response to response. Eternity as living

Love in creative outgo and outflow takes time as the learning of love seriously, from the very beginnings of groping to the final reaches of finding, from the most embryonic suggestions toward creative freedom to the most mature choices of freedom. Thus the eternal Word is no static concept, no previsaged Purpose, no merely performative Word, no directive totality. Therefore there is no all-embracing final Cause, no Truth with a capital *T*. Creation as well as history is realized rather than actualized, coming out of contingency as well as from direct Providence, created creatively from all sides, within the whole of congruence, identity, and distinction, rather than premade, manufactured, caused, determined, ordered, closely controlled. The whole creative process is open, open to the Eternal Spirit, open to the total cosmic creative process within its defined spheres of potentiality, and open to each region or part.

Consequently, final causes are there but there as suggestive, as opportunities, as potentials for possible choices, as persuasive, with persistence according to nature and circumstance, but they are not there as purposes from outside, as self-subsistent creative patterns, as willed directives from suzerainty, inevitable goals to be reached, directly, or even merely within a cybernetic process of unimaginable flexibility and variety. Creation is inherently flexible both from "beyond" itself and from "within" itself. The goals, the supreme Spirit previsaged only generally in creation, leaving freedom, creativity real and responsible, real and risky, but a kind of goals or kinds of goals where there are final causes, as flexibly, conditionally, and even creatively embracive purposes, not to be obtained as such necessarily in any of their forms, but as starts for the journey, as promptings to creative goal-seeking, as suggestions for epochal histories, as faint whisperings for cosmological processes.

Thus there are final causes ultimately, but they are neither explanatory nor descriptive, taken by themselves, but always more than either. They are not explanatory because freedom complicates the result, but they are explanatory in that the result could not have been unless they were there as genuine options, even though these options themselves could be further embroidered, and even broken and redirected, by creativity. They were definite potentialities, luring toward a goal, or goals, inviting a *finis* perhaps in particular, but also other creative *fines* as different options, with perhaps still other *fines* that were on the creative edge beyond the potential, and possible only for exceptional creative passion or insight. Thus final causes are partly descriptive, modifying normal or regular potentials, with double reference nevertheless, to the ultimate nature as such and to the organic needs or purposes that pertain to the actual routes nature, creation, or evolution has taken. As such they are both descriptive and explanatory and still also neither descriptive nor explanatory, for they are both part of a given, a final causative purpose, and also of a creative becoming, purposive but open beyond all focused purposes, seeking the ever-exhaustless new, seething with creative growth, vibrant with creative adventure.

Proximately, too, there are final causes which are both descriptive and explanatory while being at the same time also neither descriptive nor explanatory, for they spring from previous purposes, maturing in the present, and represent finite ends on the part of groping, growing creation. But they have not only being, objectification, a history as ground and goal, in the basis of identity and in its concomitant distinction; they are also a matter of non-being, of true becoming, of *ouk on* as well as *me on,* defying reason based on the past, refusing thought based on what is, eluding understanding based on being, slithering out of the gaps of interpretation rooting in process, for the root is from the past burrowing deep into the process, but the new growth is from the future, that which is not yet, that which is coming to be, that which is created as well as the creative, or perhaps even more accurately from what is being created. Thus final causes are never reducible to description nor can they give full account for anything in terms of mere purpose, and yet they are, as well as are not, and they are needed even though they are not necessary.

Accordingly finite causes are neither for mere reason nor for mere faith; they are for both. Without reason they can be neither descriptive nor explanatory, but for faith they are both descriptive and explanatory. Therefore reason must turn critical to include final causes. Reason must own its impotence in the face of creativity, or creation, which presupposes non-being, whereas faith must own its need to listen to reason as it both describes and explains what is and has come to be. Thus final causes are potential, not mostly as predictable in terms of causal chains, nor as merely conditional for the choices of freedom, but in the sense of the creation of new ends, new *fines,* new purposes, both ultimately and proximately. Possibilities are vibrant opportunities, mostly modifying God as creator and the concrete past process, or processes, but also objective to the goals of creation *ouk on,* as that aspect of discontinuous newness in terms of which reform goes over to revolution and growth to radical renewal. Creative Spirit, Love, being ultimate, there is no way possibilities can be contained or restrained. There is always that extra plus, that daring overflow, that creative extra which makes what is new always the possibility not for what is needed alone, from the point of view of present process, but what will become needed in terms of new turns, unexpected and unpredictable from within process, from within any and all previous processes, for that matter.

Possibilities, however, are negative as well as positive, or to speak metaphorically, point downward as well as upward. Non-being pulls in both the direction of creation and the direction of cessation. Continuation is persistence toward consummation or toward perishing. In other words continuation is always threatened and always thwarted from both sides. Neither the good nor the evil leaves continuation alone. It suffers violence of change from both creation and cessation. Constantly there is new growth, accretion, organic development, increase of freedom. There is biogenesis and noogenesis beyond the lower stages of cosmogenesis. Even fulfillment alters though in one sense it also respects the *status quo,* the normal flow of continuation. But there is also destruction constantly on all levels as well as development. There is coming to be and a coming not to be. Possibility is for death as well as for life. And non-being is categorically far more real than some aspect of transformation. Such concepts as the conservation of matter or the conservation of energy are misleading because they tend to deny the reality of both creation and cessation. They tend to deny the reality of non-being. They belittle the fact of death. They soften the understanding of perishing.

Time as pedagogical process and the conditions for that process is continually perishing but not merely as the constant or continual transformation of what is actual within some new continuum where time is only fulfilled. If the past persists totally in the present, the present is no longer the locus of reality in any realistic sense, for the reality of the new and of the "no longer" are then not given full status. Time becomes a matter of rekneading the dough of reality, perhaps kneading out some bubbles and kneading in others, but there is full recognition neither of creativity nor of cessation. Perhaps the word "locus" of reality saves the situation, but only if the meaning of locus is extended to mean confluence and exfluence, so to speak! The present process is not all there is, and such non-being as comes to be through time's perishing is real precisely as cessation of being. The non-being of the wasness, of cessation, is not part of the present. Nor is the future fully real in the present; even the possibilities which are not pure are not in the present in terms of being! They have no present reality until they become realized. Most possibilities never become realized. Both past and future are aspects of spirit as we have seen, but the future is real in the present only as indicative of potentiality adjectival to the total relevant reality, larger than process, especially than present process.

No matter how we treat the concepts, the conservation of energy and the conservation of matter, both can be misleading. They may be true, either or both, within some narrow scale of scope, but not within the paradigmal analysis of reality. The present process is not the locus of reality, only of the cosmological process in its time. It represents confluence of process and potentials, plus possibly some unusual possibilities at some revolutionary times and at a few radical edges of process. Reality, however, connotes primarily creative Spirit, spirit for a cosmological epoch made partly manifest in any present, and all the creative processes in eternity, within the endless creative Love of God, always immeasurably beyond human imagination, let alone measure. But even within each creative epoch and within each creative present there is cessation, or shall we say *before* each creative present, since creativity involves exclusion and destruction as well as inclusion and fulfillment. History is always perishing in a fragile precariousness, but so is nature a fortiori. The mass of nature is created and perishes constantly, before our very eyes. And such perishing is real, not merely some audio-visual fallacy of simplistic interpretation. Whatever remains of any basic dying is still not that which died. What dies, perishes, is no more. Whatever can be created can perish. Whatever can continue can cease to continue. That which can be born can die.

Take the example of a gloxinia. Growth to leaf and flower is real newness. That leaf and that flower were not there before. When that flower withers and dies it will never be there again as that flower. As that flower it is dead, it is gone, it has perished. There is thus cessation of leaf and flower as well as creation of leaf and flower. In the meantime there is a measure of continuation of creation as long as that leaf and that flower last. We must not deny that the leaf and the flower as such are real. It does us no good at all to say that here we merely have energy in a new form, but it is still only energy. No, it is energy in the real form of leaf and flower. But does not energy as such explain the leaf and the flower? By no means! The bulb is a bulb, energy in the form of a bulb, but more than the mere form. A bulb, as Zen Buddhists never stop asserting, is a bulb and must be accepted as a bulb. It is real as a bulb, not as mere potentiality for leaf and flower. But to say that a bulb is a bulb and that is that is to be equally unrealistic. A bulb is a bulb when it is a bulb and when it grows into flower and leaf it is, in some sense, a bulb growing into flower and leaf. While it was bulb without flower and leaf it was a bulb as bulb, but with the potential for flower and leaf.

Here are the concrete directives in nature for potential creation. The bulb is real, the directives for growth are real, the process of becoming, or growth, is real, the leaf and the flower are real. They are real as they are, but as they are they are more than they are. Spirit explains the unity of the total process, its identity and process for distinction. Yes, and as love, the purpose for distinction, but spirit never "explains" the distinction as though creation were not real. To "explain" the new is to deny it; it is to reduce the new to what it is not. That is why we have as new ultimates spirit, love, and personal purpose or, in other words, Creative Spirit, motivated, directing Spirit, and as such with the power *to create* the new. The new to be new must be accepted as new, thus acknowledging that we live in a creative reality. Creation is real, as continuation is real, consummation is real.

Oppositely, death is real. Cessation can happen. Possibilities are also negative. The bulb without the leaf and the flower may remain when they are dead. Then they have ceased to be. It makes no difference that the bulb remains. It makes no difference that they may now have rotted into compost or become part of the soil once again. They are not there. The energy that carried them may be there. But *it* is no longer *they*. Energy is a capacity to work, but creation is the becoming real of the created. Sometimes it is a most close relationship, as the oak to the acorn, although the registered potentials have little meaning and power apart also from the total creative process involving the soil and the sun. But acorn, soil, and sun do not explain the acorn, nor are they the acorn. An acorn is an acorn, an oak an oak, the sun the sun, and the soil the soil, while energy as neutral or as called into service of concrete potentials is energy in whatever form. In one way energy is a word we give to the general capacity to work, to grow, to be. It is spirit as the vibrant possibility for creation, for creation as well as for continuation or cessation.

No continuation explains the new, even the predictably new, the directed potential; nor does cessation explain death. Conservation of matter and conservation of energy are words we use to describe the miracle of continuation in one of its aspects. They must never be used to account for either continuation in any creative sense or for cessation as real. Thus the gloxinia bulb may send out new flowers and new leaves, but the new flowers and the new leaves are not the old flowers nor the old leaves. They are what they are when they are, however much related to all and in whatever stage of interdependence and interaction they may be. Substance thinking catches this aspect of reality. Cessation is also real, as are creation and continuation. And they are real in their own way. No consummation as such can explain the reality of the stages toward it. They have their own form and measure of being, and cause is partly explanatory but mostly directive. In this sense it is more descriptive than explanatory. Thus possibilities are not only the vibrant reality for the new, the "caused" new, the conditioned new, or the created or creative new, but they are also real as "despairing" opportunities for cessation, for predictable cessation, the daring creation that went wrong, that misfired, that blew up, that never jelled.

Whatever is born in nature, as nature, can die in nature. The supporting spirit remains as spirit, but its created form of distinction comes not to be as well as to be. Here we might venture the thought that only spirit remains, cannot die. Can the personal be so not only created as distinction but also so shared by Spirit as a capacity for enrichment of reality, that the finite may become so much more than created, so genuinely interpenetrated, so persisting in Spirit, that it may not perish with everything else in nature, but as history may enrich and be enriched by eternity?

What that may or may not mean we shall consider in relation to the final chapter: consummation. Right now, however, we ought to take a look at cessation as destruction in terms of meaning. Is cessation genuinely purposeful and thus a part, however conversely, of Creative Spirit, the reality of non-being, or can it be that such cessation can even be due to some form of anti-being? Is anti-being a reality as well as a-being? Are there not only, so to speak, irrational numbers, beyond rational explanation, "surd evils," but also anti-rational realities? Are there powers and possibilities that fight being by *nature*, seek to effect cessation? Beyond lack of being, the power for cessation, is there within the order of consummation, the satanic as well as the demonic? Yes, may there not even be creative evil, or evils directly in and of creation? Can creation itself contain anti-being? We turn then for a while to this question in nature primarily for our purposes now of understanding the order of continuation.

Reality, then, is characterized by possibility to become and to come not to be. *That* flower was not; came to be; is no more. Creative Spirit is ultimate. Creation is real. Cessation is real. Continuation is real. But, since continuation is thus real, reality is not merely a matter of power for constant re-creation or for constant cessation. Continuation consists in spirit as "basis," as the principle and power of identity which is also the principle and power of creation. Spirit is primarily qualitative power to be, to become, or not to be. Spirit as principle and power, however, is not merely for constant re-creation or continuation *ab extra*, or even co-inherently continuously, but for a continuation as a degree of self-being on the part of what continues, albeit a self-being that can be abrogated, making what is created come not to be. Such in summary is the picture we have given, but such a portrayal says nothing, so far, as to the purpose or kind of purpose which underlies not only life, which we have already discussed, or the conditions for life, inorganic nature, which we have also dealt with, in sum the whole combination of nature-history, but also right now, as to cessation, the coming not to be.

Some would define cessation in terms of evil. They would think of evil as the exclusion of possible choices, that to be definite is not to be everything, that to choose anything is to eliminate what is not thus chosen. Such definiteness for being, such possibilities for concretion, however, constitutes the very nature of the conditions for distinction, for finite being, for creation, for comparison, and for contrast. Growth on the level of freedom, or growth through riskful choice, involves accepting this rather than that. There is nothing evil in such a situation unless the good itself is defined arbitrarily as the fullest possible extensiveness and intensiveness of being at the same time, as beings being everything together, congruently. There is nothing sacred about *Alles auf einmal!* Everything at once, an entire *totum simul*, denies creation as well as cessation. The whole notion of the fullest possible being at all times in every place means more than the absence of distinction as contrast. Such a notion entails that there can be no distinction between lack of distinction and maximum distinction. The concepts become not only preposterous but meaningless. Evil cannot be lack of being as such anywhere; it can be only a lack of proper being or a distortion of being or of being where there should be non-being. Whitehead's conception of evil as necessary exclusion of being through choice was definitionally ill-considered. Exclusion of possible good itself is a most critical consideration to be judged only specifically in terms of proper situation, choice, relevance, and possibility. Otherwise we have some mathematical, metaphysical, spatialized conundrum which is merely preposterous.

There is no evil in non-being as such, nor is there any evil in the lack of anything being what it is not supposed to be. Nor again is there anything evil in the perishing of that which should not be or should no longer be. Evil must rather consist in distortion of being or destruction of needful being, or possibly is some specific lack of being, like the lack of water in a desert where there are thirsty men, or there being men where there is no water! Evil is adjectival to crative process. Purposes should modify Creative Spirit and eternal creative processes. Purpose and process should flow together as the ever outpouring of Love in creative adventures for finite satisfaction and for the satisfaction of the finite with the finite. Thus evil is basically the frustration of creative processes. What can that mean? Is such frustration a matter of anti-being or of anti-spirit?

Evil can mean lack of creative resources for choice because of the failures of previous process and processes to produce the needful conditions for further potentiality, for accumulating relevance, or even for revolutionary relevance. Such lack of resources is real, real for process and real for God, and therefore real both for time and for eternity. Such evil would be a matter of a-being; "being" meaning here, of course, not substance or process, but the objectification through spirit of the created and partially creative realm, subject to contrapletal logic by its multidimensional reality. Partiality and distortion are at least a-being. Thus there would be a true aspect of a-being in such a lack of resources for process, in such an absence of proper potentiality, and therefore also in such a limiting of the *outward* edges of radical creativity. Evil would be a matter not only of lack of seeking and of wrong seeking but also of proper seeking with no proper possibility for finding on whatever dimension or stage of process. This would amount to, so to speak, an a-possibility, or at least an a-potentiality. Evil is, however, mostly a matter of wrong adjustment or wrong choice in terms of distortion or destruction. Distortion of proper process or the destruction of it would, however, amount to more than a-being or a-possibility. Such distortion and destruction would introduce into process a frustrating factor, a resistant reality, a thwarting power that can only be characterized as anti-being.

Such anti-being would be a matter of opposing, hindering, standing in the way of proper process, and thus would be more than lack of being. It would constitute a warring factor in the way of proper creation or creative directives and therefore would be decidedly in the nature of anti-being. It would work against both proper function of being and the coming to be of proper creation. But destruction, as such would, of course, not necessarily be anti-being. Whenever there is cessation of being there is destruction of being. The fact that flowers are born and die is in the nature of an enriching variety of process. The seasons add rather than detract from satisfaction. If proper distinction is good, the cessations that operate in the processes of the creation and cessation of distinction are also good. Thus destruction as mere cessation is neither good nor bad in itself. It may be proper cessation and therefore good as part of the creative process itself.

There is, however, both destruction of the parts of the process that is timely for its purposes, and an ill-timed perishing of aspects of the process, aspects that are needful for that process in that place and at that time. These destructions or cessations are occasions not only of distortion, or of adjectivally negative anti-beings which frustrate and work against the proper development of process, but they are also the direct interfering with proper process as such. There is, for instance, in a certain community only one kind and one portion of medicine that can cure a certain illness. A chance breakage destroys the proper potential. Such destruction becomes more than a matter of a-being. It is definitely anti-being. The action creates the lack and is therefore more than mere lack. But the breakage could have come about merely through a distortion of process, some unknown weakness in the container or some uncontrollable circumstance, like a tornado destroying a hospital room. But it could also come not merely from human carelessness but even from deliberate intentions to harm. In such instances there is a new level of anti-being involved. We have more than a lack of being, when and as needed, through whatever history of previous process. In destruction both through carelessness and through evil intention we have forms of anti-being. We have culpable destruction of needed and proper aspects of process. Deliberate causing of destruction, evilly effected cessation, intensifies the nature of anti-being. Such anti-being is evil for process and for Purpose. It is both a defect and an evil effect in process. Therefore, it is evil in time and for time, and for eternity even though not in eternity. To be sure, the total perspective for defining cessation as evil must not be anthropomorphic. The untimely death of a flower on the Alpine heights where no man sees it is still cessation! A typhoon's destroying flowers no man may see is still untimely destruction. A-being and anti-being must not be classified simplistically as evil. Evil can finally be defined only from within the total process of creation, continuation, and consummation, including needful as well as useless and harmful cessation. (For the specific development of the question, compare my *Evil and the Christian Faith* and John Hick's *Evil and the God of Love*.)

We have looked, up to now, at the nature of continuation and cessation with regard to an interpenetrating symbiosis within which there is identity and initiative from one "side" and distinction and initiative from the other. We have thus a dynamic process of interaction which is at the same time intra-action. It is dynamic through and through at its "inner" dimension, at its heart, as its dominant functioning, although externally substantive or solid in great reaches of its being. It is dynamically bipolar, with the identity of aseity and the identity of distinction, the former identity rooting in whatever is, spirit, underneath all creative epochs and stages of cosmologies, and the latter rooting in the temporal actuality of whatever is as it is when it is. Even so within perfect coinherence the identities are also identical, one final identity of Spirit. Spirit is, is identical, effecting distinctions, both an entity and identical in all things. We have seen that continuation of creation is characterized by the lack of it as well, by the *cessation* of being, both partially in terms of lack or distortion of process or potentialities for process and fully in terms of destruction.

Distortion is the failure to be fully what anything ought to become and thus not only a twisting of being but a lack of being as it ought to be, the being something else, and therefore an illustration of *me on* rather than of *ouk on*. But creation is characterized by both *me on* and *ouk on*, distortion and destruction. What is, is spirit. Spirit never ceases to be in himself, itself, and for all instance of need. Spirit is, and is capacity for being. Capacity is the power of *creative Spirit* as ultimate. And capacity can be to be, being; to become, creation; and to come not to be, cessation. Later we shall discuss capacity as consummation, fully to become, or to become fully realized. Spirit in relation to distinction can maintain that distinction or let that distinction perish. Spirit can lead either to cessation or to consummation.

Thus we have creation, continuation, and cessation, and all these realities serving the purposes of consummation. Growth is goal-seeking. Process is and has purpose, or achieves purpose, as a whole and in parts. But growth can cease or go wrong as well as lead to fruition. Process can exhibit purpose, alter purpose, deny purpose, or achieve purpose. All these factors enter into the meaning and reality of consummation. Before we turn directly to this question, however, we should take one look at the stage which immediately precedes it, at least within the confines of our understanding. The totality of eternity, the full life and ways of God's love, will always remain mystery, fulfilling meaning only to frustrate it, and showing the larger possible fulfillment precisely by the power of that frustration to point beyond itself for the fuller and more creative future.

On the highest levels for freedom or within the deepest dimension of freedom or in the innermost "within" of freedom, or, again, in the most spiritward quality of freedom that we can know, the distinction is more sharp, more pronounced, more "real." The freedom that comes from personal purpose on the finite scale can differentiate its own being self-consciously from its own basis, from all else, at least in terms of some impressionist general idea, some vague groping for self-identity of distinction. It can therefore not only know difference but, in terms of free ideas and a long history of evaluations and concrete acts, can come to desire and to choose distinctions which are contrary to, and at times may even seem to be contradictory to, the meaning and nature of creative Spirit and of the common good. The self can refuse to accept itself, its very life, or the kind of choices it is offered. It can seem to destroy its own life as well as to distort it. It can forfeit its chance to choose within the future of our kind of temporal life, and perhaps forever. It can, so to speak, take its own life, destroy its own capacity to choose.

The self, furthermore, can act in deliberate opposition to what it can understand as its own good, as far as it can self-objectify its choices and choose according to some standards of what is good for the person or for the community. In such instances, we have illustrations of the kind of evil of distortion and destruction which we have just described. Even if such choices have to come within finite capacities and thus reflect demonic rather than satanic evil, or partial rather than total evil, that evil is real. Evil is real both as a-being and as anti-being. It is real as accidental or incidental frustration of process and as deliberate, chosen destruction of parts of the process. It is real as determined resistance to process or misdirection of it. All choosing of created rather than creative good, as Henry Nelson Wieman used to put it, all choices reflecting arrested development, are evil, along with the more direct destruction of self, others, or parts of process. But such possibilities merely reflect the negative side of the power of distinction, the capacity of spirit to create distinctions which are self-creative importantly and ever decisively.

On the positive side, this freedom can lead to the envisagement and appropriation of creative Spirit in such intensive forms that these become revolutionary. In human history a few people have moved the whole world, not by power or might but by spirit, like Jesus and Gautama, like St. Francis and Gandhi. Their freedom is not only just as real as that of those who have differentiated themselves most signally in terms of distortion or destruction, but even more so. In these cases the distinction that has the power to shut out Spirit and to thwart its main purpose enters instead into an understanding acceptance of the Spirit. By so doing the persons practicing such distinction realize their own selves in the fullest possible freedom. Their freedom of choice and freedom of life come together. But they come together in extraordinary openness of understanding and complicity. There is a coinherence which is chosen, a congruence which is sought, an interpenetration which is invited, in such a way that the distinction becomes consummated precociously. Such persons are ahead of their time. They have let eternity crown time exceptionally.

Such lives, however, are not only exceptional, for they exemplify the meaning of persons and the nature of the process, but they are also normative, demonstrating the experience of persons who realize history at its center. Their kind of creativity is unique, and no one can become what they are or were. Each creative life is and remains peculiarly, yes uniquely, distinct in not only the general sense of uniqueness, but also in the radical, revolutionary sense of being within a new dimension of depth, or in the exhibiting a qualitative creation which as such is both more central than that of the rest and yet also more distinct than that of the rest. The fulfillment of history is creative and never reaches any goal. History ever is because eternity ever is. Because God is creative Spirit there is no exhaustion in human history of the riches that are possible for creative adventure; and yet each revolutionary adventure, each creatively, radically new departure also opens doors.

These doors are not only doors of insight. They are not only doors of example. They are not only doors that serve to usher in the new by showing the new. They are also doors of power for new creation that comes through the open doors into history from eternity. They are doors that let in new power into history. The interpenetration of Spirit into spirit at any point colors and changes the saturation point of the whole process. When the truly great lives come, they open doors for the whole world. The world is not served so much by greatness in number and surely not so much by power in terms of thought or political pressure as it is by profundity of spirit; prayer as openness to God; meditation as transparency to creative vision; love as translucency to God and to all men, yes, to all creatures, and for all men and creatures, because definitively for God: these are the main ways in which freedom of distinction becomes cosubject with the freedom of the eternal Purpose. These are the ways by which the whole lump is leavened. These are the methods by which the deepest and most life-changing messages reach the created order.

There is a revolutionary rate of change. Thus history is not so much dependent upon those who manufacture change and counterchange, not so much upon those who evoke power and counterpower, as upon those who let in the common power for the common purpose. Help for human history comes from personalities. History depends basically upon those who live for the total reaching of the common good. The universal characters who work in the spirit from *the Spirit,* perhaps in many respects unknowingly but in reality, are the ones who prepare for the age of universal man. The age of universal man, however, is never a set goal according to any common standard. Not even the spirit as the basis in the contrapletal situation of identity and distinction seeks such a leveling communality. Not even God wants such communitarianism. The Spirit seeks creative freedom that is never exhausted and which becomes the more rich the more commonly pursued. With community of spirit comes always a richer and fuller manifestation of variety of gifts for the common good. And for the good of each! The final goal is unimunity. Thus the pioneers and perfecters of our faith make us the more real, make us the more rich in distinction, make us the more free to become creatively ourselves even as we turn from distortion and destruction to pursue the continuation that can be meaningful only because it leads to consummation.

Even within what we now call human history there can come creation which is so radical that we must call it, with Teilhard, the ultrahuman. We may be living now within a period when noogenesis may take a new turn, may achieve a radical new being. If radioactivity has been at the root of novelty in the past, what can happen in our atomic and postatomic era? Why interpret "mutation" as necessarily negative! The spirit of history is now so drastically accelerated that it may, to be sure, lead to sudden catastrophic distortion and ruination, or even to a common destruction and the ending of this creative attempt by God through our failure to respond. We seem to stand, in any case, at the end of an era. But it could also be the upsurge of a creative newness in response to our capacities within spirit in such an unexampled spiritwardness, on such a new level of evolution of the ultrahuman, in such a new kind of beings, that history itself could no longer be described in human terms. We may be on the verge of a new kind of consciousness so capacious within creative Spirit that present humanity may come to seem on a lower level than the animals and our kind of spirituality may come to be viewed as only the first trying to bud rather than any kind of flowering of creative distinctions. Then the richer the life, the fuller the freedom. We can hardly more than point to unimunity. The more we can approach unimunity, the new age of man, the more completely coinherent will be the basis of spirit and the creative distinctions. Then contrapletal logic will become both more multidimensional intensively and also the more unified at its basis of operation.

In the light of contrapletal logic we can also understand the problem of secularism far better than before. For some it means simply the nonecclesiastical, what is not under the dominance of the institutional church.

For some secularism means the contrast between the sacred and the secular, perhaps even in the form of a full dualism. Underneath lies some general notion of two substances, two realms, two areas of being and living. For some, again, secularism means the mature acceptance of this world. This world may then be the created world which God has let "come of age," from which he has withdrawn, in which he is present only indirectly, or it may be a world which is a self-sufficient process in terms of which any transcendence as such must now be defined. God may then be the God of history and have no reality except as the power and drive of history, or he may be a God who is constantly creating himself and the world as a historical process. Ronald Gregor Smith has drawn a vivid picture of such a God in *Secular Christianity*. Another form is Schubert Ogden's Eminent Relativity in *The Reality of God*. Still another such position Van Harvey takes in *The Historian and the Believer*.

A projected later volume, which will deal with man, will tackle these problems in detail; and I aim also to treat them far more fully in a succeeding work on the Holy Spirit and the Holy Community. Even here, however, it can be seen that the situation is not one of secularism or "secularity," as Ogden calls the position to differentiate it from those who make secularism a faith of scientism, denying a priori all transcendence which makes the sacred a separate, unrelated realm of reality. Creation is no qualification of the absolute, but to some extent is real in itself with a power of continuation and creativity even within the distinctions themselves. If Spirit is identity throughout all the world and its Source of Significance, we can neither just be in the world nor entirely separate from it. We are in a situation, rather, of symbiosis and distinction, or of symbiosis expressing identity and distinction. The secular realm in such a symbiosis has a degree of autonomy. We must live in this world and, in one sense, in one world at a time! We must also live for it because we are of it. But more than that. Spirit is in the world both as its principle and power of identity, of unity for community and communication, creating a universal discourse as a constant possibility, a true potential, that is partially attained. "The world" thus is both *itself* and *more* than itself. The world is in spirit and the spirit is in the world and yet the world is real and important in itself. Besides, and of decisive importance, the spirit possesses aseity, is multidimensional, ultimate, but is yet always intrinsically related to and totally for the world. The more we are in the spirit and according to the spirit, *in line with the spirit*, the more we come to be for the world. Being both in and for the world, we are in this sense men of this age, and as such at home in our world.

But being secular does not mean that we are only secular, that there is no eternal reality, that we cannot and should not transcend the world, and that we have nothing to offer the world but its own self. Those who are in the spirit are constructively secular, at home in the world, and totally for it, but they are also against whatever in the secular world is false and evil. They are against the distortions of the world and its needless or useless destruction. Moreover, they are not satisfied with the created rather than the creative good, for they live in and for the future. They are radical futurists, who, accepting with grateful responsibility the heritage of the past, and centered in living within the present, yet are faced daringly and creatively toward the total, the absolute future, with and within the creative Spirit whose nature it is always to exceed in possibility any and every actuality.

Thus God becomes completely historical, in, with, and for history without being reduced to history. Is not this a drive within Harvey Cox's *The Secular City*? We can become historical but still acknowledge that "the hinge of history," to use a term from Carl Michalson, is the creative Spirit, who is neither substance nor process but exactly Spirit, fulfilling the aims of both substance and process in terms of permanence and change, in terms of being and becoming, in terms of isness and what-is-notness, and yet also bringing that more-and-other which is needed. The whole question of what is historical, however, in terms of the dimensional view of God and the fulfilling categories of contrapletal logic, requires that the future work itself out in more adequate understanding. The future continues the present, minus its cessations, but also consummates it by the power of eternity which is ever more than time, of reality which is ever more than process. We can accept, therefore, neither the separation of the sacred and the secular nor the reduction of reality to the secular. We can never reduce reality to history. We can accept neither a God who is not through and through historical nor one who becomes reduced to some aspect of history or to history as a whole. There is a better way! And we shall follow through on it! That is the task of our concluding chapter on consummation.

One final thought remains, although the full import of it must be postponed for a bit, for it is mostly a matter of consummation rather than of continuation. When we reach the heights of human history or when, even more, we enter the age of the ultrahuman, even within the continuation of our cosmic epochs, will there not be a transcendence of subject-object relation? Over and over again we are told that religious fulfillment lies beyond subject-object relation. We must point out that such transcendence is a constant matter of coinherence. We have been speaking of cosubjects, but not in terms of any dualism, some hidden "Nestorianism" (however guiltless Nestorius himself may have been of such thinking). Coinherence is without division and without confusion in such a way as to constitute an ever more real person the more intensively the relation obtains. God is the identity both of himself and of each subject. The more he is present the more each subject becomes aware of himself as in God and yet creatively distinct, as in God and yet the more free to be himself. There is thus transcendence and yet not transcendence of the subject-object relation. The more mature we become, and thus free from God in that we are completely interpenetrated by the Spirit, the more we both transcend and can never transcend the subject-object relation. Thus in human history, at least—and the more so as history reaches the ultra-human, the age of unimunity—there is a transcendence of the object-subject relation which nevertheless, never absorbs the distinction or erases the distinction.

The more real and full the transcendence of the subject-object relation on any level of history, or in any quality of distinction as spiritwardness, the more real God becomes for our full knowledge of encounter and congruence, and the more we become men in God and therefore the more real, free, and creative the distinction. Contrapletal logic thus makes obsolescent the idea of separation of subject and object or of a merging of subject and object in term of some state of *nirguna,* a situation devoid of genuine distinctions. There is neither mere unity nor mere community. There is unity and community in a multidimensional reality which for us begins effectively with history and continues its growth toward its full fruition in consummation. There is unimunity. The highest example we now know of such consummation within continuity is the new creature, the new being who is a new creation, experienced in worship and supremely in ecstasy.

But ecstasy introduces such radical revolution, such discontinuous dimensions within continuation, that even though it constitutes the strongest bridge we have to walk on from continuation to consummation, nevertheless, since it is a matter of "inaugurated eschatology," eternity in time, the fruition of love within the processes of the growth in love, we had better at this very point change our topic and proceed to an explicit discussion of the nature of consummation.

Consummation

CREATION, continuation, and consummation belong together. Is there any consummation at all? Is there even a final consummation? If so, is what is final also permanent? Or must whatever begins in creation also end in cessation? Is non-being the only final meaning for creation? Can creation, on the other hand, not only continue, as it does, but keep continuing permanently? Can mortality "put on immortality"? Can growth, and growth in satisfaction, not only increase but become an ever-continuing experience? If it can, what can that mean? If it cannot, what does such cessation of creation, totally and permanently, involve? The only way we can answer these questions is to look at them persistently in the light of the most basic meanings we do have.

We must not look at them in terms of our feelings of hope or despair of eternal life, for some, or of dread of eternal life and of hope of death, for others. We have feelings, to be sure, and must honor them in their place, but we may not discuss the issues in terms of our preferences, let alone our prejudices, but strictly and cogently in terms of the implications of what we have found to be our most warranted faith judgment with regard to the totality of our knowledge. Our faith stance, with the most warrant, is that the most important is the most real, and that the most important is determined not aggregatively but selectively, and not statically but dynamically. We have decided, from a lifetime of investigation, that the pointing of cosmic process through the Universal Word, through the categories of spirit, love, and personal purpose, gives the fullest and truest account of the cosmic process so far, as the directive for the present and as the hope for the future. By the use of both the creative and the critical reason we must now therefore inquire and ascertain what is the most warranted faith judgment as to consummation, beyond both creation and continuation.

The approach of the discussion will be simple in structure. What does our total stance of the multidimensional Universal Word suggest most adequately as to consummation with respect to each individual, to the total created community, and to the Eternal Spirit who is Love? We concern ourselves deliberately with the legitimate and most telling implications of God's being Love, the Creative Spirit, the final giver of meaning for the total pedagogical process that we do know as well as for all possible creative processes beyond our ken. Such a stance puts before us an immediate decision of agnosticism with regard to our knowledge of eternity. By the nature of the facts we are human, within a pedagogical process utterly relative as to what we know or can know. We must therefore renounce in principle all attempts to make any predictions of ultimacy from within our own conditions or competence for knowing.

God alone knows eternity. We are continual candidates for learning in and from it. Our ways are not God's and his thoughts are not ours. Therefore we can never know as God knows, nor can we ever believe as he knows, because the finite constitutionally can never be or become the infinite. Thus all knowledge of the countless possible creations with unimaginably different qualitative capacities from ours is simply by principle beyond our ken. This fact we begin by acknowledging fully, openly, and with determination. Nor can we ever know, of course, our own process in the way that God does, who knows not only indescribably more fully what has been, what is, and what can become, but knows our pedagogical process also in relation and comparison to, for us, countless other creative epochs, both genetically and coordinately.

We need to recall and to develop concretely our previous discussion of time. We do not seek to hide from ourselves that adding more processes to ours in no way solves unresolved questions as to time. Neither God's total temporality or atemporality fully satisfies critical thinking. We can accept God as the Creative Spirit always and thus acknowledge that the logical implication of such a stance is that there never was a time when time was not, if by time we include in any sense the truth of chronology. If God ever had to have a first creation logically, our own might as well be the first. The problem in principle is the same. Therefore adding more creations, even countless creations, does not logically solve our problem.

There seem to be two ways out: one is to tackle the problem by an end run; the other is to tackle it in the middle of the line. If God is conceived of as the endless Creator who is the very abyss of being, then he can be always halfway through eternity and, as we have previously suggested, never get beyond that point. Eternity is exhaustless; therefore the infinite is supposedly neither diminished nor enlarged by creation. Creation is then only the endless turning of creative possibilities into actualities, new forms of reality within the eternal Reality. God is, in such a case, the bottomless well that can never be drained. But this view undercuts the reality of genetic division; if the new is real, do we not have a larger infinity? In some way a new and another creation also comes after the others; and logically therefore some creation must have been first. Or is exhaustlessness such that beginnings and additions have no ultimate meaning? Perhaps all we are saying, however, is that we human beings cannot conceive of eternity. Surely eternity is not basically chronological if eternity means living love and time means learning love. Still we grant that the status of the new as *adding* something to what was there before seems to imply a chronological series in some sense. Do we need to understand, as we have suggested, that the exhaustless swallows up all exhaustibles in such a way that numerical addition or subtraction has no more meaning?

Is it only we finite beings who have to make an end run around our problem; can we not tackle it at its middle by claiming that the problems of time are real only within and for time? Can we say that with God living love is no lack so that adding or enriching has no meaning in terms of numbers? Can numerical finitude limit infinite *Spirit*? A person is and is real as an event without thereby changing the nature of eternity. It is the nature of eternity to be exhaustlessly creative and ever and always to abound in love and in the creations of the conditions for love. Thus only from the view of learning love can time as a numerical, exhaustible situation have any meaning. Such threat is for insecurity alone, for anxiety alone, not for the fullness that knows no lack. By these two ways we can try either to outreach the problem or to face it straight on as unreal except in time.

Nevertheless is it not true that if all that is created ceases to be except love, and if love is not finally subject to chronology, is it not then true that creation as chronology has no final bearing on eternity? If love knows no separation, no separateness, how can numbers affect it? Is qualitative enrichment of the One *Spirit* through distinctions finally a numerical problem in the exhaustlessness of eternity, the living of love? If individuation is a term that pertains to creation and continuation only, how can we worry about eternity in terms of *chronos?* Is *chronos,* then, in the final analysis part of pedagogy, the learning of love, and never "part of" love itself? How can love have parts? Are not "parts" part of the conditions of creation, the need for separateness in order to attain distinction? Is not love a condition, a quality, a spaceless, nonsubstantial reality, a reality of spirit and not of things? Can love be measured in terms of room or duration, in terms of external relations? Is not Love itself primary and not personalities as external individuals? Why have we called God not a spiritual Personality but a personal Spirit? Why have we come to a contrapletal logic as alone capable of handling ultimate reality as well as the ultimate nature of what is in pedagogical process? Does consummation go beyond the subject-predicate reality in pedagogical terms, in the sense of time, and yet also go beyond some indiscriminate ultimate? Are not all one in Spirit as well as in themselves? We must examine the meaning of unimunity as the consummating ultimacy of both unity and community.

Can we maintain that unity and community are meaningful terms within the order of time, but lose their meaning within eternity? Can we finally come to comprehend that time as addition may be fully and importantly real for creation but cease to have meaning for consummation? Individuation has meaning for learning love but individuality in terms of separateness loses its meaning within the fullness of eternity as the living of perfect love. Distinction is real in unimunity but separateness is not. What is real for things and for personalities on the way to spiritual maturity has not the same meaning at all for the Eternal Spirit and the true distinctions within that Spirit. Life in God, life in the Spirit, eternal Life, is qualitatively different from life as we now know it who are candidates for life rather than partakers of it, in a reality where even "partaking" speaks too much of parts!

Let us at least and at last proceed to consider man's final ultimate problem of consummation. We acknowledge once again for stress that from our stance we cannot know God's eternal creations, nor our own from his point of view. We grant freely, too, that from the perspective of our kind of time we have not fully solved the problem of history in terms of *chronos* either by an end run or by tackling it in the middle, either by resorting to the category of the exhaustless, the bottomless abyss, or by denying that time has any problems except from within the context of time. What we mean to do is to show that contrapletal logic offers positive suggestions that cannot solve the problems from within our situation of pedagogical time but can offer a way of superseding positively the problems of time by the very nature of eternity. We can go beyond the categories of time in terms of both substance and process by means of the fulfilling reality of spirit in its illumination of both time and eternity. Contrapletal consummation at least offers a new fuller view on time and eternity.

If God is Love, the personal Spirit who creates, continues, and consummates, what can that mean to and for each individual? Can we talk of the individual within the context of time alone? Is not "life eternal" in some sense the persistence of the individual and of his characteristic activities? Ralph Barton Perry in his keen struggles with the problem maintained that eternal life meant nothing to the person essentially unless the individual as such persisted. Can we talk of meeting the loved ones in a world "above" and not maintain that they then retain some separateness? Tillich, we recall, came back from the Orient late in life insisting that in some sense history lost its very reality and meaning apart from some sort of persistence of the individual as such. Unity, the transcendence of the subject-object relation, for him was no longer enough. There had to be continuation as well as cessation of the person as such, to repeat the key pitch of his Ingersoll Lectures on Immortality at Harvard. Mere continuation becomes anthropomorphic. That makes this world, our kind of individuality, ultimate. Mere cessation cuts the meaning from under historic existence as such in its ultimate dimension. Whitehead, we also recall, agreed to such lines of thinking but felt that he had no resources for discussing the problem with his limited cosmological rather than metaphysical universals. What then can the full nature of God's love mean for the individual? How can we approach adequately the problem of the implications of love? Kant felt that on the level of duty there had to be life eternal as the counterpart of the categorical imperative. How else can God be understood and the moral life, he asked, even on the level of justice? But what if we move beyond that level to the reality of love?

The problem can be approached on three levels: the qualitative, the accumulative, and the finally consummating; or the qualitative, the accumulative, and the contrapletal. Qualitatively each person can be considered to be created for the rewards of love in terms of such intense satisfaction that all suffering that goes into the attainment of it or serves as the contrast for it is as nothing in comparison to that supreme moment of satisfaction, that excruciating tasting of reality. Thus the insect that is threatened and destroyed in many of its examples has nevertheless in some of them the indescribable triumph either of being the female who attracts the males, flying ever higher, soaring ever more toward the sky, or of being the males that mount after her in the utter desire to have her, higher and higher, harder and harder, until one by one they drop dead of exhaustion, dying in the blinding joy of seeking, or else, in its most selective example, mount up to catch the beloved object of desire until the consummation of sexual union takes place, even though it robs the consummated male of life itself. The species goes on and the reward goes to the strongest or to the most persistent, but for all there is the promise better than life and for some there is the attainment at the cost of life, while for the female there is the consummation in the persistence and the giving of life, both as an individual and for the species. Can all life similarly have its ecstasies, its peculiar satisfaction? Not only can it, but does it?

Both justice and love join to deny the adequacy of such a solution. Justice would insist that each creature have at least access to such satisfaction, whereas in fact only a few have the chance for it. The pleasure seems more in the line of preserving the species than of rewarding each creature. Therefore the solution would have to be at least conjunctive, even if not accumulative, let alone consummative. Love would be far more emphatic in its objection to the sufficiency of such a solution. Love would want not only each individual to have its just share but would insist that such an infrequent attainment should be made not only general but also with a chance at least for recurrence. Perhaps, for some, the finest moment was worth the rest of life but why not have all share it, as justice also would insist, and why not have more of it for each one? Why should satisfaction in an eminent degree or in a qualitatively superb sense be the rarest occurrence, or at least only rare occurrences, if Love is full, potent, and all-resourceful?

We can understand struggle, pain, and loss as leading to love, finally, as perhaps needed contrast in the learning to appreciate it at its maximum, as well as in order freely to choose it out of ample experience of backgrounds, but why should the attainment not be for all, and all that could be had of it? The best directive for life and truth, the most warranted faith on our level of description and prescription, is actually gainsaid by the small number who ever have the chance of ecstatic fulfillment. Such a contradiction would call for either a lessening of what otherwise is a warranted faith or a more resourceful and resolute carrying through with the implications for faith. We choose the second alternative. There is no content for experience from the graphic pinnacle of certain insect life, as we have indicated, to the mystic ecstasy of the saints that escapes the truth and power of the logical analysis we have offered. Such experience should finally be for all and all that could be had of it. The content is secondary; the reasoning remains the same.

Then what of accumulative meaning and satisfaction, even if we cannot reach the level of final consummation? Can the meaning of life not consist in the growth itself of each life, or of the possibilities for such growth? Can the reward of life for each constitute sufficiency? The past seeks fulfillment in the present; the present seeks fulfillment in the future; and past, present, and future are held together within the channel of one individuation which is its own end. If each life has a chance for growth, why cannot the experience of growth, we repeat, be its own reward? Many, however, do not receive the chance for growth. They die at birth or soon after. Many die deformed, retarded, practically destroyed before they start. Justice alone can debar such an attempt at solution. For love even the try is preposterous.

If love is the ultimate stance, the accumulative approach to eschatological solution stands out as the result either of incompetent thinking or of rationalization. Then, indeed, one wants to declare ultimate concern as the central perspective but not to look consistently at what should be seen from this point of view. Even to discuss it is to stand in contempt of reason. All one needs to do is to call attention to the radical inconsistency of those who call God love and then have no genuine, adequate consummation. The life we know is not characterized by a universal consummation of satisfactory growth; far, far from it! Growth itself can be good, especially if it is of the right quality, but many never have it and too much growth is wrong or unattained to any satisfactory degree, let alone worthy kind. If we limit growth to this life, we have no adequate answers to consummation.

What, however, if we accept the fact that this life is not all? Why stop with this life even accumulatively? Can the climactic accumulation not be in other and more lives than this one? Surely reincarnation is a widespread, challenging, and worthy solution in terms of unlimited growth. If one grows, one can keep on growing, and improve the kind of growth. If one refuses to grow or grows wrongly one has to face that fact in the next life, which will be appropriate to a rehabilitory situation. Growth is in the saddle. Growth is real. Growth is honored. Failure to grow is penalized, but as pruning for new growth and for better growth. Is this not our answer? It is at least a worthy reply both intellectually and morally in a preliminary sense. In many respects it accords well with the nature of the pedagogical process we know.

To sever human life, in any case, from the rest of life is fatal to any adequate answer. All life is one and must be treated as one. Life is multidimensional, but life is life. Why life should have to begin at such a low level and go through such failures and frustrations rather than to begin at higher stages is hard for us to understand. We bow before a mystery, not to avoid it, but to recognize it for what it is in its place. It seems that God may have begun peculiarly low down in the case of our cosmic epoch to see if he could not reach a new high of attainment with his new kind of experiment. There must then be some unity of life as a whole in its onward movement as well as an evolution of individuation. At what point individuation occurs is difficult to answer. But once begun, the vehicle or channel of evolution must surely have been reincarnation. The soul has survived not as an individual entity, completely separate from all else, but as a structured potentiality, a flexible, appropriating potential, which, once a particular life that bears and informs it dies, as such goes on to another life, not as consciously known or recalled, but nevertheless as the powered occasion for further growth, for new evolution of life through series of individuation. "The soul" is then the spiritual gene, the mental-moral acorn, the seed that continually loses its life and yet persists by being resurrected within new life.

How can this be? Life is one. Life is dependent upon spirit as its principle and power of identity. A distinction takes place in spirit, functioning at this point, a distinction which is accumulative toward a goal. The spirit as the inner identity persists. The particular life has as its content a background of potential which makes possible the kind of growth it can have. The content of that is the soul. Each life needs a concrete development according to its nature and to express its uniqueness in nature or history. The soul dies with each life; but spirit, as permanent, accepts only such gains as contribute to the evolution of the soul. The spirit then affords that soul, which is dead as a particular life, to be born again in new stock, in new life, where it expresses its historic or natural existence, only once again to carry into spirit whatever modicum of growth can be considered genuinely accumulative while all else perishes.

Thus life is continually dying and being reborn. The soul is ever and ever again reincarnated in more or other forms of life, as is relevant to its history. Thus the soul is a carrier through time of a structured potential. The spirit becomes "colored," has the capacity for transmutation, becomes accumulatively the basis for higher life. But if life, through the soul, can thus affect the spirit accumulatively it can also affect the spirit in the sense that, although it cannot injure or distort spirit as the eternal principle and power of identity, the One, it can nevertheless, cause to be erased from the spirit previous gains. In a way the soul is a carrier of life the way a tape is of music; it can be imprinted or erased. Thus not all growth is upward and onward even in the spirit. We might think that the spirit could leave out all but positive gains, allowing separateness not to affect permanently the acquired basis for distinction. But such treatment of the relation would injure the importance of the finite cosubject. What is gained even in the spirit in the evolution of soul is not in eternity but in time and is thus subject to cessation as well as to continuation and eventual consummation.

Especially important is this consideration with regard to the higher levels of relationship, as in the case of human freedom. Where there is moral responsibility, knowledge of spiritual choices, and some control beyond mere growth on the part of the soul, the cosubject can affect the potential for further growth as it is carried by the spirit. This cannot mean that the spirit itself can ever become imperfect. Spirit is One, the Ultimate Concern and Eternal Integrity, and nothing can change the nature of that ultimate capacity for finite differentials. But the soul can both color and erase the coloring, so to speak, of spirit, for spirit rather than Spirit, operates in time. The erasing causes a defect in spirit rather than an effect. This understanding shows how deeply Augustine had penetrated into the relation between God and the world. Such is his meaning of evil as privative. Not that evil was not real in time! Not that it had no effect on life, on nature, on history, but that, at inmost, evil could not be ascribed to God as the final giver, preserver, and perfecter of life. In this sense each man determines his own destiny by his being and doing, by his choices for life and action. While evolution of soul persists, freedom becomes ever more important. The use of freedom conditions the result ever more insistently.

Such an arrangement is perfectly just. A man is what he does and does what he is. He also understands and experiences his life in terms of what he is and does. What can be more just? Is not growth our answer at least on the level of justice? Suppose, moreover, that each life has the opportunity within eternity to reach its perfect fruition. Suppose that, however long it may take in the ages of ages, each life finally finds its full and best growth according to the way it has structured its potentials in spirit accumulatively. Would not both love and justice be satisfied with such a result? All life finds final fulfillment, but the kind of fulfillment will be according to one's life, or one's countless lives before reaching this point of fruition. Can justice rise higher in its service of love and can love be more righteous in its final rewards? No!

So it seems at least. *But* the solution presupposes that each life has the same opportunities beyond itself and that each life is only itself. The answer presupposes a disjunctive karmic order. The approach is thoroughly individualistic, substantive rather than spiritual. Life at some stages, to be sure, can be like a garden of flowers. No flower has concern for the other flowers, only for its own growth. If each and every flower found its full fruition, became its own most beautiful and fragrant self, that would be a perfect fruition *for flowers*. That would be an answer for a garden.

But no flower garden exhibits the deep, mature relation of love. The vegetable kingdom does not rise to the knowledge and glory of concerned understanding and loving interrelations. Our standard for solution— spirit, love, and personal purpose—does not come from any garden of flowers, not even in fact from the Garden of Eden. Our present discussion deals, to be sure, with the problem from the individual point of view. But that is not enough. We have soon to move on to deal with the communal level and the discussion of God himself. The accumulative ideal centered in the individual can never reach a full solution, for it must fall short of love. The accumulative ideal can, of course, go on beyond the individual as such and into the communal and the divine orders. That means that eventually we must go on to discuss the third stage of possible fulfillment for the individual and that will be in terms neither of mere quality nor of mere accumulative growth of the individual, no matter how high, but in terms of the individual in his total involvement with nature, history-humanity, and God.

Before we leave this level, however, in order to proceed to the consummatory or the contrapletal, let us freely acknowledge that the solution which holds that each life has a full history of interaction between soul and spirit, through countless incarnations or rebirths under whatever circumstance, and holds that the final destiny of each life is to become the most perfect instance of its own unique history, and then finish the process by being merged again with Life, is indeed a solution which honors both justice and love as ultimates. The result has full regard to justice at least if, in the full history of each individual, external situations become equally available to all, and also some real regard for love in that love lets each one grow to his own fullest potential. At least each life arrives at its highest own chosen development, even though it may not keep blooming forever. Love is then the flower, the best possible life, and such fruition of love comes to each and every life ever created. Nevertheless, even in such a case love need not have come into full perspective and power in the result. Why should Love let die a life of love at its best? If each life would remain its highest flowering forever, we would be spared the contradiction of love cutting down its own best achievement. Then we would not have perfect Love liquidate its children when finally they have reached the capacity for full satisfaction and contribution. If each life reached its own best development only then to be destroyed, the result would be both universal and fully intensive, and yet also fall far short of the meaning of eternal life within the understanding of our ultimates of spirit, love, and personal purpose. To discuss the individual from the point of view of our main stance we must soon go beyond the merely qualitative and the accumulative to the consummatory. But we are not quite there yet, except for a brief preview to give meaning and contrast to the intervening discussion.

Love's perfect consummation for each and all no human being can imagine. With Augustine we speak only not to keep entirely silent on the subject. If the most high is the most real, if love is sovereign, one thing is certain: the final result is immeasurably better than our most perceptive and imaginative picturing. But we do nevertheless have a few considerations to offer that can help us now from within our own perspective. These lead lines we believe to be reliable in direction although they only serve to get us started. Love's consummation in accordance with the multidimensional understanding of spirit, moved and led by creative, personal purpose, would have as its goal the perfect total unity of Spirit in the bonds of love, producing the most creative differentiations possible. The One would make the many more unique, or each and every one unique in a maximum manner and to a maximum degree.

Heaven is, then, where all both will-and-wills by love or where all wills-and-will by love. (In unimunity neither the singular nor the plural by itself will do!) Consummation is the perfect coincidence of cosubjects with yet the maximum creative, contributing distinction on the part of each and every personal spirit. Eternal life is simply life "in God," and life "in God" is always life in and for each one that he be himself in a maximum way. There is thus one Spirit, and even one personal Spirit, comprising and generating many spirits and personal spirits. Unity is then both ontological and psychological, and so is distinction; unity is through perfect oneness, identity of being in the Self, which is yet not any ex-

ternal Personality but a personal Spirit, distinguished as a cosubject as
a distinct entity, but an entity perfectly at one as spirit with all other
entities as well as distinct from them. Consummation is then a matter of
contrapletal logic in the reality of congruence of spirit which yet affords
differentiation within that Spirit. Consummation means the attainment
of perfect unimunity beyond either unity or community.

Thus consummation will be neither in terms of One, some ultimate
Self of pantheism, which undergoes experience ultimately with no final
meaning for the finite. Creation is too real for that. History is too meaningful for that. But neither is consummation in terms of many separate
individuals, however much cooperation may then be attained. Rather,
consummation will be a matter of perfect unimunity where the One will
continually remain the perfect Spirit and the many will be that perfect
Spirit, as much as that perfect Spirit is the many while remaining a distinct Entity. In consummation separation will perish. "The sea will be no
more." But the death of separation does not mean the destruction of
distinction. Rather, the doing away with separation means the enhancing
of distinction. In consummation there will be the acceptance of all being
One and also the acceptance of the One creating and consummating the
many. In this sense there will be neither the One nor the many but the
perfect reality of God the Unimunity and man the unimunity. We are
now, of course, speaking from within the necessary foolishness of the
ultimacy of our cosmic process, but its knowledge is suggestively reliable,
although always to be surpassed in the better and the fuller, the truer
and the richer. Consummation, we are sure, lies along these lines! Our
ultimate requires nothing less finally than contrapletal consummation.

The personal then is no longer a matter of personality and personalities,
but becomes transpersonal in full fact. All are one and in all, even as
God becomes all in all. All become one personal reality. We have a corporate Personal which fulfills and enhances the many. The One penetrates
and partakes of all personal entities. The entities are as much social as
personal and as much personal as social. Unimunity is through and
through transpersonal. This means that consciousness is neither merely
private nor merely public. All consciousness is one and everywhere accessible, but every entity will experience the all from its own aspect of the
all. In watching at the highest intensity a drama or a football game there
can be one scene experienced from many private angles. The occasion is
neither just public nor private. But in such a situation there is, underneath it all, false rivalry, conflict, separation. The highest form of attainment, worship, comes closer to the understanding of a public act that is
one and yet experienced from many perspectives or through many private
channels. Here the unimunal ought to begin, displacing the invidious.
But all such examples come from a world of separation and not from

the consummating reality of the perfect coinherence of consciousness and coconsciousness. The world of coinherence is the world of cosubjects. At its highest consummation, that reality is beyond separation; therefore the experience is different in kind from our kind of consciousness. Instead of coconsciousness or coconsciousnesses we had then better unite consciousnesses. Or can we find words for consciousness in terms of unimunity? Whitehead may be right that a basic problem with creative ideas is to get language to express them.

Where all wills and works by love and where all will and work by love there is neither unity nor community but unimunity. Consummation is unimunity. There the unity is ontological. There is only one Spirit. All are one in that Spirit. That Spirit alone is ultimately real. All reality has its principle and power in that Spirit always, but the Spirit is Love and therefore the unity within unimunity cannot become psychological as well as ontological until it is accepted and freely chosen. The inner nature of Spirit is always freedom; therefore there can be no unity of Spirit that is not a unity of perfect freedom.

The freedom of contrary choice, however, is only a pedagogical freedom. It helps us to become actual. It helps us to become personalities. The truer and fuller freedom, however, is the ontological freedom, or the theological freedom, the freedom of life which finally becomes coincidental with freedom of choice. Love alone can finally fulfill, can finally *free* freedom. There is no freedom that is not finally the freedom of the Spirit, in the Spirit, through the Spirit. Where the Spirit is there is freedom! Spirits become free only in freedom; they become free only by losing themselves into the One, to become one with the One, and thereby also to become one with the many. The one and the many now cease to be one and many within the freedom of consummation, within the freedom of unimunity. Where all will and works (and wills and work) by love, there God is and there is his consummation. Where love is and works, there the spirit is perfectly free, for the many are coincidentally, coinherently One while the One becomes one in and with the many to usher in the reality of the consummation of creation. The consummation of creation is thus contrapletal, unimunity.

As human beings confined within earthly existence we must necessarily speak foolishly when we try to picture consummation beyond our kind of life here. What a difference there is between animal life and human life at its highest and best. But that difference is within the same kind of existence. It is within earthly existence. What then of untold existences beyond our ken? Yet man must hope, and hope must imagine. What comes to be is no doubt vastly different, but if truth is truth and is reliable at all as to its legitimate implications, seminal suggestions are better than mere crude and less thoughtful fancies.

We might say that we deal with symbols. As we have seen in the discussion of the subject, that is always true in one sense, but some misuse words to mean that if we deal in symbols or myths, we are not aiming at the truth. On the contrary, we aim at whatever means of speech will best convey something of reliable hope even through undeniable ignorance. We always aim at statemental, "literal" truth, but always fall short of it by necessity. We aim at explorations that shall be meaningful to us now, as food for hope and as guidelines to faith, as nourishment for love and as incentives to proper action. Can we even now from our experience, then, picture some kind of consummation that suggests more than it says?

Whatever picture we draw must give us a sense of identity, of unity, which is the very best we know. Already we have suggested watching a drama of a game in rapt suspense. The self is completely forgotten, transcended, even in those who have habitual self-reference. But once the fever is gone, the drive is eased, even such a person wakes up to know that he was lost in the situation. But in such instances there is the experience of unity at the expense of distinction. Whatever ideas we form of consummation must therefore be equally insistent on the richness of the variety. Identity cannot buy off distinction! Therefore whatever imaginings of the personal we may create must be more real than any shying away from them in the fear of anthropomorphism. We play golf together and at our best are one in the sport even though each player expresses his own skill and reaps the reward of his own experiences. We can similarly be lost in a game of tennis with creative tensions of distinction on each side of the net without hostile conflict. Such experiences at their best may suggest something of what unity and distinction can mean.

Or we may work together on a project in which all are absorbed, lost, whereas each person is receiving enormous satisfaction from doing his own part. People have worked on building a church, or some decorating project, so solidly together that they never noticed time, hardly felt the need to eat, and yet each person was at his own most intensive best both in making a constructive contribution and in experiencing the reward of attainment. As a boy in Sweden I helped to plant a forest. In so doing we never thought of ourselves. The whole school was as one unit in the forestation project. And yet after fifty years I could return and remember the glow of creative participation and even look at the large trees and say to my family: "Perhaps I planted those very trees." The self was lost, but he was there!

All these references, however, speak of a world of community, of comrades at play or work. They refer to our world of egos and ego-involvements. The self is never far from the surface. He is not lost very deep in others. He soon reappears to reassert his own selfhood. He is a conscious individualist who may lose himself from time to time and in one kind of project after another. But he is foremost a self and only secondarily a socius. At best he is in community; at times he loses himself in unity; but he has not as yet attained to the reality of unimunity. Unimunity is the condition where the coincidence of cosubjects is not only so habituated but so ontologically established that the self has become graduated from the ego life and the ego-involvements of creation as pedagogical process. He is no longer a candidate in pedagogical process, learning love, but a graduate in eternity, living love. He has passed from creation through continuation to consummation.

For us at our present stage of attainment such full self-acceptance, which is beyond the acceptance of self as self, is very likely almost impossible to imagine, let alone experience. The acceptance of reality is as much the acceptance of the One as the many, and of the many as the One. There is complete identification, a perfect *tat tvam asi*, that knows a perfect *satori*. *Nirvana* is real as true suchness. The flame of ego is burned out, completely extinguished as ego, and yet for the self, the One and the many in that condition, in that aspect of the whole, in that manifestation, in that bit of reality which cannot be a bit without also being the whole, there is "perfect bliss." "Eye has not seen nor ear heard" such reality.

No wonder Buddhism contradicts itself. Its *neti neti*, its never this, never this, its absolutely inscrutable fulfillment, is yet "perfect bliss." The perfectly empty is complete fullness! Not a contradiction of opposites, but the full fruition of contrapletal logic! From this side we have the one and the many or the one or the many, but from the other side we have neither the one nor the many but both at the same time in perfect bliss. The *saccidananda* of Hinduism goes beyond all description. Words limit. There is neither contradiction nor dialectic. Here is no pedagogical logic of development. Here is process in attainment. Here is "intelligence, plus existence plus bliss." Reality is beyond our ordinary substance (or thing-personality) thinking, with external relations, limitingly relational.

The philosophic tradition itself has sought for some way of thinking beyond good and evil, or beyond time and space. But no qualitative negativity nor any time-spacelessness will do. We need the qualitative fullness of spirit as a multidimensional vehicle of transpersonal Love. We need the contrapletal logic that becomes consummated in unimunity. Where all will and work by love and where all wills and works by love, the one in the many and the many in the one, real and identical while yet real and distinct, coinhering and yet cosubjects, there consummation becomes possible in such a way that perfect unity expresses the richest, the most zestful distinctions. In unimunity is perfect freedom for each and all, but such coincidence of will as well as congruence of inmost nature that the process of living may equally well be thought of as determined as free.

The central reality of the one is completely for and with all, in inner identity and in its and everyone's distinctiveness while each and all are for and with the one. What is gone is only destructive ignorance and destroying separatism. With full access to consciousness at need and will, there need be no limiting or debilitating ignorance, and of course there is no divisive will. What life can be like in such consummating unity of both ontological and logical unity, let alone the psychological or personal, we cannot divine from this side nor envisage from within our ego-controlling kind of life. Neither unity nor community can penetrate the reality of unimunity, and therefore the consummation in unimunity must wait for the experience of it. No wonder that the most mature religious thinkers hesitate to say anything on the subject, let alone spell it out, while those deepest in faith point to some indescribable reality that alone can truly fulfill. But after this preview of contrapletal consummation we must return from the land of unimunity to explore the country that lies in between the ways to it. The preview can help us appraise the importance of the intervening stage.

Can we in any way understand how such consummation, viewed first from the angle of the individual, can be reached? From the lowest beginnings of life there very likely is some general evolution or development through ingression. Neither word fits with the relation of spirit to creation according to the way we have analyzed the situation. Neither term indicates the contrapletal nature of the process of continuation toward consummation. Both evolution and development are basically spatial and genetic. One, "evolution," goes better with the accumulative aspects of soul or individuated life, but not so well with the basis of life in spirit; the other expression, "development," goes better with transformation of quality or transmutation of kind. But neither evolution nor development hits the nail on the head. The creature is creature, but also more than creature by the capacity for spirit from the beginnings of creation and its coinherent developments through continuation. Even the word "reincarnation" is inadequate to express the process of the individuation of soul in spirit and the spirit's generating distinctiveness through the soul. All words change meaning within our new context of categories. The soul, in any case, goes back into process as far as the most lowly individuation. Its basis of permanence, its power for structured continuation, for directive potentiality, is spirit. All life is one, what we call vegetative, animal, and human. Spirit is before that and always. And spirit remains selfsame as both identity and the power for distinction. Thus spirit never "dies" although the soul does. We need a word for this deeper continuity which is contrapletal to process. Reincarnation, of course, is both continuation and cessation. Will someone coin for us the proper, meaningful word!

All life, in any case, is characterized by this process of death and life throughout the length and breadth of the pedagogical process. There is never separateness as full analysis at any stage of development nor is there the reaching of identity in consummation. The processes of nature and of history aim at individuation, but aim just as deeply at community. Teilhard de Chardin rightly speaks of the polarity of complexification and totalization. Neither can be obtained except through myriad ages or countless lives. No one knows what repetition, what newness in repetition, takes place as life develops. Here indeed is the whole of the relevant past repeated forward. But from the lowest beginnings in creation through the highest reaches of continuation there is birth and rebirth of the same soul in its total history of individuation. There is thus an evolution of soul as well as of body, and both processes are rooted in the continuum or carrier of spirit. Reincarnation is individualistic; what word goes with the process toward unimunity? Should we say that creation as continuation is a process of transmutation toward the goal, first of individuation, and then of community, and only finally of unimunity? Selfishness and selflessness seek self-fullness, but self-fullness can be had only in a preliminary sense through community. Beyond lies the consummation of unimunity.

Does the personal ever reach the point in this life that it must become permanent as conscious memory? The question may be falsely put from within the anxieties of ego-insecurity and ego-involvements. After all, I want to know my wife with whom I lived happily all my life! Can any consummation concretely be better than that? What else is heaven for, and how can it be heaven without such meeting again? But in heaven we are not given in marriage. Marriage is an institution of ego-involvement. Marriage is, at best, community on the way to but never reaching unimunity. Here is a community of an intensively high order, at least in its possibilities, and marriage serves a most important function within the pedagogical process of learning to live together intensively. But for the ego to have to remember and live in a limited set of affections throughout all eternity is to rule out unimunity by means of a limiting kind of community.

What is essential to life is not a set of conscious memories, but the highest possible potential for the highest possible unimunity. Thus we may already have lived and died many times in this earthly existence, and we may have to live countless more times until we are ready to be graduated into a different kind of existence altogether. Perhaps the approaches to unimunity will come in this life as we move into new reaches of noogenesis or pneumagenesis. We may be in for radical new forms of life in this earthly existence far more different from human life than human life is now from animal life. Perhaps not only our cosmos but even our own earthly existence will have to go on until we learn our lesson. Perhaps none of us graduates from this earthly existence until ages from now. How can we know? We may only now begin to wake up to the seriousness of life. How can such seriousness then become a hope and not a burden? Is the gospel precisely for our wearied egos to free them from the burdens of ego-involvement?

We can know, it seems certain, that the goal of attainment and release from this kind of existence may not be reached until we have attained the kind of humanity that we can reach within our own limited conditions. First we must at least reach the limits of our best possible in this kind of existence. We are what we are because of the potential with which we are born, at least as far as heritage goes, and we are going toward the goal of universal man. At this very point consummation begins to break off and to branch off from process as accumulative growth of individual life. At this point we see the shortcomings of self-realization as a goal. We are not like flowers where one or all can flower by themselves and reach or fail to reach satisfactory bloom by themselves. Human history, we repeat, is no flower garden nor even Garden of Eden. Finally, we can become right as individuals only insofar as we reach toward consummation, and consummation is measured by the relation of each to all and of all to each. That means that we may not live by ourselves and for ourselves but must, by our very nature and by the very nature of our circumstance, *both* live not only for and with others but also finally in and as others, as well as with them in one qualified meaning of the world. Consummation must become communal. It must reach community before it can become unimunity.

Thus we may have to live this life over and over again until we reach the reality of community. Universal community may be the goal of our human historic process. But unimunity may be attainable within such community by the translated few, by the ones completely in and by the Spirit, who then become the example and the power of the rest, especially as they begin to reach a high form of universal community, the age of universal man. Perhaps the reality of resurrection, beyond earthly existence, is then only for those who here reach unimunity and become ready for untold kinds of unknown adventures in different media and realities beyond our ken. One thing is certain: we must never make permanency of conscious memory an eternal characteristic, the prerequisite for eternal life. The highest potential of the Spirit for the finite is the capacity to be born and to die into ever-newer and more creative media, with full acceptance and full affection, humanly speaking, for all, in the eternal adventure of endless exploration on the part of the finite within the exhaustless riches of the infinite Love. There may thus be an overlapping of preliminary consummation of the accumulatively personal and communal in the rare few who in this life become so filled with the Spirit and fulfilled in the Spirit that even here ecstatically they have foretastes of unimunity, some mounts of transfiguration or some second heaven.

What, however, if we shift the perspective completely from the individual to the communal, from the person as such to the whole of human history? There, too, we want to treat the subject in the light of the qualitative as such, the accumulative and the consummatory. Can the whole of history at any stage we now know be considered the creation of our ultimates of spirit, love, and personal purpose? Can any genetic slice of it, at any time, be considered consistent with our main stance? Preposterous! The world as it is fully denies the ultimates we propose. Unless there is accumulative consummation not only personally but communally we may not, we must not, believe in the personal Spirit of Love, even multidimensionally or contrapletally. If this world or any world up to now, speaking in the aggregate, is all there is, all we may hope, we cannot believe in God. We cannot even be tempted to entertain the hypothesis! Either dishonesty or sloppy thinking is responsible for the limping faith that talks of God as love and then accepts also that this world is all there is.

If my own works over the years have no other merit, be this their strength that at no time and in no way have I ever suggested that we can believe in God without believing in consummation. Without "eschatological verification," to use a phrase from John Hick, there can be no vindication of any full faith in our ultimates. Even though our ultimates give the highest explanation for cosmological process and the most effective directions for conduct, personally and as social ethics, we cannot hold them unless consummation is the meaning of creation. There are qualitative satisfactions of a high order within this life, of course, and not to recognize and to enjoy them is not to love, and by that token not to grow either. The joy of human love, the creative satisfaction of meaningful work, the release in play, the sensitive awareness of beauty in nature, in life, in art and literature, the sacrificial satisfaction of costly involvement, the freedom resulting from hard and true choice, abandonment in duty, deserved rest and relaxation at the proper time and in the proper way, the unutterable ecstasies of religious devotion and worship, the power of prayer, the hope in seeking, the intellectual fruition of seeing new truth, the long and quiet living and walking with God—who can even mention the kinds of qualitative consummations that can and should be had. Not to live in the now is never to live. Not to live in the now is never to know. Not to live in the now is never to grow. Therefore to deny present consummation even on the part of any age is to deny what makes that age

livable, viable, the heritage of the next. We are not minimizing the good
there is, but only maintaining that it is not good enough or sufficient, and
that there is too much evil!

Qualitative satisfactions are rare whether we look at the question among
those who experience them or in the life of those who do. Few have them
and seldom. Then, too, the beastly contrast of shame and suffering is ever
with us. Nor is the good rewarded in all too many ways and circumstances.
The patient nation that tries to avert war must suffer ignoble defeat
because an aggressive nation catches it with its planes down. To be first in
evildoing is to catch the other at a disadvantage. What kind of world is
that? Our accumulative communal good falls far short. Although we may
not generalize without forfeiting adequacy of truth, nevertheless, as far
as human history in its collectivity goes, the poet is too far right in his
statement, "Truth forever on the scaffold, Wrong forever on the throne."

In any case, it would be a miscarriage of writing to spend much space
on even the attempt to show that no world that we now know, considered
as a whole, is even approachingly consistent with the nature of our ultimates. Besides if we had them, they would soon cease, even as we all do.
We can be thankful for the qualitative satisfactions we can have and we
can be open to and work for the best and the most of such experiences,
not only for ourselves but for others and for all. Perhaps such satisfactions
are our most real and fulfilling. Some of us can judge no otherwise from
our own experiences as well as from what we can learn from others.

But if such is the case, indeed, then we are bid to look beyond mere
quality of experience to further inclusiveness. The qualitatively communal consummation, in such a case, ought to be extended. It could be
thus extended both by being prolonged and improved from age to age and
by becoming more widespread. Let us then look at the wider panorama
for such a constructive drama. As we do so, we come to our second choice,
that of accumulative consummation. The rare and the occasional can
then be bid to become common and steady. Can an accumulative view of
consummation communally reach such a conclusion as a possible stage
and state that follows from the nature of our ultimate stance? In view of
what we have already indicated to be contrapletal consummation, what
can we learn of the stage in between that and the merely qualitative? In
the light of unimunity what can we ascertain as to the possible process of
accumulative community-consummation?

The accumulative collective cannot serve as the fulfilling meaning of
creation and the underlying drive of continuation in accordance with our
ultimate categories unless there is a personal continuum of an adequate
kind. If each person just lives and dies and that is all there is to it, then
there can be no way that we can even speak of collective consummation.
Such disjunctive disarray is what is the matter with *karma* as a doctrine.

Karma has no real social dimension nor any genuine understanding of the positive meaning of human history as a whole. But if personal life is rooted in a spiritual continuum that is both common and disjunctive within the realities of a contrapletal logic, then on every level of development, of creation and cessation, there can be an ongoing reality which conserves every gain and which affords a better chance for future history. Thus if we die only to live again, rid of concrete memories of ego-involvements, and yet abetted by what we have done in past lives, then each life as distinctive becomes a matter of utter concern and each life affects history both on the level of the common identity and on the level of the distinctive experience. The personal then becomes involved at the deepest level of the racial unconscious. History is then carried within a common continuum that is coinherently in and for all and in a distinctive continuum that is for each and through each, in and for all. In this way it is clear that each and every life matters for both the common good and for its own future. Accumulation then becomes the chief channel for genetic improvement. Accumulation, *in depth,* in "causal continuity," is then the key to human history, the most basic meaning of its ironic conspiracy. Each and every age then matters profoundly to all coming ages as well as to the kind of final result of each cosmic epoch or each distinctive creation within eternity. The book of Hebrews suggestively indicates that "they [previous generations] without us should not be made perfect."

At the same time no life lives unto itself. We have not now abandoned the personal. But no life is separate. All lives are one life and are together at their depth in creation, continuation, and consummation. Thus in one sense the old Hebrew concept of a collective personality, so to speak, is true. The personal is as much communal as it is individual. Especially is this the case on the pedagogical level. Finally, of course, and be this fact recalled again and again and ever more intensively, we are heading for neither unity nor community, but unimunity. Finally the result is neither individual nor collective. The ontology of coinherence and the logic of contrapletal fulfillment go beyond the old substance, thing, or personality way of thinking. We are beyond the old dilemma of either subject-object relations or no subject-object relations. But on the way to consummation our lives are not only accumulative as persons but also as communities, especially as communities of faith.

Pedagogically we must learn to live in and with others through the living with and for others. The individual becomes real and effective as a life by the criterion of the universal community. The more he lets his life become a part of the largest concern possible the more he advances as a life in the proper pedagogy of life's worth and meaning, the more he is more than himself. The more, similarly, each group becomes not only intensively and constructively creative but also inclusively and constructively concerned, the more that group becomes accumulatively important. The result is not only coordinate but genetic, and not only genetic but coordinate. Each person affects both his time and the future by the way he opens himself freely and widely to the full meaning and significance of life. Thus life and history both become intensively exciting and challenging. Personally and communally the way we are and what we do matters profoundly. Such are the communal meaning and reality of accumulative consummation.

One aspect of the accumulative consummation becomes especially important from within our present kind of analysis. What of guilt in history and moral judgment as far as the community goes? Can it not be that those who particularly hate and despise certain groups are born, for their own good, for their own needed training, into this very despised group in their next life? Could not even a person who becomes degraded to a persistent abuse of animals be made to experience the life that he persecuted? He no doubt needs to return in his development to primitive levels of learning. Although we cannot know the details of such training, such retrogression is consistent with our own moral choices. The persecutor of Negroes is born a Negro, the despiser of women, a woman, the cruel and callous to the mentally retarded himself mentally retarded in his next line of experiences. God's mills grind slowly and exceedingly fine. And they grind justly and to the advantage of the learner. God has all the time there is and he never fails to do a thorough job.

Perhaps communally, too, we may have to become the groups we oppose or the kind of groups we pride ourselves on not being. May not the extreme liberal community of concern have to suffer through the passions of the Daughters of the American Revolution and those daughters in turn have to be born into families and circumstances where they are inclined to a fuller humanity? Perhaps masses are thus trained? Perhaps whole communities of faith change roles? Is this why there is little or no full achievement in any group? May not Jews become Arabs and Arabs, Jews? Is this the reason that there is a lag in all groups? Human nature is stubborn, they say, but may it not be more than stubborn? May it not have to experience collective guilt both personally and communally? What then happens to the base of relevance? The relevance is then not to individual *karma* and to mere continuation in our chosen channel but to God's determined training and to the needs of persons, and perhaps even more to communities. Guilt in history is then not a matter of conscious consequences, understood merely or mostly on a conscious level, but is rather a matter of the deeper assignment through their basis in spirit rather than their actualization in soul, to whatever tasks man needs to meet in his long run or larger training.

Yet what then of consummatory fulfillment, of contrapletal consummation, to drive home our main theme? What of full contrapletal consummation of community? What of consummation finally in unimunity? Already we have discussed the topic preliminarily. There the personal and the communal come together. The communal and the personal both eventuate in the full identity that is always characterized by the maximum individuation that is consonant with inner sameness and allness. Each person and community of concern, so to speak, joins the original Holy Trinity. God is fully the One and the Many; each one becomes now through participation consistently one and many, one and all. What that can mean we cannot begin to grasp from this end of seeing except through faith, hope, and love, the realities with which we shall conclude this work. The religious imagination can grope, and finding a beckoning light in the distance, reach toward that light. But into that light we cannot now enter. That must be both *neti neti* and *tat tvam asi* and *tat tvam asi* and *neti neti*. That must be in line with the highest and fullest meaning of Christ as the Universal Word. That must mean the full realization of the purpose and the power of the Logos. Such full identity where God is all and in all, and all in all, but where yet each one will be even as Christ is, is a state so symbolically suggestive and eschatologically promising that here the potential Word becomes only a road sign to further travel.

What is important is that the final result will be according to both personal and communal realization. God, the Eternal Spirit, the Great Experimenter, the Loving Ground and Goal of all creation, works toward the fuller realization of creation in freedom. In eternity he lives and works, he lives and loves, but the result of each of his creations includes seriously the kind of response God has received in time. The living of love finally includes the way love was learned. Time matters to eternity. Thus there may be countless judgments on the way to unimunity, both personal and with all others. The "self" is now personal and universal, open and accessible, replete with public feelings and with consonant private feelings. Only coinherent cosubjectness can contrapletally comprehend public and private consciousness at the same time, at need and will, at need and wisdom. The self, beyond being a soul, is fully open without separation yet distinctively conscious within the total "Self" who is personal Spirit, who is Love, who is Unimunity. The public is congruent and consistent. The private is distinctive and consistent. There is no enmity, beyond the pedagogical and preliminary. Thus the "self" as focused consciousness persists, but is beyond both good and evil in the pedagogical sense of struggle, and is beyond the subject-object dichotomy in the same sense.

The subject-object division is done away, and gives way to the subject-subject fulfillment. Subjectivity becomes the truth without either separation or the abolishing of enriching distinctions. The Self becomes the All while the Self, as the All, is the fulfilling identity of the many; and the many are the One in the fulfillment of creative diversity. There is one

total Consciousness in which all participate and focused distinct consciousnesses open to the total. No wonder eye has not seen nor ear heard! We
may make anticipatory suggestions knowing full well that in the light of
reality all such suggestions pale into thin, unseeable shadow, but even so,
those shadows are too bright to seem shadows. Only as we explore the
subject in the light of our ultimates of spirit, love, and personal purpose
can we come to such suggestions of the transpersonal consummation of the
spirit of love in the living of love, the seeing of the brilliance of eternity
from within the shadows of time.

Will there, then, be fulfillment of the personal beyond the communal,
not only as quality and not only as accumulation, but also as contrapletal
consummation? Yes, and again, yes! The reducing of the personal focus
does injustice to the reality of the personal in our ultimates. The personal
will be not dimmed, but made more brilliant. But we are not now personal in the sense of love and spirit. We are now mostly egos who seek
self-protection and self-promotion. We are hardly ready to talk of love.
We are not ready even for justice in any mature sense. We live too far on
the animal level or on the level of the pedagogically human which must
be categorically transcended and done to death. Therefore we must continue in the stage of training. Therefore we must live in the pedagogical
process. Therefore we must experience in time. Therefore we must be
reborn time and time again in this world until we reach the contrapletal
dimension of development and fulfillment.

Even in this life some may begin to find the reality, at least anticipa-
torily. They may then be ready to be born into some further stage of
continuum, whether in some body or not we do not know. Perhaps there
are many glorious stages awaiting on planets or similar continua, world
without end, in regions not yet even glimpsed by man. What of God's
infinite universe, the creation of his infinite love? But the difference between the contrapletal dying and being resurrected is that when the personal no longer separates but enhances, when the personal becomes truly
contrapletal congruence and distinction, then, the personal can continue
beyond death. Then dying becomes a means only of transformation. Then
dying is creatively a cessation and continuation.

Our present ego dare not even hope for such reality. We dread it because of our present harrowing ego-involvements. We style it anthropomorphism. But when the contrapletal personalities come, even in basic or
conclusive anticipation, they know that in heaven there is neither a taking
nor a giving in marriage even while God is not the God of the dead but
of the living, and the final life in God is always qualitatively generative of
realities of experience beyond our ken, always consummatory beyond
community in unimunity, and always a participation in the reality and
the utter bliss of the Eternal Spirit. The power of lives like those of Jesus

and of Gautama, and of a few other charismatic personalities that have changed the world, is the power of contrapletal living, of participation in the reality of the will of God beyond ego-involvements or in victory over ego-involvements, within the release of the Holy Spirit, the Spirit of the All in all.

Therefore their lives count for the bettering of the world more than all external acts of do-gooding no matter how good, and more than all the words of wisdom of mere human understanding no matter how wise. This is the love that builds up, this is the truth that we can never finally do anything against, this is consummation, and for a few the reality begins in this life. This is the reality of ecstasy, of being taken in this world into the second heaven whether in or out of the body. This is the reality on the mountains of transfiguration. This is the final and true power of resurrection, not a resuscitation of life of our kind, but an encounter beyond death of a contrapletal life, a consummated life, on the way to the fuller ascension of the eternal process of consummation, which is yet reached as the decisive way of attainment. In such lives and in such experiences we have the true prophecy of things to come; we have the divine foretaste of eternal life.

From God's point of view the writing becomes ever riskier. How can we speak at all? We have kept repeating that we do not presume to speak from God's point of view as though we can speak of what he sees. Such speaking is categorically, apodictically, impossible. Never to all eternity shall man become God, or understand as he understands. We are finite and freely acknowledge the fact, governing ourselves accordingly. And yet we must also try to see in line with whatever is central. Therefore we must try, not to become God or to give his inner seeing, but to think God's thoughts after him. We must assume that some wholeness is given to man to seek, and for our purposes reliably to find. Thus we speak symbolically, imaginatively, suggestively, ever openly, as we grow into truth by whatever means it becomes available. Above all, we depend upon participation. We are coinherently in God and he is determiningly our cosubject; and thus we speak in God and for God, not by our own power, but by his, indeed, by his presence and inspiration. Inspiration alone counts when we speak of God and of God's perspective.

Then we speak not as we see, but as he lets us see. We see by means of his presence and power in us. How, then, does our subject of consummation appear if we try to speak his truth in relation to our three aspects of the qualitative, the accumulative, and the contrapletal? Except for linguistic awkwardness we should speak of consummatory consummation since there is no other word for the highest except the highest. Truth, as we keep defining from Spinoza, is the criterion both of itself and of error. And we can approach the highest adequately only from within its own circle. Consummatory consummation, however, is a clumsy and redundant phrase, but nothing less or else can say what we want and must have said. Contrapletal consummation is the alternative and rhetorically it is a better term. Therefore we use it. What we are after is that nothing less than the full consummation fact, not only in logic, will ever even begin to indicate the nature of the final fulfillment of the Universal Word. Only in such consummation can we understand the authentic nature of the Potential Word.

From God's point of view, then, if speak we must, not to remain silent at the critical center, qualitative fulfillment is real in itself. What is, is. What is, is what it is, when it is, as it is. There is true suchness. But true suchness is not only descriptive but also prescriptive. It is not only actual but real. It is not only potential, but also normative. Thus any good experience is as it is when it is, and *that far* qualitatively good. Consummation is a present experience as well as a future hope. Consummation is an immediate fact as well as a driving potential. It is real for finite experience; and it is real for God. It is real in the distinction; and it is real in the identity. It is real in the self as soul; and it is real in the Self as Spirit. But when it is as it is, it is not only itself. All is related, and even when the false finite separates itself on the level of the finite, it cannot sever the relation to the root of its being, in which the being is real and for which it is also real. God is not unconcerned at any point nor unrelated. Even when he becomes personally absent he is present as the carrier of all experiences, on all levels of life, and of all the conditions for life. Even when the finite shuts God out through freedom, God is present in and for freedom as the creative absence which yet is the only reality of identity and continuity.

The evil as such cannot enter God. God is not unaffected by it; he permits it in its place. He lets it remain for what it is and what it can do within the pedagogical situation. He allows the consequences of evil to become actual and to affect nature, life, and history. But such time cannot enter eternity, even though eternity can enter time, to be with it, correct it, support it and fulfill it. Thus there can be qualitative consummation in God in any present that does not yet allow the concomitant of evil to become copresent. Thus even qualitative disjunctive and conjunctive attainment and satisfaction are real to God. Evil cannot reach high enough to touch heaven, so to speak, but heaven can reach down, stoop down, to touch earth and to heal it. God can oppose evil, where that is needed, without becoming evil or without admitting evil into his own proper being as the eternal Spirit of Love.

Thus consummation can be real and is real in God qualitatively. It matters profoundly to God as well as to persons and communities how each individual chooses in life to be and to become. Each qualitatively acceptable choice, each attempt, effects consummation in God. Whatever good an individual accepts and becomes, becomes part of God's experience in eternity, which is the living of love, without thereby letting time as the learning of love enter eternity to spoil it. Thus all qualitative consummations in creation, prehuman, human, and posthuman, are consummations in God whether from a personal or communal source.

In the same manner accumulative consummation counts. God is concerned with how we grow as communities, especially as communities of faith or communities of ultimate concern. Whatever affects community-consummation not only qualitatively but accumulatively affects God. God is the ground and goal of all consummation. Whatever is consummated in distinctions is consummated in the base of identity. All positive attainments in the many affect the all. Thus God is consummated along with creation in becoming as well as in being, in growth as well as in fruition. Accumulative consummation makes history real and urgent.

Accumulative consummation whether personal or communal is real and urgent to God because he is care, concern, love, creative spirit. Thus God entertains as well as envisages qualitative satisfactions, however occasional and incidental. All good is good to God. He is "pleased" with whatever is generated in creation and human history, but he is especially concerned with growth because he is personal purpose. Thus we may not leave the matter of consummation with "true suchness," or with what is as it is insofar as it is good. The relational God, the God of process, the dynamic purpose cares for what also leads to further good. He "appreciates" extrinsic and instrumental good as well as intrinsic and endful good. Growth is real to God and becoming is of especial importance to him, and the more so the more it pertains to high eventual good and widespread or universal good. God works to gather all gain into the middle of the channel which carries forth the past toward the future for that person, for that community, for that civilization, for that cosmic epoch, for the main purpose of creation.

God is a gathering God. He gathers from the past for the future and he gathers in the present for the whole. And he experiences consummation in the process as well as in the goal of process, in the becoming as well as in whatever becomes. He is the God of the spring as well as of the summer and of the summer as well as of the autumn. Even the winter of cessation and change of seasons has its meaning within his purpose and within his satisfaction. True suchness should then be not only of being but also of becoming and not only of the timeful but of the timely. God is the creative Spirit and the creative Spirit is eternal. To live love is not only to enjoy love, but to be creative in its reality and power.

To be sure, there is a difference between the general kind of growth where spirit is the bearer of accumulation in such a manner that there is as yet no continuity of consciousness from one life to another. All such accumulation is preparatory, merely, but importantly, pedagogical. Thus, God is concerned both with the experience and with the accumulative result in spirit of the experience. All that lives and grows matters to God and all that supports life matters to God. Not a sparrow falls to the ground nor a blade of grass withers without his caring in the fullest sense of participation according to the circumstance and the need. Nothing is purposeless in God. Even what is useless rather than needless evil serves the purpose of an open, free universe, where God wins finally by persuasion and understanding rather than by command and force. Thus there is constant consummation in God as the affirming of his own experience, his own purpose, in creation, in continuation, in cessation, and in growth's fulfillment and love's fruition.

Such consummation, however, is different in kind from the consummation that comes when God can become the cosubject of sustained growth through life and death, or through the kind of permanent participation in his life that knows resurrection but no further death. Eternal life at its highest becomes life without end, utter bliss, "beyond this, beyond this," *saccidananda,* final true suchness, heaven, *satori, moksa, nirvana.* The wheel of our kind of life is broken. There is cessation and yet continuation. Personality as ego-drive ceases; conflicts are over, quiet growth in God sets in. But in some sense the qualitative and the accumulative persist as they are transformed and fulfilled. *Nirguna* as qualitativeless existence is the denial of existence. If the denial of our kind of existence, then well and good; if of the final reality of love, spirit, and personal purpose, then woe to all human thinking at its highest.

Nevertheless here we face the wall seemingly. Here we seem to be led to the dead end of human thinking. If that means an acknowledgment finally of human finitude so that our thoughts cannot be the same as God's, then power to such a dead end! Then hail the wall we face! Let God, then, be the wall that only he can remove in his time and in his way; and let us stand confronted with eternity believing where we cannot see. Our best thinking has then brought us to this impasse. Our most warranted faith has in such a case led to this dead end. But the obligation of reason, creatively and critically, is to go as far as God and truth let us. We must be daunted by no cry of speculation. We must trust truth to the end and, trusting our most warranted faith, live believingly.

As honest human beings and as committed thinkers, under God and for humanity, we dare do no less. Is then this question of the reality of growth with relation to God a blank, impenetrable wall? Is this road of pursuit a dead end with no chance to see some future road that can never be built? Are we at the foot of a mountain with no pass through it? Are we at the edge of the ocean with no hope forever of proceeding? Where are we? We can understand why the main tradition has spoken of God's timelessness, his being categorically beyond space, his being *nirguna*. All relations in God have been taboo because creation and relation to creation introduce the problem of growth in God, and how can the infinite grow? How can the perfect improve? How can the absolute change? Better, they say, to deny creation and end up in *maya* than to end up without essential being. Better to deny qualities in God than to end up with the reality of creation and human history; and have no God. Better then, they say, to become agnostic about God than to affirm the kind of God that will never solve the ultimate problem of time and eternity, of being and becoming, of permanence and change.

Our process thinkers cry shame. Why not accept merely this world? Why insist on any ultimate? Why have any eminent being? Must not eminent being become absolute, and must not the absolute become unrelated, according to our best thinking, and if so, why invoke the name or reality of God at all? Choose instead an existential atheism, with Sartre, as alone consequent thinking. Then acknowledge that to accept the reality of this world, especially of human freedom, is to court and wed humanism. Choose being, some say, and God, but then not a related God, what Whitehead calls a "barbarous" God. Or choose becoming, others say, but then no ultimate reality in terms of aseity. Abandon the category of eternity and live in time alone. Why not accept the ultimacy of relativity? Why not make process with eternal interrelations and interactions primary? Why not, with Schubert Ogden, worship the Eminent Relativity as ultimate Reality? Have no worry about the nature and reality of relations; only accept them and interpret them within this flow of flux. No permanent reality; only constant relations! Why not, indeed?

Or make God half absolute and half relative. Go with Charles Hartshorne in establishing some necessary ultimacy, comprehensively relative, because the ultimate is not unrelated but constantly in relation to a dynamic process. Why not simply accept Charles Hartshorne's "Ar," the absolute in some respects and the relative in some respects? There are many proposed solutions (and we have discussed them philosophically in *Reason in Religion* as well as in *The Christian Understanding of God*), but if we work with our chosen and established ultimates: love, spirit, and personal purpose, these ultimates can be eternal not as substances or personalities with external relations, and not as adjectival to process or inherent in process with internal relations, but as what ultimately is that by its very contrapletal nature contains fulfillingly the truth of both substance and process thinking within itself, at need and wisdom, being characterized by both internal and external relations. The very nature of the Christian faith, shorn of its conditioned, historic elements, offers us a new and fuller answer whereby God is indeed both absolute and relative, both eternal and temporal, both beyond the world and related to it, and that creatively, responsibly, urgently, and fulfillingly.

According to substance thinking, the world taken seriously limits God, makes him finite while, according to process thinking, God is by nature relative, or in some cases where process thinking is modified, ultimate and relative. According to substance thinking, the Supreme Being had no need to create, but he chose freely to do so in the only instance we can know. He can then perfect this creation and add that to his eternal richness. But substance thinking has always blushed at the idea of God's growing by creation. The infinite, the perfect, cannot grow. He already is; he is perfect; he cannot change. Thus relations, potentialities, have been dangerous, uncomfortable words in this way of thinking. They have been man's chief problems. According to process thinking, on the other hand, becoming is ultimate, but nothing is as such and nothing can then, either, become as such. Thus process or becoming is really begging the question of being, of ultimacy, of aseity. From this point of view it is better to stress how a God of love cannot by nature be unrelated, how the creative Center, Envisager, must be internal to his creation and operative within it. But now ultimate reality, aseity, what becomes whether as ground or fruit, become problems to be solved. The best attempts are by those who, like Whitehead, Hartshorne, Pittenger, and Cobb, frankly or unwittingly compromise process thinking in favor of process plus classical assumptions.

With some of these thinkers the problems are more understood and acknowledged than with others, but no one escapes from such compromise. The eclectic ultimate, however, is needless if we accept instead the ultimates of spirit, love, and personal purpose, which provide all the power for identity and distinction human thought, as far as we can see, can need, and bear. Within these ultimates reality is of such a nature that identity or permanence is established while creation is not arbitrary but inherent. Creation, too, has adequate purpose and promise of consummation.

But those of us who now or in the future choose such an ultimate still face the problem, what of the permanence of creation? Is not the new, in all ways of thinking, always a contradiction in terms? Can God grow? This is the paradigmal problem of human thought. Those who believe in eternal life as persistence, under whatever terms or forms, and those who deny to man eternal life in such terms must ultimately part company right here. Have we then come to our final wall or is there a peephole in it? Have we reached our final dead end of decision? Can we promise some further release for warranted faith? If we have been consistent with the fullest fact and the most coherent thinking up to this point, can we carry the potential Word beyond this point?

As far as consummation goes, there can be no consummation in the proper or plenary sense without creation and continuation. There can be sporadic satisfaction. There can be occasional enjoyment. There can be a purpose with intermittent attainment. But consummation involves reaching a goal, going somewhere, and that requires some mediating continuation. Thus properly speaking we should not speak of qualitative consummation if we mean only the unpurposed entertainment of satisfaction now and then. It is well before we proceed to remind ourselves of this point. Let us not deny the reality and the meaning, the partial fulfillment of life, even in this manner. This is the reason we have termed even qualitative attainment "consummation." From this point of view, of course, there is no problem of becoming or growth. Nothing really becomes ever. What is born in nature and history passes away. All creation ceases. We do not want to deny the reality and satisfaction of whatever values there are when they are as they are. It is good that they be. It is good that they be enjoyed. In this world of experience both good and bad are, and always are. We cannot tell why or how. From this point of view, furthermore, given all chances possible this universe is as likely as any other to be accepted for what it is and to be enjoyed for what it can be. Experience can, we know, teach some wisdom as to how to choose and as to how to accept what can come.

As soon as we admit an accumulative wisdom, however, we introduce the reality of more than the random. There is now some preference of values and some predictable way to approach their entertainment. Now we have abandoned mere chance and introduced the category of mind and purpose, of knowing and decision, and therefore, at least in part, a meaningful order of being and life. Thus there can be accumulative consummation of experience and choice, for man and for God if he is the sum total of all, in whatever way that may be. God and man may then cooperate toward some fulfillment that can, up to that point, be called consummation. Nevertheless, unless there be a final harvest of attainment, from such a stance ultimately life is defined by death, meaning by meaninglessness, being by nothingness, history and nature by *maya*, reality by illusion, because all is vanity and disappears. It is still good to live for those who live when they live, if they have enough satisfaction to make life worthwhile. Men disagree at this point. Many choose not to be and others keep suffering indecision, hanging on in some hope for the better or dreading the possible consequences of taking one's own life, for others or for themselves, beyond death. But there is not enough continuation of creation within this new to create an acute problem for thought. Life is; is good and bad; and includes some possibility for consummation in terms of a partial, accumulative experience in wisdom, growth, and decision.

When, however, there is a history of creation and when love is seen as a basic directive for life and thought, as at least suggesting a warranted faith, the entire question becomes new and different. For those who deny meaning, who deny the reality of any history of creation as establishing an accumulative basis for interpreting life, who do not invoke love as a reliable directive for life or thought, the main problem of consummation does not appear. But if history means anything at all in terms of life's meaning and the meaning of our cosmic epoch, if the center of our promise in process is warranted, then we are faced head on with the hardest of all problems. What is the nature of consummation with regard to the nature of what really is? What is the relation between consummation of life and history and consummation in and of God? If life is defined by death, being by non-being, purpose by purposelessness, ultimately, then thinking upon these problems and discussing them has no final meaning or value. It can be a matter of curiosity and incidental satisfaction, and thus far good, and truly good that far, but it cannot be a matter that affects the very nature of man and his universe in any consummatory sense that is proper and plenary.

For those who attempt to reconcile the knowledge that we do have with its fullest consequences and involvements, there is, however, a constant challenge to deal with the nature and reality of consummation in history, in God, and in the relation between them. Some hold that anything constructive that we do in human history, although we cease to be human beings, forever in every sense, is yet contained in God, for satisfaction and for further use for others in the future. Both God and man then attain a partial fulfillment that is meaningful, and can be zestful. To be sure, one could wish there might be more of such attainment and that those who help make it possible would share more fully in it, but such considerations have little or no meaning unless one assumes the adequation of value and existence, or of the most high and the most real. Whitehead, while holding that further consummation both for persons and for God had in the main to be worked out on the theological level, in general held a view of consummation in terms of history's good affecting God and becoming accumulative in him, as did Tillich increasingly at the end of his life. The third volume of his *Systematic Theology* bears eloquent witness to this fact. From one point of view, however, such a God is more barbarous than the unrelated God because he profits from all lives and alone retains the profit. Some of us shudder at the thought. But then such criticisms can be partially allayed by his suffering with creation and by his making available his gain for future lives. God does the best he can under the circumstances!

Our problem, however, persists: If such accumulation is real in aseity, in the ultimate, then something new, something real, is added to God that was not there before. But then logically there must be a time when the first new addition came to God. Before that, in such a case, he must have been unrelated, a "barbarian"! Why then did God ever begin to create? But let us say immediately such additions do not have to be substances, things, personalities; only qualitative enrichment of spirit. But either such enrichments are or they are not. If they are and become real, we have the mathematical numerical problem. Even a distinction that was not there before, in some sense must be, and therefore must add to the whole. How else can creation be real? What else can genuine becoming involve? Eternity, of course, is not a matter of numbers. The nature of deity is always to exceed in possibility any and every actuality. Only by becoming can being become what it is. Is not, then, creative Spirit itself the aseity that is never limited and is therefore exhaustless? God is then always halfway through eternity and never nearer the beginning or end than before. God is the abyss of being, the bottomless pit of possibilities. Some of us can see such an analysis and still feel deep inside that Kant's antimony has not been adequately solved. We are still up against a wall, however much the peephole may afford some suggestion of the fuller beyond. Accumulative consummation fails as a dimension to solve our problem.

The point is, however, that unless we become total agnostics, rejecting the final intellectual problems, or unless we resign ourselves to meaninglessness in the final matters of thinking, living practical hopes and helps, and never reaching beyond that, as soon as we have any accumulative value, any enduring purpose, not only in man but also in God, we are up against this final problem of the reality of the new and the meaning of time in some sense of addition, even though *exhaustless addition*. To have no aseity solves nothing. To have only eminent relativity, on the other hand, is to mix terms and solve no problems. It is better in that case to be honest and not to cover up the problem. Or is it perhaps better to deny it by insisting on the unrelated, timeless God who is essential reality whether in Hinduism or in classical Christian theism? Some will call the problem paradox. Others will bull their way through, mixing categories, mixing Christian presupposition and substance or process thinking, denying the sensitivity and trustworthiness of reason.

The sensitive, honest, and competent thinker, however, must still, we think, be plagued by this problem or solve it in some new way. That spirits may attain eternal distinction and a life of utter bliss in God without cessation is, however, no more of a problem than that the values we see and choose become part of God and go to help the future of the world. Finally the problem is the same. In the former case, however, we have proper and plenary consummation while in the latter we have only partial and arbitrary consummation; we have consummation of the Self at the expense of all selves, of the All at the expense of distinctions. Let us see if there is still further light on this problem; or must we leave our analysis with the fullest consummation we can see, albeit with an unsolved question as to the nature of the genetic aspect of consummation? What of consummation in terms of the fullest realization of each potential in creation, first with regard to lives and then with regard to the ages? May we not continue to develop a solution along previous lines?

Can it not be that God will be consummated, or ever keeps being consummated, or if some prefer, keeps consummating his creation, by accepting their lives into his perfect memory? When a beautiful dog companion is run over and killed, is that life fulfilled, as C. S. Lewis suggests, by our remembering it, if we did so constantly? When we have beloved children who die in childhood, does it really matter since they are remembered in our affection? Even so our lives remain, some say, if we are remembered in God's boundless love! We human beings must find some way to say something on the subject of death's finality, it seems, as far as human experience goes. This approach is even touted as God-centered. The paltriness of it, however, screams at us. Had it not been better if the dog companion had kept living and the child had its chance for fuller life? And either God remembers us as we were (and what a frustration that would be! And how could that accumulative frustration ever enter eternity, since time as time cannot?) or he must ache to transform us, give us a chance to mature. What, too, of God's having to remember all "evil" lives? If God cannot do better than the present world through all eternity with all the means at his resources, he is to be pitied, not loved and honored. What a callous, frustrated, unconcerned God that would be!

We cannot take seriously such a dodge from all profundity! To be remembered by God is a miserable position as to consummation. We dare not accuse God of such a hard heart as well as being such a poor hand at creation. For anyone who claims God to be integrity and concern, spirit, love, and personal purpose, such a way out can be deemed only a false start. God's remembering only the good, however, and making any creative progress available to the future gives God a central function and makes our lives of importance. But is the next life in principle and fact any more important than our lives now or the lives of those who preceded us? God then makes means of some lives. If he suffers with them and can do no better, being caught in the way things are, we can respect and honor him for doing his best without claiming any real arriving at consummation. If God enjoys himself at the expense of the process, he is callous and cruel, but at least of some use to those who come after us, though in some views like that of Whitehead's, life is still basically tragedy, and it were better if it were not. Some good, yes, some real good, yes, a partial solution, yes; but a result, a kind of consummation quite unworthy of the God of love, of our basic stance.

The main evidence, however, the central pointing of the cosmic process, is toward life, toward higher, more complex, more sensitive life, toward mind and purpose, however mixed and unfinished our present process or product may be. Accumulation can be a matter of exhaustless cocreativity, of endless pursuit of creative adventure, of daring novelty, on the part of a perfect coinherence of the One and the many. Man is a preliminary stage, surely; we cannot picture the ultrahuman that may start in this life or in future ages; it may continue on countless planets with adventure beyond all imagination, save God's; it may go on beyond all time, in the living of love beyond the learning of it, with contrapletal unity and zest of distinction in "the paradise of the spaceless," where what to us is invisible knows that all objectification belongs to the crudities of pedagogical process and processes. God is then always the senior partner, the eternal cosubject, the same in all and the all in the others. Thus God, the eternal Spirit, the eternal Love, the eternal Creativity, finds fulfillment in the success of his creation, sharing its joys and being part of its attainments.

The same can be said for the accumulative in community. God thus grows, fosters, perfects communities of faith, communities of concern, on the way to unimunity; and then within unimunity, the eternal Love may work in terms of nexus or continua of "history" that we cannot now know except for the fact that the One is not concerned with the other as an individual alone, but with all others as well as with each, or as Augustine put it, with each as though he were all and with all as though they were each. We have, then, more than a consummation of concomitance. We have a consummation of coinherence with concomitance, of neither unity nor community but of unimunity, of neither individual striving nor of cooperation, but of unicooperation.

We have the choice for thought that God can perfect each person and each age—to use our present measures rather than designations that surely will change with the development of God's purpose—until it reaches its own maximum fruition. God's resources may be exhaustless, but for finite growth there must be final limits. Such is the case with individual distinctions and groups of distinctions. We have no words for the creative new and must therefore use words from our world which surely are inappropriate to the larger future. Final limits must be reached by finite histories, personal and communal. Only the eternal is exhaustless, at least so it seems. Or can the Exhaustless always creatively reconstitute even a finite occasion through all eternity? Suppose, however, we grant that the finite definiteness can, at long last, exhaust relevant possibilities, that potentiality is a limiting category, as possibility need not be. Then there can be a final flowering of conscious life even for finite love.

When God has perfected each distinction and also the whole creative epoch, the cosmological age, may it not be that this perfection may have such richness of distinction and yet such perfect identity, too, that the distinction simply coalesces with the all, with the eternal Spirit, finding its fruition in perfect satisfaction within the Spirit of its origin? Or can it be that such perfection which is a perfection of Love, within personal Purpose, within the identity of Spirit, will now so join God in his creative zest eternally that it reaches out again, to participate basically in worlds being created? Can it not be that Love, having reached full distinction creatively in the finite with perfect identity, now yearns for its own condescension, its own mission of incarnation? Do such spirits, being perfected, join in some new creative age, some new cosmic epoch, trying forever to see what can be accomplished with a better start?

Is consummation from God's point of view an eternal drama of Love trying to produce the ever-better communities? Such a living of love, and a going out in the many to learn love, can be the occasion forever, where time itself is the constant living of Love, as eternity, and the learning of love is time's pedagogical definition. Perhaps God simply wipes out countless ages, the way our own may perish, as not worthy of his creative love and care, remelting us into the common spirit and making us begin again. Can he learn from such false starts? Can some of the lessons from these false starts make up the concrete potential for the ongoing learning of love within the eternal living of Love? One thing is certain: not pleasure, nor rest, nor aesthetic appropriateness is ultimate, but love, and love means sharing, giving, aiding, suffering, conflict, victory by lure and persuasion, by sacrifice and identification.

Accordingly, creative ages which may be concomitant with the ages of attainment or with the perfect inner bliss of eternity, may not contradict but rather express the ultimacy of love, spirit, and personal purpose. God is multidimensional and is real in all respects, but in all respects he is Love, in eternity where time cannot enter and in time where eternity enters, to perfect it by its own self-giving and constructive identification. God is multidimensional, real and perfect in attainment and real and perfect in his incarnation, but real and perfect as love whether in utter bliss or in the suffering symbolized by the Cross. Thus the consummation is ever the consummation of the universal Word, of the eternal *multidimensional* Love. It is true both that heaven is always heaven and that contrapletal logic accepts the realities of creation, continuation, and consummation, qualitatively, accumulatively, contrapletally. How, however, can we from our point of view more than guess at what can be? Such guesses can only serve to refute and refuse unworthy views and to release the realities of the religious imagination. Faith, in the service of love, turns to hope. Hope that can be clearly seen, moreover, is no longer hope. In this world we have to live by faith, hope, and love.

We have come to the end of our discussion of the Potential Word, in creation, in continuation, and in consummation. In looking back on it there are three considerations we must keep in mind. Our main stance is the ultimacy of spirit, love, and personal purpose. Such is the nature of the Universal Word. Such is the heart of a theology for a universal faith.

No theology can be anything but faith. To live is to be a believer. To live in the midst of a cosmic process is necessarily to live by faith, whatever faith we may then claim to live by. There can be no full knowledge of ultimates in a plenary and proper sense within an incomplete cosmic process, or within the very history of the universe which is the basis of our common knowledge, and the history of man which is equally common property. We build our faith on our best, on our central knowledge, forced to choose, to be sure, but not to choose the way process points. We must choose between past, present, and future, and only the past and present as focused toward the future can for us constitute the basis of a warranted faith. We live by faith, but by the faith that is the most amenable and adequate to knowledge possible. Only such faith can produce warranted hope.

Thus our whole undertaking is the seeking of faith for clarity and conviction that is authentic and helpful. The mind lives as much by the practical as by the intellectual, for mind must be in the service of the whole of life. Thus we must use the creative reason as well as the critical; to cope with our final problems as human beings; every hypothesis and every heuristic adventure, to be sure, is speculation, but all speculation must be brought back and to heel at the needs of the whole man and of all men. Thus our venture in examining the Potential Word is an act of faith, using reason, respecting knowledge, serving man. Faith must be both prescriptive and predictive, or directive for both life and thought.

Obviously our own experiences matter. If a man has known ecstasy, or walks closely as well as humbly with his God, that life will know experiences he cannot in honesty deny which go beyond the ordinary and which reinforce his faith. But faith cannot do without seeing as well as experiencing and no private person has the right to dictate truth to the public. What a man has seen and knows within, he has an obligation to clarify and to make available to all interested and competent coseekers. Faith must give reason for its hopes; it must state the grounds for its being genuinely a warranted faith. Then, having confessed from experience and from his most creative and critical seeing, the theologian must leave his witness in the hands of God and those who read him. For himself he must go on living his faith and examining it ever more carefully and helpfully.

Faith as faith settles no intellectual problem, but faith is the way life must finally entertain and use knowledge. Life depends upon the quality of our faith: the kind of faith we have and how we live it as whole-response. Faith, however, needs hope. Hope is expectation. It is living faith while looking for its fruition. Hope is no mere choice of directions or roads. Hope is looking for flowers along the road and for anticipated scenery around the curve. Man is actually nourished by hope. Hope feeds man on the journey of life. A theoretical faith in life after death is, therefore, rather useless. It may become escapist. It may be compensatory. Faith must include hope, the hope that practically walks over the boundary into heaven, while waiting expectantly for the fruition of faith. To lessen faith is to diminish life. To kill hope is to kill life. The totally hopeless life is a burdened, an unwanted, life. The Potential Word should give man concrete hope. When the Word is God's universal Love man should take all needed hope. He should "abound in all hope," in joy and peace in believing. When man really hopes for God's fulfillment in the large and long future the tenor of his whole life improves. Hopeless theology is a contradiction in terms. Hopeless Christian theology is the denial of it. And beyond all sectarian theologies lie the promises of the Universal Word.

Hope, however, must be not only believing but realistic. True hope is expecting from God with regard to the concrete world. Faith sees not only the promises of God but also the evil state of the world. No hope, like faith, is right that does not face up to the facts. Hope, therefore, must also be two-dimensional. No easy solution of a quick heaven and all is well can do for an adequate Christian theology. Hope can be cheap as well as grace! We must learn the long, long time of the unimaginable future. Thus we have tried realistically to deal with the process of going beyond egos and ego-involvements through a long process of discipline carried mostly in the context of Spirit. Realistic hope must center in God's long last. It must endure the agonies of waiting and of being deeply hurt by disappointment. True hope comes hard. It is no easy happiness in expecting. It must groan and give, agonize and attain. It must live now in the face of all relevant facts. Then it must keep on growing, growing accumulatively. After that can come that persevering growth in the distinctions which beyond the accumulative can become contrapletally consummatory.

Nevertheless if such discussion of long-range endurance lessens life, if it dims hope, if it makes life more of a burden, the whole discussion is wrong. We must be realistic and our discussion must be consonant with the facts we know. We cannot escape reality into futile hope. The hope we give must rather be such as to provide a real incentive and a genuine lift to life. Hope must have as well as expect, it must find as well as seek, it must deepen within the realities of the gospel. It must grow strong with the forward journey in the experiences of God's promises. More fulfilled than frustrated, more real than disappointing! Our faith must find hope, true, growing, gaining hope.

But "the greatest of these is love." This whole work is about love. That love is *theos,* the ultimate fact; it is *logos,* the universal meaning. God, the Spirit of Love, is multidimensional. Only contrapletal logic begins to afford some adequacy of dealing with him who remains sovereignly himself, creating eternity—the living of love, for eternity is adjectival to God, not God to eternity—and creating within eternity the adventures of time, the learning of love and the conditions for learning love. Time is cosmic within eternity. Between them there is a semipermeable membrane through which eternity can enter time, to perfect it, but time can never enter eternity to spoil it.

Love that knows the best possible outcome, considering its being conditioned by human freedom, can remain joy at its inmost being and sharing, and also go out to suffer with and for creation. Not hedonism's permanent pleasure, and not tragedy's constant frustration, but love's reality multidimensionally, before, above, with, and through, yes, and after, all creative suffering and sorrow—such is the ultimate that is full of peace and zestful with adventure. Eternity is qualitatively in a different category, a different kind of reality, in its depth and power, strong and real enough to remain its own satisfaction while at the same time lending to creation its drive, its strength, its hope, its courage, and its attainment. Thus love is the ground and love is the goal, not simply, to be sure, but in grand complexity, the whirlwind's heart of peace, the no-voice that is yet the meaning of the earthquake and the wind.

Such love calls for faith; for faith, as Brunner insisted, is the affirmation of love. Faith is the heart of all meaning, the conviction that meaning can be trusted. Faith at its best is the daring to live love, beyond fear of hurt, within frustration of misunderstanding, through stages of unresponsiveness, from most if not from all sides. Faith at its most mature life is the acknowledgment that *theos* is *logos* is *agape*. Faith is the assurance, not yet made evident, that truth can be trusted, and truth comes at its center from the Universal Word, the word of God's unconditional Love, God's concern no-matter-what. Genuinely to accept love is to become fully and constantly open to integrity, to all truth, and to use one's mind as critically as well as creatively as possible.

Wise faith is trusting our minds when they seek the full universal truth, with the knowledge that learning, thinking, wondering, if detached from life, become matters of pride and curiosity, of vanity and division, but when they are in the service of life, they become part of the love that builds up and is the final goal of all seeking. If such be the case, however, faith must turn to hope because love lives by the concrete tokens of concern. Love in hope lives expectantly. Love lives hopingly, scanning the skies for the better day, awaiting the morrow for the more rewarding relationship, hoping for the future what cannot be seen or had today. Love lives in persistent hope. It dares not think that it can fail finally. All finite hopes can deceive, but when love knows Love to be ultimate, love dares "hope against hope," for the full fruition of its seeking. He who loves always hopes. For him who loves, hope cannot be quenched. To quench hope is to quench the Spirit, for finally love is of God who is

Spirit, and whose personal purpose plans eternally for all ages. Hope always has its heart in heaven, but its eyes scan the way there, burning with expectation and yearning for concrete indications that heaven is no fancied goal but the ground of love's every undertaking and the power for all finite and final fruition.

Thus love is the theme of a theology for a universal faith. Love is the personal Spirit, the Universal Word. The world stands in need of the true universal that the more it is made known and the more it is lived the more it proves to be the truth. The world needs a universal directive for conduct, as free as the Spirit and as definitive as God, affording guidance in principle, and yet open for creative responsibility and mature moral growth. The world needs a source of significance that can illumine and motivate all true value. The world needs a vision of beauty that can draw all outside themselves, not by running away from themselves, but rather by the finding of themselves in the all, and in the many. The world needs a Glory to worship that shall be so utterly free from all seeking to worship, that the very fullness of that freedom, that fount of outgoing love, constrains irresistibly the spontaneous and unreserved worship of all creatures.

The world needs a fullness of truth, so overflowing, so overbrimming, so overwhelming, that when the creatures find it they truly sell all else to become partakers of that treasure. Such truth cannot be possessed. It is open to all. It cannot be exhausted. It is as eternal and rich as God. It is as real and concrete as every fact, meaning, and problem. Only such love can be the theme for a universal theology, the faith for all the world. Religions come to such faith and die. Religions come to such faith and are reborn. Religions come to such faith and rise again in the newness of the life of the fuller truth, which is truth in and for life, even the truth of the living God.

In this life we must do what we can to know as well as to live. Thomas Aquinas upon his third experience of ecstasy, gave up writing. Nothing mattered now that he had tasted more of the fullness. Those who have experienced ecstasy and dare not deny the experience can never be the same again. They can indeed be tempted to stay on the mount of transfiguration, rather than to return into the plateaus and valleys of ordinary life, but most of us, whatever our experience, believe that basically we have to live one life at a time. Faith and hope finally become fulfilled when they are in line with love, and love is at its heart a present experience. Love cannot postpone its concern. Love is always that center which cannot without destruction be moved back into the past or forward into the future. Love is living, and life is ever present. Thus those who have seen in faith the promised land or who have pondered the possible implications of love must yet walk in and toward it in the now, life upon life.

Theology is a trying to learn more of the love which is the heart of life. Theology seeks to understand the Universal Word. To do so we must think. But thought is from and for life. Thus love dare never escape into the past or into the future, but rather accepts the road as it is, humbly and helpfully to walk in it. At the last, all true thinking and all genuine ultimates lead to love, and all love leads to life. Life and love, again, lead to God who stands ever ready to share both and to give life a new zest.

Those who know love are ever less inclined to argue about the reality of God. They long instead to learn more of love, to live it more genuinely, that they may transcend the preliminaries of time and by participating in God become translated into the fulfillment of eternity. Such eternal life never flees time, but lives humbly and helpfully within it, allowing faith and hope to find ever-fuller fruition within the final reality of love.

INDEX

Index